DRIVING TOURS
CANADA

Macmillan • USA

Written by Carole Chester

Edited, designed and produced by AA Publishing.

© The Automobile Association 1991.

Maps © The Automobile Association 1991.

Reprinted 1995, 1996.

Published by AA Publishing

Published in the United States by Macmillan Travel
A Simon & Schuster Macmillan Company
1633 Broadway
New York, NY 10019

Macmillan is a registered trademark of Macmillan, Inc.

ISBN 0-13-917626-8

Cataloging-in-Publication Data is available from the Library of Congress.

Color separation: L C Repro & Sons Ltd, Aldermaston, England

Printed and bound in Italy by Printers SRL, Trento

Title page: *Niagara Falls, Ontario*

Opposite: *Boathouse on Maligne Lake*

CONTENTS

INTRODUCTION

This book is not only a practical touring guide for the independent traveler, but is also invaluable for those who would like to know more about the country.

It is divided into 7 regions, each containing between 3 and 5 tours. The tours start and finish in major towns and cities which we consider to be the best centers for exploration. Each tour has details of the most interesting places to visit *en route*. Side panels cater for special interests and requirements and cover a range of categories—for those whose interest is in history, wildlife or walking, and those who have children. There are also panels which highlight scenic stretches of road along the route and which give details of special events, crafts and customs. The numbers link them to the appropriate main text.

The simple route directions are accompanied by an easy-to-use map of the tour and there are addresses of local tourist information centers in some of the towns *en route* as well as in the start town.

Simple charts show how far it is from one town to the next in kilometers and miles. These can help you to decide where to take a break and stop overnight, for example. (All distances quoted are approximate.)

Before setting off it is advisable to check with the information center at the start of the tour for recommendations on where to break your journey and for additional information on what to see and do, and when best to visit.

ENTRY REGULATIONS

A valid passport (but not a British Visitor's Passport) is required, except for citizens of the US, who need only proof of citizenship such as a birth certificate, though obviously a passport would prove that too. You must also have a return or onward ticket and evidence of adequate funds for the duration of your visit. Visas are not required for citizens of Britain, Eire, Australia, New Zealand or the US. Persons under 18 years who are not accompanied by an adult must bring a letter from a parent or guardian with permission to travel in Canada.

CUSTOMS REGULATIONS

There are no currency restrictions but there are limits on duty-free liquor (40 fl oz) and cigarettes (200), or cigars (50), or tobacco (1kg/2.2 lb). Also, there are strict controls on agricultural materials, fruits, vegetables, meats and plants and on any products using any part of an animal belonging to an endangered species.

EMERGENCY TELEPHONE NUMBERS

Police, fire and ambulance: 911.

HEALTH

There are no specific health problems for visitors, nor are any special vaccinations needed, though tetanus shots are recommended, as they are for travel anywhere. If you are camping, it is wise to boil water from lakes and rivers.

Emergency help (ambulance, etc) can be obtained by calling 911 from any phone, or potentially serious medical problems can be taken directly to the emergency ward of the nearest hospital. Traveler's health insurance to cover the duration of your stay in Canada is strongly recommended, as medical services are expensive.

CURRENCY

Canadian money is divided into cents and dollars with 100 cents to the dollar. Coins are one cent, five cents (a nickel), 10 cents (a dime), 25 cents (a quarter), 50 cents (half-dollar). The notes have different colors to allow instant identification: $2 are brown, $5 are blue, $10 are purple, $20 are green, $50 are red and $100 are beige. The $1 is no longer being printed and its place is being taken by a golden-coloured $1 coin called the Loonie, after the bird depicted on the back.

CREDIT CARDS

All major credit cards are accepted throughout Canada. It is useful for visitors to carry at least one, particularly for hotel and car rental payments.

The Canadian Museum of Civilization at Hull, Quebec

BANKS

The trend for Canadian banks is away from the traditional business hours of 10.00 to 15.00 hrs Monday to Friday and towards extended hours and Saturday morning openings. Many banks offer automated tellers at any hour.

All banks have foreign currency departments and will exchange bank notes and travelers' checks.

Many stores, hotels, restaurants and tourist sites will also take US currency but usually give a less favorable rate than a bank.

POST OFFICES

Post offices are open from 08.00 to 17.00 (18.00) hrs, Monday to Friday and sometimes on Saturday mornings. Canada is not noted for the speed of its mail delivery but that has not kept the cost of mailing letters down. Stamps can be bought at hotels and stores and there are small branch post offices in many shopping malls as well.

TELEPHONES

Coin-operated telephones are available almost everywhere, just follow the instructions on the phone box. Local calls usually cost 25 cents and can be dialed directly. If you don't reach your number, your money is automatically refunded when you hang up.

For long-distance calls, make sure you have plenty of change unless you are calling 'collect' (reverse call). You can dial most places in the US directly from almost everywhere in Canada.

International calls from Canada can be dialed direct using these codes: Britain 01 44; Eire 01 353; Australia 01 61; New Zealand 01 64, followed by the area code (dropping the initial 0) and the number. For the US dial the area code and number.

TIME

Canada spans six time zones, with only $4\frac{1}{2}$ hours separating Newfoundland from Yukon.

Newfoundland Standard Time: Newfoundland – GMT minus $3\frac{1}{2}$ hours.

Atlantic Standard Time: The Maritime Provinces, Labrador, part of Baffin Island and Anicosti Island – GMT minus 4 hours.

Eastern Standard Time: Quebec, most of Baffin Island, Ontario east of 90° longitude – GMT minus 5 hours.

Central Standard Time: Ontario west of 90° longitude, Manitoba, the eastern half of Saskatchewan and the Keewatin district of the Northwest Territories – GMT minus 6 hours.

Mountain Standard Time: the rest of Saskatchewan, Alberta, northeastern corner of British Columbia and the Northwest Territories north of Saskatchewan and Alberta – GMT minus 7 hours.

Pacific Standard Time: the rest of British Columbia and Yukon – GMT minus 8 hours.

MOTORING

Documents

The only document necessary is a valid driver's license, unless you bring your own car, in which case you will need a valid registration or ownership form and proof of insurance.

Drivers from the US taking their car into Canada should get a Canadian Non-Resident Inter-Province Motor Vehicle Insurance Liability Card which is available from insurance companies in the States.

Canada's best-known fishing village, Peggy's Cove, Nova Scotia

PUBLIC HOLIDAYS

1 January – New Year's Day
Good Friday and Easter
   Monday
Monday before 25 May –
   Victoria Day
1 July – Canada Day
1st Monday in September –
   Labor Day
2nd Monday in October –
   Thanksgiving Day
11 November –
   Remembrance Day
25 December – Christmas
   Day
26 December – Boxing Day

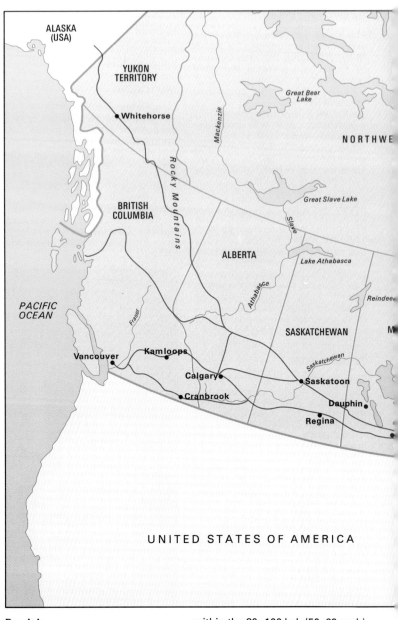

ELECTRICITY

Electrical power is 110 volts,
60 amps, AC with appliances
requiring twin-pronged, flat-
tongued plugs. An adaptor
is required for most
overseas appliances.

USEFUL WORDS

The following is a list of
common Canadian words
and expressions:
Canadian English
Anglophone English-
   speaking person
apartment flat
candy sweets
cookies biscuits
elevator lift
fender wing
Francophone French-
   speaking Canadian
gas petrol
Inuit Eskimo
kayak low light canoe
logging lumbering
lumber timber
panning separating gold
   from gravel by washing in
   a pan
saltchunk ocean
tuque French Canadian
   knitted winter cap

Breakdowns

In the event of a breakdown, pull
over to the side of the road, if
possible, and put up the hood
(bonnet) of your car as a signal of
distress.

Car rental companies will replace
vehicles if there is a breakdown
and a number of firms provide
towing and emergency road
services; all of them are listed in
the Yellow Pages under Towing.

If you are an AA, AAA, AIT or
RAC member, the Canadian Automobile Association (CAA) can
provide club services.

Accidents

If you are in an accident, stop. Call
the police immediately and describe the nature of assistance
required.

Always report immediately to
your insurance company (or car
rental hire firm) any accident in
which your car is involved, no
matter how trivial it may seem.

Speed limits

Speed limits vary from province to
province, but they are generally
within the 80–100 kph (50–62 mph)
range on open highways and 50
kph (31 mph) in many cities and
towns. The open highway speed
limits are: Alberta – 100 (62);
British Columbia – 80 (50);
Manitoba – 90 (56); New Brunswick
– 80 (50); Newfoundland – 80 (50),
90 (56) on Trans-Canada Highway;
Northwest Territories – 90 (56), 80
(50) at night; Nova Scotia – 80 (50);
Ontario – 80 (50); Prince Edward
Island – 90 (56), trailers 80 (50);
Quebec – 100 (62) on Auto Routes,
90 (56) on other hard-surfaced
highways; Saskatchewan – 80 (50)
and Yukon – 90 (56).

Driving conditions

Driving is always on the right, with
passing on the left. The use of seat
belts by at least the driver and
front-seat passengers is required in
all provinces except Northwest
Territories and Yukon.

The use of child restraints by
children under a certain weight or
age is mandatory in all provinces
except Northwest Territories,
Prince Edward Island and Yukon.
Quebec is the only province with
toll roads.

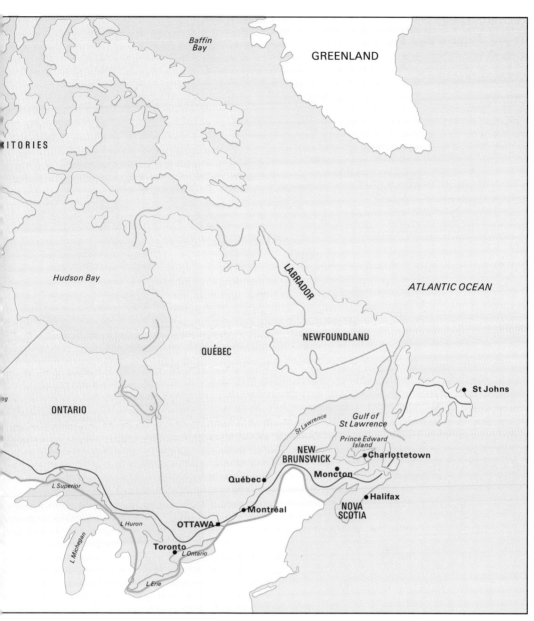

In a number of places you will have to take a ferry to get where you are going by car.

Distances on road signs are in kilometers.

Car rental and fly/drive

The minimum age to rent a car in Canada is 25 (21 with a credit card), and you must produce identification, a valid national or international driver's license and be able to pay either with cash, travelers' checks or credit cards. Keep a copy of your rental contract with you.

Fly/drive package rates vary considerably, as do conditions. Some packages offer an unlimited number of miles free, with others you get a specified number free, then you must pay an additional charge per mile over that.

If you are traveling in areas where the roads are poor or unpaved, check conditions of car rental to see if this is permitted.

The spacious beautiful Bas-St-Laurent region, south coast of the St Lawrence in Quebec

ATLANTIC CANADA

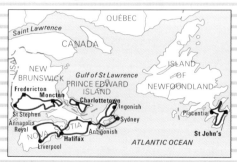

The Micmac Indians were the first inhabitants of the maritime provinces. The first white explorers were the Vikings, in 1000AD, who established a settlement in Newfoundland, although John Cabot was the first officially recognized discoverer in 1497.

The earliest communities in all four provinces (Nova Scotia, New Brunswick, Prince Edward Island and Newfoundland) were English and French, constantly in dispute with each other for possession of territory, until the 18th-century defeat of Nova Scotia's Fortress Louisbourg by the British. Traces of French influence, known as Acadian, still exist, most especially in new Brunswick, where both English and French are official languages. In the 1800s large numbers of Scottish Highland pioneers arrived, which is the reason why so many Gaelic customs and crafts still flourish in many parts of these provinces.

Many pioneers were fishermen, and fishing is still a way of life in this region of Canada. Basque whalers were attracted to Newfoundland's shores, and the waters are still marvelous for seafood, especially cod. Canada's smallest province, Prince Edward Island, just over 5,000 sq km (2,000 square miles), may not compare in size, but its seafood is renowned – Island Blue mussels, Gulf Queen crab, Malpeque oysters and of course, lobster. Lobster is a favorite wherever you go, and lobster community suppers are common, not only on Prince Edward Island, but in Nova Scotia, the province shaped rather like that crustacean.

In addition to boating, outdoor pursuits in photogenic surroundings are big news in Atlantic Canada. In Nova Scotia you will never be further than 56km (35 miles) from the sea, but the rugged Cape Breton Highlands are a hiker's and motorist's delight, and the orchards and farmland of the Annapolis Valley are a scenic inspiration. Neat little rectangular New Brunswick boasts almost 2,400km (1,500 miles) of sea-washed coastline – seascapes that vary from gentle waters and lengthy stretches of sand in northeastern bays to the awesome tides of Fundy dashing waves against rocky cliffs. Yet you are never far from farmland green, forests of spruce and pine, or the lush St John River Valley (North America's 'Rhine'). In Newfoundland there are only four people to every square mile so there is plenty of space and room to breathe.

Throughout this region of Canada there are small inns and guest houses or farms in which to stay. Community spirit is strong, especially in the villages that dot the coastline and nestle in the hills. A wealth of legends, folklore and traditions have resulted in good-natured friendly annual festivities, even if nightlife neon and razzmatazz are not in evidence.

Halifax:
Halifax is a vibrant seaport and regional hub, twinned with Dartmouth on the other side of an exceptionally fine harbor, where the celebrated *Bluenose II* sailing schooner is based. On the waterfront, the Brewery and Historic Properties have been converted into shops and restaurants, and the **Maritime Museum** houses fascinating seafaring exhibits. Overlooking the city, the **Citadel** is a prime historic site, with re-enacted fort life and an **Army Museum**, while the **York Redoubt**, on its high bluff, was the first defense effort in 1793. Architectural gems include **Province House** (Canada's oldest provincial legislative building); and worthy museums include the **Nova Scotia Museum**, also on Summer Street, and the **Art Gallery of Nova Scotia**, on Hollis Street. Don't miss the **Old Town Clock** (an 1803 landmark) or the **Prince of Wales Martello Tower** (1796) in Point Pleasant Park.

Moncton:
Moncton, New Brunswick's second largest city, is a major urban centre on the southeast shores with its pedestrianized, brick-paved downtown area. A major sight, the **Tidal Bore** – a fast moving wave that literally raises the River

Petitcodiac's surface by almost 9m (30 feet) in less than an hour – can be seen twice daily from Bore View Park. Another curious phenomenon is **Magnetic Hill**, at Mountain Road. Put your car in neutral, release the brakes and you appear to roll uphill! A mini steam train, game farm, and the **Wharf Village** shops and restaurants next door, are other attractions. Museums include the **Moncton Museum**, on Mountain Road (for historical exhibits); venerable buildings include the **Free Meeting House** (1812) and the **Thomas Williams House** (1883). A major collection relating to Atlantic region Acadians can be seen at the **Acadian Museum and Art Gallery**, on the campus of New Brunswick's only French-speaking University.

Charlottetown:

Charlottetown, the only official provincial city of Prince Edward Island, is a harborfront capital, and site of an 1864 conference, that led to the unification of Canada (in **Province House**). The **Confederation Center Art Museum** displays over 1,500 paintings; its large theater stages summer musicals. Imposing buildings include **Government House** (1834) and **St Dunstan's Basilica**, one of Canada's largest churches. For shopping, try Confederation Plaza

The downtown business area of Halifax, Nova Scotia, with its sophisticated waterside frontage

around Grafton, Queen and Richmond Streets, the City Mall, or **Island Market Village**, a 2-hectare (6-acre) amusement area to the west of the city center. Food is simple, but seafood abundant.

St John's:

St John's is an old, historic city, where steep hills clustered with colorful wooden houses rise sharply from the harbor. The best view is from **Signal Hill**, a natural fortress with an annual Military Tattoo, topped by **Cabot's Tower** (1897), where Italian inventor Guglielmo Marconi received the first transatlantic wireless signal. **Quidi Vidi Battery**, an 18th-century French fortification, overlooks the tiny **Quidi Vidi Village**. Old downtown buildings include **Commissariat House** (1818), **Old Garrison Church** (1836) and **Colonial Building** (1850); and museums include the **Newfoundland Museum** (for history) on Duckworth Street, which, with George Street, is good for restaurants. There are lively pubs on Water Street and fashionable boutiques in Murray Premises.

5 days – 1,223km (762 miles)

A HIGHLAND TRAIL

Halifax • Truro • New Glasgow • Port Hawkesbury • Isle Madame • Sydney • St Ann's • Ingonish • Cheticamp • Baddeck Antigonish • Sherbrooke • Halifax

Don't be surprised to hear the bagpipes somewhere on this tour. Scottish music, tartans and Highland Games are all alive and well in Cape Breton Island, where the first Highland pioneers settled in the 1800s. Scenically, this is a wonderful part of Nova Scotia; whether you are hiking through the National Park or motoring along the Cabot Trail, it has all the charm of small inns and friendly communities.

SPECIAL TO . . .

1 West of Truro, where the Economy River enters Minas Basin, is the tiny community of **Economy**, which boasts the world's best clams. It marks the division between Minas Basin and Cobequid Bay, headwaters of the Bay of Fundy, and tides here are among the highest in the world, often reaching more than 15m (50 feet).

ⓘ Old City Hall, corner Duke and Barrington Streets, Halifax

*From Halifax take **Highway 102** north for about 66km (41 miles), branching off to **Highway 2** just after Exit 12, signed for Truro.*

Truro, Nova Scotia

1 Truro is the best place to watch the tidal bore, a 'wall of water' that rushes into the Salmon River filling it at one foot a minute. This phenomenon is due to the high tides in the Bay of Fundy. When the incoming tide enters a narrow channel it cannot spread out, so it rises into a 'wall'

Cheticamp's Acadian Cultural Center preserves the region's proud Acadian heritage, traditions and crafts

sometimes several feet high. This sizeable town once boasted the largest settlement of Acadians, but after they were expelled from the province in 1755, settlers arrived from Northern Ireland and New Hampshire. Today, Truro is mainly a manufacturing center, but **Victoria Park** is a wonderful natural playground, with picturesque waterfalls, walking trails and a picnic area. There are plenty of tourist facilities here and several museums, including the **Colchester Historical Society Museum** on Young Street which has changing exhibitions and depicts the area's human and natural history.

ⓘ Victoria Square

*From Truro follow the signs to **Highway 104** via Bible Hill, and head northwest to New Glasgow, about 66km (41 miles) away.*

New Glasgow, Nova Scotia

2 At one time New Glasgow was a great shipbuilding port; later, it became a steel-making center, and one of the first steam engines to run on steel rails in America, *The Samson*, is on display at the **Pictou County Historical Museum**, which also houses a good collection of early Trenton glass. Pictou, 21km (13 miles) north on **Highway 106**, is a harborside fishing center known as the birthplace of New Scotland; it was here, in 1773, that the first boatload of Highlanders landed. Mid-July is Lobster Carnival time, and this is always a good place for lunch. While you are here, look in at the **McCulloch House Museum**, furnished as it was when illustrious local resident, Thomas McCulloch, the first president of what is now Dalhousie University, lived here in 1806. The **Burning Bush Center Museum**, which displays two centuries of church history, is free, as is the **Northumberland Fisheries Museum**.

Step into the past at the Fortress of Louisbourg, reconstruction of an 18th-century town

ⓘ Off rotary at town limits

*Return on **Highway 106** until it meets **Highway 104** which you take east until you reach the Canso Causeway. Cross, then go south on **Highway 19** to Port Hawkesbury; 110km (69 miles).*

Port Hawkesbury, Cape Breton Island

3 Port Hawkesbury is pleasantly situated on the shores of the Strait of Canso. The 21km (13-mile) long, 1.6-km (1-mile) wide Strait links the Gulf of St Lawrence with the Atlantic and, until the Canso Causeway or Road to the Isles was built in 1955, separated mainland Nova Scotia from Cape Breton Island. Building of the causeway created a deep-water, ice-free Atlantic superport. The Festival of the Strait takes place in this major service center during the last week in June.

ⓘ Port Hastings, on the right after crossing the causeway

*From Port Hawkesbury take **Highway 104** east, then **Highway 320** south across the Lennox Passage Bridge to Isle Madame.*

Isle Madame, off Cape Breton Island

4 This 44 sq km (17 square-mile) Acadian island is easily seen via a scenic loop of paved road (**Highways 320 and 206**) in less than an hour. The island is wooded but there are picnic spots and swimming beaches on its shoreline. Arichat, at the junc-tion of **Highway 320 and 206**, is now the center of island business, where you can see a restored 18th-century stone blacksmith's shop at LeNoir Forge Museum. The oldest settle-ment is nearby **Petit-de-Grat**, a fish-ing center founded in 1713. From the colorful harbor of **Little Anse** a hiking trail leads to Cap Rouge, with its view of Green Island, gateway to the Strait of Canso; and from the lookout at **Babin's Hill** you can see Jerseyman's Island.

*Having circled back to **Highway 104**, follow **Trunk Highway 4** by the side of Bras d'Or Lake northeast to Sydney.*

Sydney, Cape Breton Island

5 Between 1802 and 1828 Scottish Highland immigrants arrived here in droves, and today Sydney is Nova Scotia's third largest community, so there are plenty of visitor services, making it a good base for Louisbourg and Glace Bay. The latter may be reached by continuing on **Highway 4** for 16km (10 miles). The main reason to visit is **The Miners Museum**, open year round. You can tour **Ocean Deeps Mine** and visit the **Miners' Village**, with reconstructed dwellings of the 19th century. Of interest in Sydney itself is 18th-century **St George's Church**, which has a chair from the wardroom of Nelson's ship *Victory*.

ⓘ 20 Keltic Drive, Sydney River

*Take **Highway 125** until it joins **Highway 105**. Continue west to Exit 11 at South Gut St Ann's, start of the Cabot Trail going north.*

FOR CHILDREN

9 The **Alexander Graham Bell National Historic Park**, at the eastern end of Baddeck, is a fascinating museum for all ages. The Scottish-born inventor, teacher and humanitarian spent 35 years in Baddeck and original artifacts on display here show his experiments in the fields of medicine, genetics, communication and his work with the deaf. The museum has activity programs and workshops.

SCENIC ROUTES

Much of this tour incorporates one of the most beautiful drives in North America: the **Cabot Trail**. Named for the famous explorer who sighted Cape Breton Island in 1497, the circular route from South Gut St Ann's to Baddeck has tremendous mountain and sea views. Among the most picturesque stretches are those around St Ann's Harbor, Cape Smoky's hairpin bends, between Pleasant Bay and the Cheticamp River and the Margaree Valley.

RECOMMENDED WALKS

Cape Breton Highland National Park covers 958sq km (370 square miles) between the Gulf of St Lawrence and the Atlantic, and the hiking trail network is large and diverse. Recommended ocean view trails include L'Acadien, Le Butereau and Skyline. The Bog Trail is suited to wheelchairs, and an 8km (5-mile) trail along the northern coast atop Cape Smoky has worthwhile views.

St Ann's, Cape Breton Island

6 In the 1820s a sudden storm brought a group of Scottish settlers, bound for the US, into St Ann's harbor, where they and their descendants stayed. The Great Migration from the Highlands has given Cape Breton its unique Scottish character: an account of it may be read in the **Great Hall of the Clans** at the Gaelic College, located between South Gut and North Gut St Ann's. The College not only keeps the Gaelic language alive but teaches Highland dancing, Gaelic singing, clan lore, bagpipe playing and handweaving; and you are welcome to look at the family tartans in the **Celtic Arts Center**. The Gaelic Mod, a seven-day festival of Celtic culture, takes place in the first full week of August. Look in at the **Highland Pioneers Museum**, where the personal belongings of local giant Angus MacAskill are displayed. He was almost 2.4m (8 feet) tall, and traveled for a time with equally famous Tom Thumb. The drive around rugged St Ann's harbor is particularly photogenic, with high bluffs and exquisite sea views.

Continue north on the Cabot Trail for 73km (46 miles), past Cape Dauphin and the Bird Islands to your right, and later past towering Smoky Mountain to Ingonish.

Ingonish, Cape Breton Island

7 Many people think the few miles between Cape Smoky, so called for the shroud of mist that hovers over the massive rock, and Ingonish Beach is the most impressive section of the Cabot Trail. This is certainly a place to stop and perhaps take the chairlift up the northern slope of the Cape for the panoramic views. Ingonish Beach is the main entrance to the **Cape Breton Highlands National Park**. Its name is believed to be of Portuguese origin: there was a Portuguese community here in the 16th century. The village itself sits on beautiful Warren Lake.

Continue around Cape Breton Highlands Park on the Cabot Trail for some 106km (66 miles) to Cheticamp.

Cheticamp, Cape Breton Island

8 This Acadian fishing village on the Gulf of St Lawrence may prove an alternative overnight stop; there is another entrance to Cape Breton Highlands National Park just before Cheticamp. **St Peter's Church**, in town, was built in 1883 with stone hauled by horse and sleigh across from Cheticamp Island, and the nearby **Acadian Museum** features a small display of artifacts relating to the early settlers.

Look out for signs for the **Acadian Hiking Trail** on the fringe of Cheticamp near Petit Etang: it will lead you to the top of the Highlands for a spectacular view. In summer, whale-watching boat trips depart daily from Cheticamp harbor.

Continue south on the Cabot Trail for 43km (27 miles) until you reach Belle Cote, then turn inland through the Margaree Valley towards Baddeck, about another 52km (32 miles).

Baddeck, Cape Breton Island

9 A little gem of a village which is the starting (or finishing) point of the Cabot Trail. Its name, derived from the Micmac Indian word *Abadak*, means 'place with an island near', and that island is Kidston's, in Baddeck's harbor. This is a good base for touring the western portion of Cape Breton Island. Many famous people have, in the past, built summer homes in Baddeck, including Alexander Graham Bell, whose lovely house *Beinn Bhreagh* (not open to the public) may be seen from the government wharf and from **Bell National Historic Park**. Keep your ears open for the sound of Gaelic – still spoken in these parts.

ℹ Local community center

*Take **Highway 105** all the way south to Port Hastings, where you cross back to mainland Nova Scotia and continue on **Highway 104** to Antigonish; 144km (90 miles).*

Antigonish, Nova Scotia

10 Much of the day-to-day activities in this major town revolve around **St Francis Xavier University** in whose library the Hall of the Clans is dedicated to the area's founding Scottish families, and whose theater presents a summer season of plays and musicals. Antigonish stages some of the best Highland Games of the province every mid-July. For the best beaches, follow Bay Street out of town.

ℹ 56 West Street

*Take **Highway 7** south past Lochaber Lake, to Sherbrooke, a distance of just under 78km (49 miles).*

Sherbrooke, Nova Scotia

11 This resort on St Mary's river will be much appreciated by salmon fishers. It was originally a fur-trading post, built by the French in 1655 and settled by pioneers in the 1800s. Think of a village in the boom-and-bust Victorian era and you have pictured Sherbrooke, restored to its 1800s heyday. Costumed guides will escort you into the past as you watch craftsmen at work, peep into the jail or drop in for tea at the old tearoom. Not far away from Sherbrooke, the **Liscomb Park Game Sanctuary** shelters moose and deer and its waters are ideal for canoe and fishing trips.

ℹ Sherbrooke Village

*Continue for 16km (10 miles) south on **Highway 7**, then head west for about 175km (109 miles) back to Halifax.*

Halifax – Truro **79 (49)**
Truro – New Glasgow **66 (41)**
New Glasgow – Port Hawkesbury **110 (69)**
Port Hawkesbury – Isle Madame **53 (33)**
Isle Madame – Sydney **137 (85)**
Sydney – St Ann's **91 (56)**
St Ann's – Ingonish **73 (46)**
Ingonish – Cheticamp **106 (66)**
Cheticamp – Baddeck **95 (59)**
Baddeck – Antigonish **144 (90)**
Antigonish – Sherbrooke **78 (49)**
Sherbrooke – Halifax **191 (119)**

Lives and fortunes have been lost trying to find Captain Kidd's treasure on Oak Island

ℹ️ Old City Hall, corner Duke and Barrington Streets, Halifax

Take **Highway 333** to Peggy's Cove.

Peggy's Cove, Nova Scotia

1 The most popular and appealing of the province's fishing villages, this preservation area's rugged appearance, spreading from a narrow ocean inlet against a granite backdrop, has attracted many artists, notably Finnish-born William deGarthe, who lived in Peggy's Cove from 1926 until his death in 1983. His last work is in the memorial park named for him – an impressive rock sculpture depicting fishermen and their families and the legendary Peggy (an early settler after whom the village was named). Two of deGarthe's murals can be seen in **St John's Anglican Church**: one portraying Christ walking on the water in a Peggy's Cove setting, the other of fishermen in turbulent seas. The **lighthouse** no longer operates its beacon; it has served as a summer post office for almost two decades.

Highway 333 *winds north to the crossroads with* **Highway 3** *at Upper Tantallon. Head west on* **Highway 3**.

Chester, Nova Scotia

2 One of Canada's most scenic summer resorts, this town is situated on a peninsula at the head of Mahone Bay, whose coves and harbors were once the hideouts of pirates. Founded in 1760, Chester has enough accommodation and sport facilities to make it a good overnight base. Summer events include **August Race Week** and a festival at the local theater.

Chester's charm is best appreciated on foot: a leisurely stroll past lovely old South Shore houses to the **Town Bandstand** (summer Friday evening concerts are given here), to the old train station, now a **museum** displaying items from the town's past and exhibiting local artists' work. Further along **Highway 3** is Oak Island, where Captain Kidd reputedly buried his treasure (small admission charge).

Highway 3 *continues to Mahone Bay.*

HAUNT OF THE PIRATES

Halifax ● Peggy's Cove ● Chester ● Mahone Bay ● Lunenburg ● Liverpool ● Annapolis Royal ● Wolfville ● Windsor ● Halifax

Many a photogenic fishing village nestles along the coast of the southern shores, and many coves and harbors were once pirate retreats. This route should be taken slowly: allow browsing time in the small craft shops and galleries along the way. When the tour turns inland it takes you through the farmland and orchards of the Annapolis Valley and to the untamed beauty of Kejimkujik National Park, where the keen hiker can follow Indian ghosts down wilderness trails.

Mahone Bay, Nova Scotia

3 Set amid rolling hills that stretch to the bay's edge, this community's name is said to have derived from the old French word *mahonne*, for the low-lying craft used by pirates.

Sailboat and harbor cruises may be taken from **Mader's Wharf** while **Kedy's Landing** (a 1799 heritage building), at the eastern edge of town, is a good place to shop and eat. The history of the early settlers (many of whom were German) is best learned at **Settlers Museum and Cultural Centre**, which contains artifacts from the past, including found-

It is easy to see why Peggy's Cove has become a haven for artists, craftspeople and photographers

SPECIAL TO …

Many of Nova Scotia's festivals relate to food. Among the most interesting on this tour route are the **Annapolis Valley Apple Blossom Festival**, celebrated everywhere between Windsor and Digby. Events include parades and fireworks, barbecues and art shows. Each Thanksgiving Day in Windsor, the **World Pumpkin Festival** is held; thanks to Howard Dill and his 'Dill Atlantic Giant' pumpkin seeds, enormous pumpkins are grown in and around the town. Strawberry or lobster suppers are quite common throughout Nova Scotia.

6 **Fort Anne National Park** is Canada's oldest, although what you see today is the fourth fort on the same site; the first was erected around 1643. Today's fort is a fine example of early 18th-century earthworks. What in 1797 was the British Field Officers' Quarters is now a **museum** (open year round). It comprises a Nova Scotia Charter Room, the Queen Anne Room, Acadian Room and rooms relating to the former British garrison, maintained here until 1854.

6 **Port Royal National Historic Park** (off Highway 1, about 13km (8 miles) from Annapolis Royal) was one of the earliest European settlements in North America. Here there is a reconstruction of the first French fur-trading post (1605–1613) where guides, in period dress, tell you all about the lifestyle and events of this pioneer colony.

4 The **Fisheries Museum of the Atlantic** on Lunenburg's waterfront is likely to fascinate children. Tours are given of two ships: a trawler and a schooner. The *Theresa E Connor* was the last of the salt-bank schooners and today features the story of *Bluenose*.

ing father Peter Zwicker's personal belongings and major pieces of the Percy Inglis-Quilan ceramics collection.

Highway 3 continues to Lunenburg.

Lunenburg, Nova Scotia

4 This busy fishing port is most famous for the schooner *Bluenose*, built in 1921, undefeated champion of the North Atlantic fishing fleet, and depicted on the back of the Canadian dime. All the major attractions here are to do with ships and/or fish: the **Fishermen's Memorial Room** in the Community Center off Green Street is dedicated to those lost at sea; and the **Nova Scotia Fisheries Exhibition and Fishermen's Reunion** takes place every September, when dory racing and scallop shelling are among the many popular activities. The town site was originally an Indian encampment, then a French fishing post, but in 1753 Germans and Swiss founded Lunenburg, and even now, surnames and architecture reflect their influence. Escorted tours are given of **St John's Church** (1754), Canada's second oldest church. One of its most interesting possessions is the Queen Anne pewter chalice.

ⓘ Blockhouse Hill Road

Highway 3 continues to Liverpool.

Liverpool, Nova Scotia

5 The tree-lined streets of this South Shore tourist center boast many fine old houses. Like its British namesake, it sits on the Mersey River and is quite industrial, with paper mills, foundries and fish processing

In Lunenburg, past and present are bound up with fishing and the lure of the sea

plants. Settled by New Englanders in 1759, it has the oldest town crest in Canada. Privateering is a part of Liverpool's past. A cairn at **Fort Point** by the harbor pays tribute to the daring men who sailed the *Lucy*, *Rover* and *Liverpool Packet*, vessels which roamed the northwest Atlantic during the American Revolution and the War of 1812. Major historic sites include 1766 **Perkins House**, now a museum; **Trinity Anglican Church** (1822) and the **Anglican rectory** (1820); and the **Old Settlers' Cemetery** on Main Street, some of whose headstones date to 1761. Liverpool has all the amenities you would expect and is a good base for deep-sea fishing, duck shooting, and visiting **Kejimkujik National Park**, a 45-minute drive away.

Highway 8 leads north to Annapolis Royal.

Annapolis Royal, Nova Scotia

6 Canada's oldest settlement was founded in 1605; the original site is actually 15km (9 miles) down the Annapolis River. Local life these days revolves around the weekly summer Farmers' Markets, but visitors come to take the self-guided or escorted walking tours of the old properties. The **O'Dell Inn** (1869), on Lower St George Street, is today a museum displaying Victorian costumes and furnishings, and the **Robertson–McNamara House** (1785), on the same street, features early school items. The Georgian-style **Adams–Ritchie House** (1712) has been restored to its original appearance.

ℹ️ The Railway Museum, Victoria Street

Highway 1 leads east to Wolfville.

Wolfville, Nova Scotia

7 Despite its former name, Mud Creek, this is an attractive university town with some delightful small inn accommodations and restaurants on its tree-shaded streets.

Settled in the 1760s by New England planters, Wolfville sits by one of the world's smallest natural harbors. Early history is contained in **Randall House**, on Main Street. Gaspereau Avenue leads to the **Gaspereau River** (popular for tubing), which winds its way through the Acadian settlements of Gaspereau and Melanson. Highland Avenue climbs up Wolfville Ridge to Stile Park for the best view of the valley.

Acadia University, founded in 1838, dominates the center of town and is also home to the Acadia Repertory Theater.

Highway 1 continues to Windsor.

Windsor, Nova Scotia

8 This gateway to the Annapolis Valley is on a site aptly named *Piziquid* by the Micmac Indians, for it means 'meeting of the waters' – as the St Croix and Avon rivers do. The town was settled in 1703 by the Acadian French, who reclaimed land from the sea.

The main historic site is **Fort Edward**, erected in 1750, of which some portions are still visible. It was here that preparations were made to expel the Acadians in 1755. Here, too, Flora Macdonald (friend of Bonnie Prince Charlie) stayed briefly with her husband in 1779. An interpretive display explains the fort's history. Canada's first agricultural fair was held at Ford Edward in 1765: it now continues as the **Hants County**

The remains of an old French fort are preserved at Fort Anne, Annapolis Royal – a former British garrison which was named after Queen Anne

Exhibition each September. Several Windsor natives later found fame but for varied reasons. Judge Thomas Chandler Haliburton created the fictional character Sam Slick, and with him, such phrases as 'raining cats and dogs' and 'quick as a wink'. His home is now the **Haliburton House Provincial Museum**, furnished in Victorian style. The Shand family had several successful businesses in Windsor. Their home, **Shand House**, built in 1890, is open to the public, and is typical of the large homes built in Nova Scotia, when shipbuilding was in its heyday.

Return to Halifax.

Halifax – Peggys Cove 39 **(24)**
Peggys Cove – Chester 67 **(42)**
Chester – Mahone Bay 23 **(14)**
Mahone Bay – Lunenburg 10 **(6)**
Lunenburg – Liverpool 61 **(38)**
Liverpool – Annapolis Royal 115 **(72)**
Annapolis Royal – Wolfville 97 **(61)**
Wolfville – Windsor 31 **(19)**
Windsor – Halifax 60 **(38)**

SCENIC ROUTES

The first part of this tour takes in part of what has been designated the **Lighthouse Route**, for the jagged coast is dotted with lighthouses and is famous for its white sand beaches. The section of **Highway 333** around Peggy's Cove is especially rewarding, and the Oak Island Passage from the Head of the Bay to Mahone Bay is a must for a true southern shore flavor.

Highway 8 leads through beautiful inland countryside, especially around Kejimkujik National Park; and the Annapolis Valley, which extends between Digby and Windsor (on and around **Highway 1**), is scenically at its best at apple blossom time in late May or early June.

RECOMMENDED WALKS

Kejimkujik National Park (**Highway 8** at Maitland Bridge) has walking trails and picnic areas, as well as hiking trails and canoe routes for the more adventurous, providing access to the wilderness area of the park. Kejimkujik is at its most colorful in the autumn but has more interpretive nature programs in summer. It is open year round and cross-country ski trails are maintained for winter visitors.

BACK TO NATURE

Some of Nova Scotia's notable lakes are located in **Tobeatic Game Sanctuary**, off **Highway 8** at Caledonia, where the headways of the Mersey, Jordan, Roseway, Clyde and Tusket rivers meet. The park is home to beaver and white-tailed deer.

3 days – 494km (308 miles)

THE FAIREST ISLE

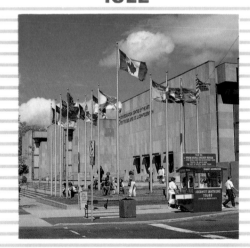

Charlottetown • Orwell • Eldon
Pinette • Murray Harbour • Montague
Pooles Corner • Georgetown • Souris
St Peter's • South Rustico • Cavendish
Stanley Bridge • New London • Malpeque
Summerside • Victoria • Rocky Point
Charlottetown

This tour covers a good portion of the tiny, crescent-shaped Prince Edward Island, where whitewashed houses and village churches stand out against red sandstone cliffs. The island was the fictional home of Anne of Green Gables and the factual home of author Lucy Maud Montgomery. PEI is relaxed and rural; no wonder Jacques Cartier described it as 'the fairest land 'tis possible to see', and laws against billboards protect that old-world beauty!

SPECIAL TO ...

15 Prince Edward Island is known for its lobster suppers and fêtes. One of the liveliest celebrations takes place in July in Summerside. During the Lobster Carnival you can watch fiddling and step-dancing contests, a beauty pageant and sporting events.

14 Not far from Malpeque, in the Tyne Valley, an **August Oyster Festival** also features country music and oyster-shucking contests to go with the seafood suppers, while the **Murray River's Northumberland Provincial Fisheries Festival** (late July) throws in races and a softball tournament.

ℹ️ Oak Tree Place, Charlottetown

*Take **Highway 1A**, then **1** to Orwell.*

Orwell, PEI

1 Just before the small town of Orwell itself (signed off **Highway 1**), you reach **Orwell Corner Historic Village**, a re-creation of a late 19th-century rural crossroads, which is as calm and quiet now as it was then. You can visit the 1864 farmhouse, which was also the post office, along with the general store and dress-

Charlottetown's Confederation Center of the Arts Building is a home for local culture

maker's shop; the local church, blacksmith's, shingle mill and animal barns complete the picture of village life, raising crops and livestock in much the same way as a century ago. Summer highlights are the Wednesday evening ceilidhs (musical evenings).

***Highway 1** continues southwards to Eldon.*

Eldon, PEI

2 In 1803, Lord Selkirk brought over a number of poor Scottish crofters to this area from the Isle of Skye. The Provincial Park named for him, at Eldon, contains one of the country's largest collections of hand-hewn log buildings: the **Selkirk Pioneer Settlement**. These include a smokehouse, weaving shed and settler's home. Not far away, in the farming community of Belfast, there is a monument to the Selkirk settlers. The stones at its base were some of the ballast in *The Polly*, one of the ships they traveled with. You may wish to drop into the privately owned **British Royalty Collection** (signposted on Highway 1), which features over 200 commemorative pieces of china, starting with Queen Caroline (1820).

***Highway 1** continues to Pinette.*

Pinette, PEI

3 A good place for one of the islanders' favorite activities – clam digging, at its best at low tide. Keep an eye out for small round holes in the sand that seem to eject streams of water when you walk by them: these are the burrowing clams. You can picnic in **Pinette Provincial Park** and take an excursionary drive along **Highway 209** to Point Prim, site of Prince Edward Island's oldest lighthouse (1845), still in use.

*From Pinette, **Highway 1** continues along the shore via Wood Islands, where ferries cross the Northumberland Strait to Caribou, to Murray Harbour.*

Murray Harbour, PEI

4 This delightful fishing village has several craft shops and small guest houses. The **Log Cabin Museum**, on **Highway 18A**, contains American antiques such as old spinning

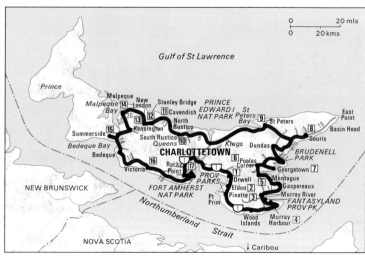

The native name for Murray Harbour is 'fishing place', and this small village is still home to a thriving fleet

wheels, plus a doll collection dating from 1850. On **Highway 4** at Murray River the **Northumberland Mill and Museum** is a replica of a country store which stood on the site until early this century, serving the then busy ship-building industry.

> **Highway 17** *leads north from Murray River to Montague.*

Montague, PEI

5 You might wish to stay here overnight, after a champagne and mussel cruise on the river from Montague Wharf. The key attraction is the **Garden of the Gulf Museum** on Main Street South, which features a collection of woodworking tools, textiles, military equipment and uniforms as well as crafts. Most of the collection pertains to local history.

> **Highway 4** *continues to Pooles Corner.*

Pooles Corner, PEI

6 Stop at the Visitor Information Center here, at the junction of Highways 3 and 4, for an overview of King's County. Displays, maps, photos and artifacts tell you everything you need to know about the region's history, architecture and resources.

> **Highway 3** *leads directly to Georgetown.*

Georgetown, PEI

7 Georgetown has one of the best harbors on Canada's eastern coast, but it is better known for its **King's Playhouse** where summer plays and concerts are staged. Lovely little **Holy Trinity Church** here is one of the province's oldest, and anyone is welcome to make a brass rubbing of facsimiles of English medieval brasses, found in the crypt.

ⓘ Junction of Highways 3 and 4

> *Retrace your journey on* **Highway 3** *until the sign for* **Highway 311** *heading for Cardigan North, Launching Place and beyond. From Dundas, follow* **Highway 310** *until it joins* **Highway 2**, *where you turn eastwards for Souris.*

Souris, PEI

8 This lively community was founded by the French in the early 1700s. Its French name means 'mouse': plagues of the field variety made frequent attacks in the 18th century. Today, it is considered a service center for the immediate region and there is a ferry link from here to Iles-de-la-Madeleine in Quebec. Island sandstone was used to build **St Mary's Roman Catholic Church**, which overlooks the harbor, and the beach along the Northumberland Strait is great to pause for a swim.

ⓘ Souris Beach, on Highway 2

> **Highway 2** *west leads to St Peter's.*

FOR HISTORY BUFFS

7 Near Georgetown at **Brudenell Point (Highway 319)**, an early French settler, Jean-Pierre de Roma, established a little town in the hope that it would become a commercial fishing center. His dream was short-lived: war broke out between the British and the French, and today only a cairn marks the site of that original De Roma settlement. Scottish immigrants settled on Brudenell Island in the late 1750s; their names are inscribed on a stone memorial in the cemetery there.

FOR CHILDREN

4 Off **Highway 4** at Murray Harbour, **The Toy Factory** gives summer tours. Its 60 different models of wooden toys and ornaments may tempt a parting with pocket money. Just east of the Murray River (on **Highway 348**), in **Fantasyland Provincial Park**, popular storybook characters take on statue form. The park is home to several deer and has slides and swings for the more active youngsters.

FOR CHILDREN

11 Several Cavendish attractions are ideally suited for children: **Cranberry Village's** waterslides twist and plummet, and smaller children will delight in the scenes from popular fairy stories at **The Enchanted Castle. Rainbow Valley's** park activities cater for toddlers – their own slide, a talking owl, a magic show – and to those slightly older – with giant water slides, motorboats and seabikes. In **King Tut's Tomb & Treasures** there is a full-size replica of the Egyptian tomb. The young king's story is explained with the help of computerized projectors.

SCENIC ROUTES

This tour incorporates sections of specifically designated scenic routes: the **Lady Slipper Drive** is joined around Summerside, and the **Blue Heron Drive** encircles Queens County in the middle of the island. The northern section travels by white sand dunes, the southern by distinctive red shores. The **King's Byway Drive** passes acres of berries and tobacco in the southeast and more rugged country in the northeast.

St Peter's, PEI

9 When the French occupied Prince Edward Island it was known as Ile St-Jean, and St Peter's village was a main center for fishing. (Shipwrecked French sailors settled here in the early 1700s.) The wooded hillside overlooking **St Peter's Bay** is a particularly pleasant picnic spot.

Highway 6 travels east to South Rustico, bordering Prince Edward Island National Park.

South Rustico, PEI

10 There are plenty of facilities in this major holiday base including a golf course and horseback riding, and the Rustico area is extremely attractive. The Old Acadian community was named for René Rassicot, a settler from Normandy in 1724. In town you will see a monument to the Rev Georges-Etienne Belcourt. It stands between **St Augustine's Church** (where he was parish priest between 1859 and 1869) and the **Farmer's Bank,** which he founded in 1864. The bank used to be the smallest chartered bank in Canada, but today the little building contains a museum commemorating the priest's work and exhibiting the bank's own $5 bills. If you are here in July or August, you can also visit **Jumpin' Jack's Country Store Museum** (on Highway 242), a 19th-century country store where you will find cracker barrels, fish barrels and other paraphernalia.

Highway 6 continues to Cavendish.

Malpeque, in Prince County, is famous for its oysters which take five years to 'fatten' and farm for the table

Cavendish, PEI

11 Besides being a seaside resort with a full range of facilities, this is Green Gables town. Lucy Maud Montgomery spent much of her life in Cavendish, raised by her grandparents, who ran the local post office out of their farmhouse home, and spent a good deal of time with her cousins, the Macneills at Green Gables. She used that house and the countryside she loved as the setting for her popular novel, *Anne of Green Gables*. Today, the public are invited into the house (just west of the intersection of **Highways 6 and 13**), including Anne's room, with its apple blossom wallpaper, where Lucy Maud wrote the children's book. In the grounds are the Haunted Wood, Babbling Brook and Lovers' Lane. The author died in 1942 and is buried in Cavendish Cemetery.

🛈 Off Highway 6

Highway 6 continues to Stanley Bridge.

Stanley Bridge, PEI

12 There is plenty of family entertainment here: the **PEI Marine Aquarium** features live specimens of local fish and shows how oysters are cultivated; seals may be watched in an outdoor pond and there is an exhibit of 700 mounted birds (open mid-June to mid-September). Children love to explore the full-size reproduction of a space shuttle in **Cap'n Bart's Adventure Park**, a park which also features sports for the young, a dinosaur alley and nostalgia museum.

Highway 6 continues west to New London.

The yacht club and marina at Summerside are an important part of local life

New London, PEI

13 Lucy Maud Montgomery was born here, and the modest green-and-white-trimmed house, which overlooks New London's harbor, is open to the public in season. Inside, among the Victorian furnishings, are copies of the author's short stories and poems, and personal items, including her wedding dress and scrapbooks.

*Take **Highway 20** to Malpeque.*

Malpeque, PEI

14 No one should leave PEI without sampling Malpeque oysters! Every year over 10 million of them are harvested in Malpeque Bay, and they were as well known to the island's early pioneers as they are to us. While you are in the village you could pay a visit to the **Keir Memorial Museum**, housed in the former Keir Memorial Presbyterian Church in the center of Malpeque, where exhibits depict 19th-century life. A little way out of the village (on **Highway 20**), at the **Malpeque Gardens**, hundreds of varieties of dahlia, rose gardens and floral arrangements represent scenes from *Anne of Green Gables*.

*Take **Highway 20** as far as Kensington, then follow signs to Summerside (**Highways 2** and **1A**).*

Summerside, PEI

15 This is the island's second largest town and the main port for the export of potatoes; nevertheless, it is small enough for enjoyable walks through its historic streets. In the waterfront shopping complex is the **Eptek National Exhibition Centre** and **PEI Sports Hall of Fame**, honoring well-known athletes. A somewhat more unusual museum is the **International Fox Hall of Fame and Museum** on Fitzroy Street, dedicated to the fox farming industry, started on the island over a century ago. In the

Acadian Museum of PEI, on Highway 2 a few miles west of town, Acadian culture is traced from the first settlement at Port la Joye, through expulsion and resettlement to present times. You will see everyday artifacts and ancestral pictures of 23 of the original families. Ask to see the 15-minute audiovisual about the Acadian people.

ⓘ On **Highway 2**, about 1.6km (1 mile), east of town

*Leave via **Highway 1A** as far as Bedeque, then **Highway 10** to Victoria.*

Victoria, PEI

16 Small inns and lobster restaurants often entice travelers to stay in and around this charming village, whose **Main Street Playhouse** offers local entertainment. In summer, schooner trips are available from the harbor.

ⓘ 812 Wharf Street

*Take **Highway 19** to Rocky Point.*

Rocky Point

17 This is a stop for history buffs, for it is the site of **Fort Amherst/Port la Joye National Historic Park**, where the first Europeans permanently settled. Also on **Highway 19** is the **Micmac Indian Village**, illustrating what life must have been like before the Europeans arrived.

Return to Charlottetown.

RECOMMENDED WALKS

11 One of Canada's smallest national parks, **Prince Edward Island National Park**, boasts some of Canada's finest saltwater beaches, high dunes, bluffs, salt marshes and freshwater ponds, and is home to more than 200 species of birds. **Rustico Island**, within the park, is home to hundreds of blue herons. The park is open year round and provides winter visitors with cross-country ski and snowshoe trails, but the summer months are when interpretive nature programs and guided walks are given.

BACK TO NATURE

4 & 5 Seal-watching cruises depart from **Murray River Wharf** daily between July and October, to see the seals at Reynolds Island in Seal Cove, and from **Montague Wharf** to a colony around the reef at Whitman's Point. In summer and fall, you can join deep-sea fishing charters as a participant or observer and, in March, helicopter tours offer transport to the ice fields of the **Gulf of St Lawrence**, home to thousands of baby seals.

3/4 days – 828km (515 miles)

THE PICTURE PROVINCE

Moncton • Shediac • Aulac • Hopewell Cape • Alma • Sussex • Saint John St George • St Andrews • St Stephen Fredericton • Oromocto • Moncton

This circular tour takes in a variety of seascapes, cities and lush rural inland. You will see wooden houses – a New Brunswick feature: plain old saltbox types, some built in Victorian ginger-bread style, some cheerily colorful. The route takes you through the Saint John River Valley, following the footsteps of Indians, explorers and settlers of the past, and offers curious natural phenomena such as the tidal bore in Moncton, as well as opportunities to watch for whales and other wildlife.

ℹ️ Off Main Street, Moncton

*Take **Highway 15** to Shediac.*

Shediac, New Brunswick

1 The locals say their home town is the world's lobster capital, and hold a July festival in honor of that popular crustacean. This South Shores small town boasts one of the province's finest saltwater beaches at Parlee

The dramatic tidal changes at The Rocks Provincial Park are a natural wonder of the world

Provincial Park, with water temperatures as high as 80°F (28°C) in summer. The area is good for sailing and windsurfing and there is a golf course nearby.

***Highway 15** continues to Port Elgin, then take **Highway 16** south to Aulac.*

Aulac, New Brunswick

2 Fort Beausejour, near Aulac (on Highway 2), is historically very important: after their defeat here the French ceded sovereignty, held since the early 17th century, to the British. It is one of the few Canadian fortifications at which fighting actually occurred. It was declared a National Historic Site in 1926.

ℹ️ Near the New Brunswick–Nova Scotia border

*Take **Highways 2**, then **106** back towards Moncton. Just before the city, branch south on **Highway 114** to Hopewell Cape.*

Hopewell Cape, New Brunswick

3 The Fundy tides (the highest in the world) have made the curious rock formations here, known as **Flower Pot Rocks**. If you have the time, it is worth watching the dramatic change from high to low tides in the **Rocks Provincial Park**. This phenomenon has been described as a wonder of the world.

*Continue on **Highway 114** to Alma.*

Alma, New Brunswick

4 Located at the base of **Fundy National Park**, this is a service area for visitors to this rugged coastline, complemented by woodlands, inland lakes and abundant wildlife. During low tide it is actually possible to walk on the ocean floor. The community center in town gives summer arts and crafts classes.

*Continue on **Highway 114** and **Highway 2** to Sussex on **Highway 1**.*

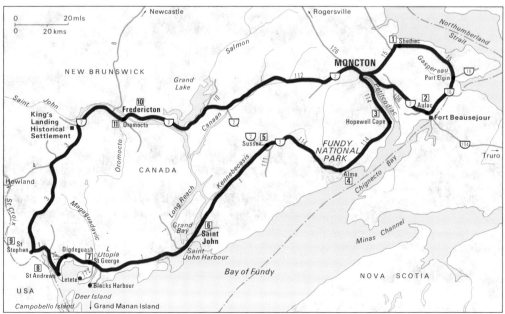

Enjoy the host of activities Fundy National Park has to offer – or just enjoy

Sussex, New Brunswick

5 Founded in 1786 by Loyalists, this could be the best place to stop for souvenir hunting, since it is a well-known center for handicrafts. Visitors are welcome at most of the artisan studios. A **museum** portrays agricultural history and the **town park** welcomes visitors who can also enjoy the **mineral spring** at Church Avenue. Just outside town, **Animaland** has unusual sculptures in concrete of animals including dinosaurs and a gigantic lobster. **Queen Street** is a flavor of olden days.

*Continue on **Highway 1** to Saint John.*

Saint John, New Brunswick

6 New Brunswick's largest and Canada's oldest incorporated city is a great place to stay overnight. Saint John claims to have had the first police force in North America and the first newspaper and bank in Canada, but the city has aged – and added the new – gracefully. The United Empire Loyalists landed in 1783 at **Market Slip**; in the next century, **Market Square** was built overlooking it. The 19th-century façade now conceals fashionable boutiques, restaurants and night spots. During the late 19th century, numerous Irish immigrants arrived at the port, many of whom were quarantined on **Partridge Island**, which these days is a historical site with its own museum. You can take a harbor cruise from the Market Slip Wharf, and since the city stands at the mouth of one of North America's most scenic rivers, all kinds of watersports and boating are possible in the area. Sightsee on foot and you will see **Barbours General Store**, stocked as it would have been in 1867, together with an early **barber's shop** and **Loyalist House**, and much more of architectural interest. The tourist office provides three 1½-half hour routes to follow. Use your car to visit the **Carleton Martello Tower**, built by the British in case of American attack, and still standing guard at the western end of the harbor. Inside the tower, artifacts from the 19th century are displayed. A good place to take children is **Rockwood Park**, where there are bumper boats and other outdoor amusements, plus the **Cherry Brook Zoo**.

ⓘ City Hall

*Continue on **Highway 1** to St George.*

St George, New Brunswick

7 Whether or not the legendary monster lurks in **Lake Utopia** here is a matter of debate, but it is certainly an area for sighting salmon on their way upriver on the Magaguadavic, and for watching ospreys swooping for fish. Just before St George (off **Highway 1** at Blacks Harbor) is the ferry terminal for **Grand Manan Island**, one of the most beautiful islands in the Bay of Fundy. From Letete (south of St George) a free ferry operates to **Deer Island** in summer, an ideal spot for outdoor activities – and a toll ferry crosses to **Campobello Island**, another lovely isle in the Bay of Fundy. Unusually, until the 1800s, the island was still a feudal fief of Welsh seamen. It then became a fashionable summer place for wealthy Americans, including Franklin Delano Roosevelt, whose former summer home is a key feature of the park named after him.

*Take **Highway 1** to Digdeguash, then scenic **Highway 127** to St Andrews.*

St Andrews, New Brunswick

8 This favorite coastal resort's resemblance to a New England town is due to the United Empire Loyalists who settled here in 1783 and brought their houses with them from Maine by barge. The **Ross Memorial Museum** on Montague Street is a Georgian building housing a variety of decorative art and porcelains, and other historic landmarks include **Charlotte County Courthouse**, **Greenock Church** and **St Andrews Blockhouse**. One of the most fascinating places to visit is the **Huntsman Marine Science Centre Aquarium and Museum**, where you can really learn about life in the Bay of Fundy. Its 'Please Touch' tank will appeal to younger members of the family, and a walking trail leads to the shore. Throughout the summer, whale-watching and sightseeing cruises leave from the wharf.

***Highway 127** north leads back to **Highway 1**, which heads west to St Stephen.*

SCENIC ROUTES

Highway 114 is specifically designated a scenic route and its highlights include **Hopewell Cape, Fundy National Park** and **The Rocks Provincial Park. Highway 127**, from Digdeguash to St Andrews and back up to **Highway 1**, is a particularly pleasant section of the route, with coastal scenes, **Chamcook Mountain** and **Dochet's Island** along the way. In the Saint John's river valley region, you may well want to take some of the side roads off the **Trans-Canada Highway (Highway 2)**.

SPECIAL TO ...

9 St Stephens hosts one of the most unusual of New Brunswick's many summer festivals: the Chocolate Fest. Anything and everything related to chocolate takes place including chocolate meals and tours of the **Ganong candy factory** which has been selling chocolate bars since 1910. In the **Chocolatier** shop, in front of the factory on Milltown Boulevard, old sweet-making equipment and the world's tallest jelly bean display can always be seen, as well as demonstrations of chocolate-dipping.

FOR HISTORY BUFFS

6 Canada's first museum, the **New Brunswick Museum** on Douglas Street, was founded in 1842 by distinguished scientist Dr Abraham Gesner. There is something of interest for everyone: national and international art treasures, a natural science gallery, historic artifacts and national and provincial memorabilia. Among those items of maritime interest are a series of model ships preserved from the 1880s, including one of the *Marco Polo*, the fastest vessel in its day.

FOR CHILDREN

10 King's Landing **Historical Settlement**, just off the Trans-Canada Highway, is an educative theme park, a superb re-creation of Loyalist life in New Brunswick between 1820 and 1890. There are 60 old buildings and over 100 costumed guides to demonstrate daily life in those days. During the summer, events include Scottish dancing, tossing the caber and performances in the Kings Theater. Work goes on in a blacksmith's shop, a grist mill and the Joslin Farm.

RECOMMENDED WALKS

7 There are many places in New Brunswick which walkers will enjoy but **Grand Manan Island** in the Bay of Fundy (accessible by ferry) should not be missed. There are 19 walking and nature trails on this peaceful island, following the shore to landmarks like Hole-in-the-Wall. The trails vary from short ones taking half an hour to those taking several hours. Rockhounds like to take advantage of the unusual geological formation: one side volcanic, one side sedimentary.

BACK TO NATURE

4 & 6 **Fundy National Park**'s rugged coastline and inner woodlands are home to a variety of wildlife. Park staff conduct nature interpretation programs and outdoor pursuits include hiking, fishing and bird watching. Twice daily in Saint John, the high Bay of Fundy tides pressure the Saint John River to flow the other way, creating the **Reversing Falls Rapids**, a curious natural phenomenon. Two lookouts provide the best viewing spots. The Bay of Fundy is also renowned for whale-watching – North Atlantic right whales in particular come to the Bay to mate in the summer and early fall. Humpbacks and fin whales are also regularly seen.

Described as the Queen of Brunswick, Fredericton is a gracious city of tree-lined streets and historic houses

St Stephen, New Brunswick

9 There have never been any hard feelings between residents of this border town and their US neighbors – they even lent them gunpowder for 4th of July celebrations despite being at war with them! Local history may be viewed in the **Charlotte County Museum** and a saltwater beach is to be found in **Oak Bay Provincial Park**.

Highway 3 takes you to the Saint John River Valley region and to the capital, Fredericton.

Fredericton, New Brunswick

10 As handsome and stately a capital as its nickname, City of Stately Elms, suggests, Fredericton is a fine place to stay, eat or shop. The main areas for all three are Queen and King Streets, though there is a craft area around Regent Street – don't miss breakfast croissants and a browse at **Boyce Farmers' Market** on Saturday mornings. Local artisans favor working with pewter and a good choice of items can be found in the work studios and craft shops.

This riverbank city was named in honor of King George III's second son, and was at one time an important military base, as you will see on a visit to **Officers Square**, where the 'guard' still changes in summer. The old Officers Quarters are today the **York-Sunbury Historical Society Museum**, housing relics of Fredericton's past. The statue in the middle of the square is of Lord Beaverbrook, one of the city's great benefactors, who financed the **Beaverbrook Art Gallery**, which is probably Eastern Canada's most impressive showcase of art. Overlooking the city is one of North America's oldest colleges – the University of New Brunswick (1789), on whose campus is Canada's first astronomical observatory, the **Old Arts Building**, and a restored one-room schoolhouse. The central city five-block area, compact for easy walking, covers most of the historic sites, and in the **Legislative Assembly Building** (1880) there is a rare copy of the original Domesday Book, as well as some Audubon bird sketches. Among the historic churches, **Christ Church Cathedral** stands out not only for its Gothic architecture, but because it was the first new cathedral foundation on British soil since Norman times. Free guided walking tours of the town leave quite frequently from City Hall. River activities are part and parcel of the annual summer **River Jubilee Festival**, and a replica paddlewheeler offers river cruises from the wharf at the base of Regent Street.

Take Highway 2 east to Oromocto.

Oromocto, New Brunswick

11 Site of a large military training area, Oromocto is located at the junction of the Saint John and Oromocto rivers. The **Blockhouse** is a replica of one built here in 1777, and military buffs will not want to miss the museum at **Canadian Forces Base Gagetown**, which displays arms, uniforms and vehicles to explain the military history of the area.

Follow Highway 2/112 back to Moncton.

The Stationer's Festival at Carbonear is one of the town's lively attractions

ⓘ City Hall, New Gower Street, St John's.

*Take **Highway 20** to Pouch Cove.*

Pouch Cove, Newfoundland

1 The small community of Pouch (pronounced *pooch*) Cove used to be illegal. Law in the 17th and 18th centuries forbade permanent residence in Newfoundland, so those who settled at Pouch Cove in 1611 chose it for its dangerous harbor to keep the policing ships away. It is one of the oldest settlements in the province, and its history is documented in the local museum in the **Town Hall**. The scenery is a spectacular bonus, especially when you continue on Highway 20 to **Cape St Francis**, whose lighthouse was installed in 1887; but drive carefully – the road to this headland is a rough one.

***Highway 60** winds along the coast to Brigus.*

Brigus, Newfoundland

2 American artist Rockwell Kent had a summer home and studio in this scenic setting early this century. The community was the birthplace of Captain Bob Bartlett (1875), a navigational pioneer who lived at **Hawthorne Cottage**, which still stands. Nearby **Cupid's** was the site of the first official attempt at colonization, when Bristol-born John Guy tried to establish a plantation.

***Highway 72** passes fishing villages in striking settings before rejoining **Highway 70** to Harbor Grace.*

Harbor Grace, Newfoundland

3 The French named this community *Harve de Grace* (from which it takes its present name) in the early

Early settlers of Pouch Cove relied on its dangerous harbor to ward off unwelcome visitors

A JOURNEY BACK TO NATURE

St John's ● Pouch Cove ● Brigus ● Harbor Grace ● Carbonear ● Heart's Content Placentia ● St Mary's ● Trepassey Ferryland ● Witless Bay ● St John's

The Avalon Peninsula is only a small part of the province of Newfoundland, but one which is rich in wildlife. Its museums and historic sites tell the story of early hardy adventurers, who came to fish and farm here in the 18th century. Its tiny communities will appeal to photographers, as will the vast colonies of seabirds nesting in the cliffs along the land's edge. Avalon is home to thousands of caribou and puffins and in summer is carpeted with blueberries. It is a great escape for nature lovers who enjoy wild beauty and the quiet life.

16th century. In the 17th century it was the headquarters of a famous pirate, Peter Easton, whose stronghold stood where the **Customs House** now stands. The latter houses a museum which depicts local history, including aviation: many early attempts at flying used Harbor Grace as a departure point. The first suc-

SPECIAL TO . . .

In Newfoundland on July 1 (Canada Day) are celebrations including special activities, music and dance. The best places to be are **Butter Pot Provincial Park, Cape St Mary's** and **Castle Hill National Historic Park**. Newfoundland festivals do tend to be very localized, but one fun occasion (usually late June) is the annual **Conception Bay Folk Festival** in Carbonear, with events, handicrafts and entertainment. Blueberry pies and mooseburgers are featured at the annual **Brigus Blueberry Festival**, held on a weekend in early August.

FOR HISTORY BUFFS

6 Castle Hill National Historic Park, fortified by the French in 1662, was the site from which they attacked the English capital of St John's three times. Though forced to retreat on each occasion, they captured the main fort twice and burned the city. When the British moved into Placentia in 1713, they upgraded the defenses here, helping them to recapture St John's, which shortly thereafter became the colony's capital. Today, from the Castle Hill ruins, there is a magnificent view of Placentia Bay, and, in the Interpretation Center exhibits tell the story of the French in Newfoundland.

FOR CHILDREN

Children who are interested in nature and wildlife will find marvelous opportunities to study and learn in Newfoundland. Theme and amusement parks, on the other hand, are scarce.

SCENIC ROUTES

The whole of the Avalon Peninsula's shoreline is of scenic interest and almost every small community a subject for photographers. Highlights include the winding **North Arm** from Holyrood to Brigus and beyond; the areas around **Conception, Trinity** and **Placentia Bays**; and between **Ferryland** and **Bay Bulls**. **Cataracts Provincial Park**, on **Highway 91** (west of Salmonier), has been attracting motorists since the 1920s for its beautiful deep river gorge with cascading waterfalls.

cessful flight took place from here in 1927, and Amelia Earhart left here in 1932 to become the first woman to fly solo across the Atlantic. Several major fires prevented the town from growing into a second city, but some of its old buildings have survived, such as Newfoundland's oldest stone church St Paul's (1835), and Victoria Manor, furnished to era with its own museum and craft center.

Highway 70 continues to Carbonear.

Carbonear, Newfoundland

4 The French may have burned the place down in 1696, but the undeterred inhabitants took refuge on the small fortified island you can still see in the harbor (now designated a National Historic Site). The town is lively and hosts several festivals, and motel accommodation is available. Trail and carriage rides are offered by **Earles Riding Stables** at O'Keefe Place, and in **Shades of the Past** private museum, on High Road North, you can learn about the history of the Conception Bay area (summer only). Just up the coast are two sandy beaches.

Highway 70, then *74* continues to Heart's Content.

Heart's Content, Newfoundland

5 This is an area much taken up with the heart: just beyond are the communities of Heart's Desire and Heart's Delight. The first successful transatlantic cable was brought

ashore here in 1866 and the small place served as a major cable relay station for over a century. The old cable station may be visited in summer, when costumed guides explain the equipment and Heart's Content's role in communications.

Highway 80 then *100* take you to Placentia.

Placentia, Newfoundland

6 Because of its strategic position, this beach front community used to be the French capital of Newfoundland. It was a focal point for the British and French fight to control the colony and its fisheries. Placentia Bay is dotted with islands, and you may well persuade one of the local fishermen to take you on an afternoon's trip to one or more of them. Just beyond Placentia, **Point Verde Lighthouse**, built in 1876, overlooks the sea from its cliff-edge position: the cliff is being eroded by 1m (3 feet) a year.

Take Highway 91 east, then 90 south to St Mary's.

St Mary's, Newfoundland

7 This community will remind you of Ireland, especially if you stop and listen to the accent. The descendants of the original settlers who came here to fish and farm carry on the old Irish traditions and customs.

Take Highway 90 then 10 which continues to Trepassey via St Vincent's.

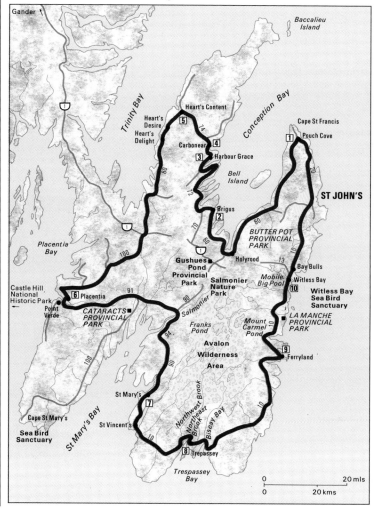

Trepassey, Newfoundland

8 Despite its name, which means 'the dead souls', this is a good place to stay overnight. The town was the ancient seat of Sir William Vaughan's Welsh colony, which collapsed in the 1620s, and was more recently the starting point of early transatlantic flights. The **Trepassey Area Museum** includes a history room, with pictures of the first transatlantic flight and Amelia Earhart's stay in the town, and a fishermen's room which has a replica of a banking schooner used in the 1930s. Highlights include the local Catholic church silver and a sideboard with a punched-nail design of native flora and fauna. In July and August, the Northeast Brook, Northwest Brook and Biscay Bay rivers are prime fishing spots. Don't be surprised to see caribou wandering by the highway – they head south in spring and summer and are often seen around here. Much of the interior of the peninsula is taken up with the **Avalon Wilderness Reserve** (between **Highways 90** and **10**). This unspoiled barren land is 'home to a wide variety of wildlife. Active visitors will find numerous hiking trails and a canoe route.

Although entrance is free, you do need an entry permit, available from the Parks Division in St John's.

Highway 10 continues to *Ferryland*.

Ferryland, Newfoundland

9 Sir George Calvert, later Lord Baltimore, established a colony here in the early 17th century. After he moved to warmer Maryland, Sir David Kirk took charge, fortifying

War Memorial, St John's: a fishing village and modern city with a turbulent past

Ferryland's rocky cliffs. When the fortifications were removed it was easy for the Dutch to capture the town in 1763. From the **Community Museum** in the courthouse the view is breathtaking – over the harbor, Ferryland Downs and Isle aux Bois. Among the exhibits the fishermen's room shows how those tough men survived after Lord Baltimore's departure in 1629

Highway 10 continues to *Witless Bay.*

Witless Bay, Newfoundland

10 Off the coast of this tiny, photogenic community is the renowned **Witless Bay Seabird Sanctuary**. Every summer thousands of seabirds flock here, and the reserve has what is believed to be the world's largest nesting colony of Leach's petrels as well as puffins, razorbills, gray kittiwakes and black headed murres. Further south along the shore, **La Manche Provincial Park** teems with wildlife and attracts many nature enthusiasts.

Return to St John's.

RECOMMENDED WALKS

The **Avalon Wilderness Reserve** is particularly recommended for serious hikers, and one of the best places for a close-up view of Newfoundland's flora and fauna is in **Salmonier Nature Park** at Salmonier Line, 12km (7 miles) from **Highway 1**, where sections of the trails have been leveled to make walking easier. Although the park in total comprises 1,214 hectares (3,000 acres) of wilderness, the special 40-hectare (99-acre) exhibit area allows close encounters with nature not usually feasible for the average person (open June–Labor Day).

BACK TO NATURE

6 Off **Highway 100** a 16km (10-mile) gravel road leads to the **Cape St Mary Seabird Sanctuary**, where Newfoundland's largest colony of gannets nests. The actual lookout is half an hour's walk from the lighthouse, a vantage point that overlooks a sea stack. Besides gannets, you will spot kittiwakes, guillemots and razorbills. The best time of year to view the most birds is between June 15 and August 15.

QUEBEC

Montreal:
Montreal is an exciting city which is home to over a third of the population. It is both fashionable and a gastronomic center. Named after its own mountain, Mount Royal, but originally known as Ville-Marie when founded in 1642 by the Sieur de Maisonneuve, Montreal has excellent hotels, and is sometimes called the Underground City for its superb shopping complexes, such as Place Ville-Marie, Place Bonaventure and Complexe Desjardins.

The old quarter, around flower-filled **Place Jacques Cartier**, is best seen on foot or by horse-drawn *caleche*. Among the historic buildings are **Notre-Dame-de-Bon-Secours Chapel** and **Maison Calvet**. Fine squares include **Place d'Armes** and **Place Royale**. Of the many neighborhoods, don't miss **Sherbrooke Street** downtown; 'the Golden Mile' for art and antiques; **Sainte Catherine Street**, city heart and shopping hub; **Crescent Street**, for sophisticated wining and dining; **Chinatown**, whose main street is De La Gauchetiere, Old Quarter and **St Denis**, the Latin Quarter. Night-life in Montreal is late and varied.

Quebec is not like any other province in Canada: it is European, French and full of *joie de vivre*. It is also the country's most historic province and its largest, covering 1,500,000 sq km (579,150 square miles), and more than twice the size of Texas. Half of it is not land mass at all, but lakes and rivers, and the majority of the population continues to live along the St Lawrence River, where the first settlements were founded, and where the weather is more temperate.

One has to remember that here the population is French-speaking (most are bi-lingual) and that while a golden leopard, symbol of the British Crown, is part of the coat-of-arms, there are three *fleurs-de-lis* in memory of France. It was only after Wolfe's armies besieged Quebec City and Montcalm's troops were defeated on the Plains of Abraham in 1759, that the King of France gave Canada to the British, who flooded in to settle the New World.

Naturally enough, with so much undeveloped territory – some of it quite desolate, like the frozen tundra around Ungava Bay – those 750,000 lakes and virgin forests, Quebec suits lovers of the hardy outdoors, but the effervescent cities and their pleasant suburbs will appeal even to the most widely traveled cosmopolitans. In addition to the two major metropoli, Quebec is divided into 17 other tourist regions.

There are, for example, islands, and there are mountains (the Laurentians), favored by skiers. There is the region they call 'Maple Country', known for its fall colors; and the region of Outaouais, dotted with pretty villages; or off-the-beaten-path Abitibi-Temiscamingue, both of which attract hunting and fishing enthusiasts. There is the peaceful countryside of the Richelieu Valley, spectacular Saguenay, dramatic Duplessis and the vast wilderness of the Far North. And everywhere there is great food and hospitality.

Although this is a province on a grand scale, it is easy to get around, thanks to an extensive network of well-built and maintained roads. You might well opt for the Chemin du Roi (King's Highway), Quebec's oldest inter-city route; you might follow the Loyalists Route to the Eastern Townships or take the Forest Route to lumberjack country. You could follow in the footsteps of the legendary fur trappers and traders to the western woodlands, shaped by the rounded hills of the Canadian Shield, or see the region declared a 'world reserve of the biosphere' by Unesco.

Whatever your interests, they will be fulfilled in Quebec, whose every corner brims with wildlife, vitality, great escapes and wonderful discoveries.

The best views are from **Mount Royal Park** and beautiful **St Joseph's Oratory**. For fun, visit **La Ronde** amusement park on Isle St Helene. Top museums include the **Fine Arts** in Sherbrooke Street West, the **McCord Museum of Canadian History** and the **Château Ramezay Museum** (Notre-Dame Street East).

Quebec City:

Quebec City, on Cap Diamant overlooking the St Lawrence, is North America's only fortified city. Founded by Samuel de Champlain in 1608, this picturesque historic center is split level, and the easy way to reach the Lower Town is by funicular, from Terrasse Dufferin. The heart of this quarter is **Place Royale** and the **Petit-Champlain** quarter, where the many 17th- and 18th-century buildings have now become boutiques and restaurants: the focal points are **Notre-Dame-des-Victoires Church** and the **old port**. The major link street to the Lower Town is Notre Dame, at the end of which ferries cross the river to Levis. The core of the city is handsome **Place d'Armes**; tiny **rue de Tresor**, off the square, is an outdoor art gallery.

Some of the oldest structures in the Upper Town include the **Ursuline Convent** (1639), the **Hôtel-Dieu Hospital** (1644) and the **Seminaire** (1678). The major landmark is the turreted **Château Frontenac Hotel**.

One sightseeing must is the **Citadel**, a star-shaped fortress with summer Changing of the Guard; guided tours are available, including the **military museum**. The Promenade des Gouveneurs follows the Citadel's outer walls to the plains of Abraham, these days called **Battlefields Park** – a green belt to Gilmour Hill. Major artworks are displayed at the **Musée du Quebec** in the park. Also see the **Musée de la Civilisation** on Dalhousie, which focuses on five themes: the human body, matter, society, language and thought; the **Artillery Park National Historic Park**, with its scale model of the city and its restored fortress area, the Redoubte Dauphine; and **Cartier-Brebeuf Park**, with its replica of Cartier's ship *La Grande Hermine*.

From the St Lawrence, a view of Quebec City dominated by the Château Frontenac Hotel

3/4 days – 629km (391 miles)

MOUNTAIN MAGIC

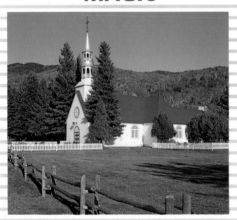

Montréal ● Saint-Jérôme ● Val-David
Sainte-Agathe-des-Monts ● Saint-Jovite
Mont-Laurier ● Maniwaki ● Hull
Saint-Eustache ● Montréal

This is the forest route to the Laurentian Mountains, land of year-round magic. Les Laurentides are noted for scenic beauty, particularly in the fall, when the trees blaze with color, but the views are splendid at other times, too: from hikers', riders' and drivers' points of view. The resort area begins 32km (20 miles) north of Montréal and boasts over 150 vacation centers within a 145km (90-mile) radius. Many of the inns and luxury resort lodges stay open in winter for the ski season, as well as providing summer activities. In spring, it's 'sugaring-off' time, when many 'sugar shacks' offer maple syrup-based meals.

SPECIAL TO . . .

3 Sainte-Agathe-des-Monts is very much a festival center. The **24 heures de la voile** (24 hours of sailing) in July is interesting for those who love the sport, with its competitions on Lac des Sables; and there is also a summer **Le Nord en Fête** and a winter **L'hiver en Nord**.

7 Hull has its share of festivities, such as the July **Folkloric Festival** and the August **Cultural Festival of Hull-West**. The biggest event is **Winterlude**, which takes place in both Ottawa and Hull each February.

FOR HISTORY BUFFS

7 The Chaudière Falls were the first big obstacle for canoes headed up the Ottawa River. In Hull's **Brebeuf Park**, as you follow the riverside path, you will see remnants of an old portage trail used by the Indians for thousands of years, and later by European explorers. A statue commemorates 17th-century missionary and martyr St Jean de Brebeuf, who traveled up the Ottawa River to work with the Huron Indians and was tortured and killed by the Iroquois in 1649.

Mont-Trèmblant is as well known for its food as for its exceptional winter sports

ⓘ 1001 rue du Square-Dorchester, Montréal

*Take **Highway 117** northwards to Saint-Jérôme.*

Saint-Jérôme, Québec

1 Gateway to the Laurentians, founded in 1830 by Curé Antoine Labelle, Saint-Jérôme played an important role in the colonization of the north. You cannot forget the curate: his statue stands in the park opposite the cathedral. Take a walk along the riverside promenade from the rue De Martigny Bridge to the rue Saint-Joseph Bridge, and read the descriptive plaques along the way; and visit the **Centre d'exposition du Vieux Palais**, the old courthouse, which houses a visual arts exhibit. Sport possibilities include golf, riding, hunting, fishing and, in winter, snowmobiling.

ⓘ 280 rue Labelle

*Take **Highway 117** north to Val-David.*

Val-David, Québec

2 A delightful, well-known tourist center that has become an artists' colony. Many of these artisans have shops and welcome visitors to watch them work as well as buy the products. There are the boutiques, cafés,

A spectacular display of fall foliage in the Gatineau Hills

high quality restaurants and charming inns, and plenty of year-round outdoor activities over and above the ski centers of **Mont-Alta** and **Vallée-Bleue**.

ⓘ 2265 rue de l'Église (open mid-June to Labor Day)

*Continue on **Highway 117** to Sainte-Agathe-des-Monts.*

Saint Agathe-des-Monts, Québec

3 You may want to stay in the oldest of the Laurentian resorts, located on the shores of Lac Sables and often called The Metropolis of the Laurentians. Its 26km (16 miles) of beaches attract swimmers and dedicated watersport enthusiasts, especially sailors. Chair lifts operate year round for panoramic views. The nearby **Village du Mont-Castor** features new but typical Québecois homes – the owners are so proud of their recreated turn-of-the-century village that they have no objection to slow driving, admiring tourists.

ⓘ 190 rue Principale Est

*Continue on **Highway 117** to Saint-Jovite.*

Saint-Jovite, Québec

4 An appealing resort with small inns, restaurants and boutiques, where the summer action is quite lively along rue Ouimet. Saint-Jovite is located on the road to **Mont-Tremblant**, a famous winter resort that borders on **Parc du Mont-Tremblant** (Mont-Tremblant Park).

ⓘ 305 chemin Brébeuf

*Continue on **Highway 117** to Mont-Laurier.*

Mont-Laurier, Québec

5 This regional capital on rich forested land was named in honor of the first francophone Roman Catholic Canadian Prime Minister, Sir Wilfrid Laurier (1841–1919). Admire the architecture along rue de la Madone, visit the typical Québecois **maison Alix-Bail** (1819) on rue du Portage, home of one of the first settlers, and stop off at the **Abbaye des Moniales Benedictines**, on boulevard Albiny-Paquette, which has one

of the province's largest goat-breeding farms, and sells goat-milk chocolate. The **Monument to Loggers** is a fine piece of sculpture in parc Toussaint-Lachapelle.

ⓘ 177 Boulevard Paquette

*Take **Highway 117**, then **105** south to Maniwaki.*

Maniwaki, Québec

6 The main service center for northern Outaouais is in the heart of the Gatineau Valley. Like many towns in this region, Maniwaki's history relates to the lumber industry, and the piece of sculpture in **parc de la Drave**, at the entrance to the town, recalls the history of the log drives on the Gatineau and Desert rivers. Irish timber merchant Charles Logue built the granite **Château Logue** on the banks of the Desert River in 1887, and it has since become Québec's first interpretive center, focusing on forest conservation.

*Continue south on **Highway 105** to Hull.*

Hull, Québec

7 A stop at this major city on the shores of the Outaouais River (Ottawa River) is usually combined with a visit to the federal capital of Ottawa (in Ontario). It was founded in 1800 by Loyalist Philemon Wright, who saw the potential of the Outaouais forest. Until recently Hull was *the* place for nightlife for visitors to Ottawa, who had to cross the river to get a late-night drink and music. **Place Aubry**, with its cafés and bars, continues to be an attractive place on a summer's evening.

The most impressive buildings are the **City Hall**, with its 19m (63-foot) glass wall, where theatrical and community or special events are put on, and the **Museum of Canadian Civilization**, also on rue Laurier, rising up to face the Parliament Buildings on the opposite bank. Among the museum's highlights are the exhibits on the Indian people; to see this new museum properly you will need at least three hours. It also houses an **Imax-Omnimax theater**,

FOR CHILDREN

2 **Le Village-du-Père-Noël**, on **Highway 177**, near Val-David, gives children the wonderful world of Santa Claus in summer. Here he has his chapel, Kingdom of the Animals, automatons and mini-gym (open May to October).

In the Laurentian region, you will find water slides at **Sainte-Adèle** and **Saint-Saveur-des-Monts** open in summer. Hull's **Museum of Canadian Civilization (7)** has its own Children's Museum, where children are invited to explore and discover ideas and objects in a hands-on experience.

SCENIC ROUTES

To take real advantage of the Laurentian scenery you need to follow the meandering back roads. They will take you through farmlands, dairy farms and past Québecois homes among rolling hills and turn-of-the-century manor houses. You might deviate right off **Highway 117** at **Saint-Janvier**, for example, on your way to Saint-Jérôme, and you might deviate north off **Highway 158** to **Highway 329**, after passing **Lachute**, both suggested for panoramic views. Much of **Highway 117** itself is considered picturesque. In **Mont-Tremblant Park** a winding touring road stretches for 160km (100 miles) between mountain and forest, with many vantage points along the way.

RECOMMENDED WALKS

Mont-Tremblant Park, not far from Saint-Jovite (4), offers numerous scenic hiking trails with names like day du Diable, Croche, aux Rats Falls, de la Roche and de la Corniche. An easy walk is the one through the **parc regional de la Rivière-du-Nord**, at Saint-Jérôme (1), whose paths lead to Wilson Falls. Not far from Mont-Laurier (5), at Lac-du-Cerf, **Le Petit-Castor** ecological trail, a gentle 3.5km (2-mile) nature interpretation trail, is accessible from the lake, with descriptions of the local plant life along the way. The trail passes huge pines and waterfalls to a panoramic belvedere.

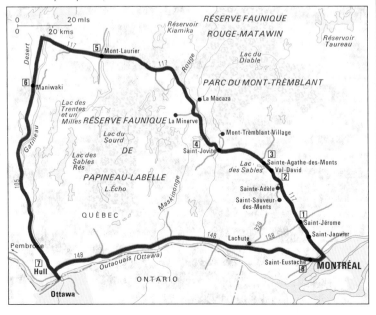

BACK TO NATURE

Réserve faunique de Papineau-Labelle, reached via **Highway 117** to La Minerve, is a wildlife reserve named after the curate, Labelle. You will find information on the different sections at the hospitality station. In addition to the flora and fauna, this is an ideal place for camping, fishing, hiking and berry-picking. **Réserve faunique Rouge-Matawin**, reached via **Highway 117** at La Macaza, covers 1,635 km (631 square miles) of lakes and forests. There are ample opportunities for outdoor activities, and more moose than anywhere else in Québec.

which plunges visitors into a 360-degree round of action. From here you can stroll to **parc Jacques Cartier** for a river cruise.

Thirty-minute tours from the tourist office to the 24th floor of the **Portage 1 Building** are available June–Labor Day. From this vantage point you can see the administrative complexes of **Place du Portage** and **Terrasses de la Chaudière**, where over 25,000 civil servants work: the view extends up and over the **Chaudières Falls** across **Parliament Hill**.

A two-hour walking tour will take you around **E B Eddy's sulphite tower and paper mill** (1900), part of Hull's heritage, and through streets which retain their turn-of-the-century architecture, such as **Champlain**, many of whose Victorian houses are now art galleries. **Place Aubry** and **promenade du Portage** are both lively; **parc du Ruisseau-de-la-Brasserie** and **parc des Portageurs** are islands of greenery.

ℹ 25 Laurier Street

*Take **Highway 148** east to Saint-Eustache.*

Saint-Eustache, Québec

8 This was the site of the worst fighting of the 1837 rebellion, when Dr Chenier led 250 patriots against 2,000 soldiers under the

Parliament Hill looms in the background behind the teepees at Hull's Museum of Civilization

command of General Sir John Colborne. The subsequent looting and burning of the village earned the general the nickname Old Firebrand, and the trace of bullets his soldiers fired can still be seen on the façade of the local **church** on rue Saint-Louis. It is worth walking around the streets of old Saint-Eustache.

One of the most historic buildings is **Moulin Legare**, Canada's only water mill, which has been in operation since it was built in 1762. It continues to provide flour (visitors may watch the process during year-round, 45-minute guided tours), which is used by many of the local restaurants.

ℹ 600 rue Dubois

*Return to Montréal via **Highway 148**.*

Montréal – Saint-Jérôme	**35 (21)**
Saint-Jérôme – Val-David	**36 (22)**
Val-David – Sainte-Agathe-des-Monts	**5 (3)**
Saint-Agathe – Saint-Jovite	**30 (19)**
Saint-Jovite – Mont-Laurier	**144 (89)**
Mont-Laurier – Maniwaki	**65 (40)**
Maniwaki – Hull	**125 (78)**
Hull – Saint-Eustache	**169 (106)**
Saint-Eustache – Montréal	**20 (13)**

This hot dog stand belies Beloeil's charming historic streets and its impressive old quarter

ℹ 1001 rue du Square-Dorchester, Montréal

> Take **Highways 10** and **112** to Chambly.

Chambly, Québec

1 A historic town in the Monteregie region, known as The Garden of Québec, Chambly has a canal on the Richelieu River whose first three locks are located where the canal crosses Bourgogne Street. This important street is noted for its 1820 **St Stephen Anglican Church** and the 1815 **Thomas Whitehead House**.

Richelieu Street is also notable: famous Canadian painter Maurice Cullen had his studio at Number 28; **Manoir Salaberry** (1814) was the home of Battle of Chateauguay hero Michel de Salaberry; and **Maison Vadeboncoeur** at Number 10 sheltered 400 men during the war of 1812. Follow this street to see Chambly's most famous site, **Fort Chambly Historic Park**. The original log fort; razed by fire, safeguarded against Indian attack. The town is also a useful base for cruises on the Richeieu River.

ℹ 1566 rue Bourgogne

> Take **Highway 112** to Granby via Rougemont.

Granby, Québec

2 Stop on the way to Granby at Rougemont, to pick apples or sample the local apple juice, cider or pie. There are many orchards here, and you can learn everything about apples at the **Centre d'interpretation de la pomme** (Apple Study Center). Nestled in the foothills of the Appalachians, this town site was part of the land granted by King George III to John Manners, Marquis of Granby, so, as you might expect, its first settlers were Loyalists.

Granby boasts fine period houses, including **Brownies Castle** on Elgin Street and **Vittie House** on Dufferin Street, which is the local history museum. Well laid out with parks, sculptures and fountains, the town is a noted gastronomic center within the Townships.

ℹ 650 rue Principale

> Continue on **Highway 112** to Magog.

THE LOYALIST ROUTE

Montréal ● Chambly ● Granby ● Magog
Sherbrooke ● Melbourne ● Drummondville
Saint-Hyacinthe ● Beloeil
Montréal

The Loyalist Route takes you through the Eastern Townships (Estrie); it was here that those colonists remaining faithful to England at the time of the Declaration of Independence took refuge. Here you will find sleepy riverside hamlets, lavish Victorian houses and covered bridges. You will find large farms in rolling countryside, a patchwork of wooded valleys and huge lakes in this French version of New England. This area is renowned for its lodging – romantic inns and little hotels – and has the largest concentration of golf courses to be found in the province.

Magog, Québec

3 This resort at the northern end of Lake Memphrémagog, not far from Mont Orford, is used for alpine skiing in winter. The region is good for all kinds of sports from horseback riding to golf and has an excellent selection of accommodation and places to eat and drink. **Centre d'Arts Orford** is an arts center hosting a mixture of art exhibitions and musical presentations. The best spot for outdoor activities is the **parc de récréation du Mont-Orford**. You can take a cruise on Lake Memphrémagog or visit the health spa, **Institut Andreanne**, which specializes in hydrotherapy, or visit a nearby vineyard.

ℹ 1032 rue Principale Ouest

> Take **Highway 108** to Sherbrooke.

SPECIAL TO ...

This tour circuit is a very festive one with something going on almost everywhere on the route. One popular occasion is Granby's **Gastronomic Festival** (2), from the end of September to the end of October, when various restaurants highlight their specialities. The town also hosts a fall **Song Festival**. Magog's **September Festival of Colors** involves a parade and a variety of competitions and displays (3). The province's largest big band festival takes place in Sherbrooke in May, and this city is equally busy in July with its **Fête du Lac des Nations**, and in August with an amateur theater festival, plus a regional fair **Expo Plus** (4). Traditions from all over the world are celebrated in July in Drummondville's **World Folklore Festival** (6).

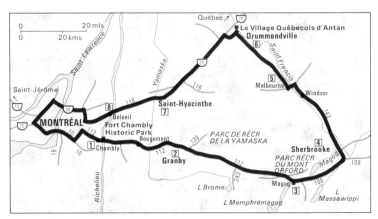

FOR HISTORY BUFFS

1 Fort Chambly National Historic Park can be visited any time of year. The French, under Jacques de Chambly, chose this strategic position on the shore of the Richelieu River to repel Indian attacks in 1665. The stone fortifications you see today date from 1709. Here you will see how garrison life was between the 17th and 19th centuries.

6 Le Village Québecois d'Antan re-creates typical 19th-century life in the Drummondville area as a living pioneer museum. Costumed craftsmen demonstrate their various trades, from boot-making to bread-baking and wool-spinning in many of the 70 buildings (open June–Labor Day).

FOR CHILDREN

2 The best bet for children is Granby's **zoo**, where hundreds of animals and birds are on display: reckon on half a day (open May–October). Children should also enjoy the fare in the rustic sugarhouses: crêpes, baked beans and ham, with plenty of maple syrup.

SCENIC ROUTES

Of particular panoramic interest is the touring area around Magog (**Highway 112**) and the stretch between Sherbrooke and Melbourne (**Highway 143**).

RECOMMENDED WALKS

Nature lovers will enjoy walking in **Parc du récréation de la Yamaska** (Yamaska Park) in Granby (2) and in the **Mont-Orford Park** at Magog in the foothills of the Appalachians (3). In Sherbrooke, they will enjoy a stroll through the **Old North Ward** and along the banks of the **Magog River** (4).

A mist rising up from the valley of the Saint François River at Melbourne, near Sherbrooke

Sherbrooke, Québec

4 Sherbrooke is a major metropolis, home to the majority of the region's population and nicknamed Queen of the Eastern Townships. Walk up King Street Hill and you will find plenty of green space in the parks of **Jacques Cartier**, **Victoria** and **Blanchard**. In the latter, the **Maison de l'Eau** offers films and displays on the aquatic environment, as well as nature interpretation tours. You can downhill ski and waterski in the heart of Sherbrooke.

The city has first-class accommodations, restaurants and art galleries. Don't miss the **Fine Arts Museum**, downtown on Palais, or a look at the period architecture (Victorian) in the **Old North Ward**. The **Natural Science Museum and Seminary**, on rue Marquette, is another good rainy day suggestion. Look up the **Historical Society**, based at Domaine Howard, formerly the estate of Senator Charles Howard. The Society has developed heritage tours of the city that include the **old courthouse**, **St Peter's Church** and **St Michel Cathedral**.

ⓘ 2883 rue King Ouest

*Take **Highway 143** to Melbourne.*

Melbourne, Québec

5 Make a quick stop here for a picture of locally celebrated **St Andrew's Church**, which until 1967 was pictured on the back of the $2 bill. The century-old **Musée de la Société d'histoire du Comte de Richmond** is an old farmhouse which re-creates a typical household of the era and illustrates the settlers' way of life.

*Continue on **Highway 143** to Drummondville.*

Drummondville, Québec

6 This large industrial city is actually located in the region called the Heart of Québec. Founded in 1815, it takes its name from Lord Drummond, who was Canada's governor at the time. It expanded industrially after dams on the St Francis River and the Hemming Falls produced electrical energy. Overlooking the river is the **parc des Voltigeurs** where, in 1812, the Voltigeur regiment defeated the American army; today it is ideal for camping. Close to the city is the outdoor recreation center of **Loisirs**, where you can spend the day sailing, canoeing or hiking; the admission price varies according to chosen activities.

ⓘ 1045 rue Hains

*Take **Highway 20** to Saint-Hyacinthe.*

Saint-Hyacinthe, Québec

7 Québec's Capital of Food Growers is a large heritage city, which holds an annual July Regional Agricultural Fair and a weekly livestock auction. The best way to see Saint-Hyacinthe is to start at the western end, where the **Porte des Anciens Maires** stands – a gateway that is carved with maple leaves and a French cockerel. Near by, the **Louis-Cote Terrace** borders the Yamaska River, and on Girouard Street both the steepled **cathedral** and the **Bishop's residence** are handsome examples of Victorian architecture. **Maison Casavant et Frères** is renowned for making organs sold throughout the world for more than a century, and used in countless churches.

ⓘ 780 rue Hôtel de Ville

*Continue on **Highway 116** to Beloeil.*

A more traditional view of the pleasant town of Beloeil

Beloeil, Québec

8 Beloeil is a splendid town to wander around, with views of the Richelieu and Mont Saint-Hilaire. One of the most historic streets is **rue Richelieu**, with its 1895 **church**, an old **windmill** and **Maison Guertin**. The oldest structure of all is the 1772 **Maison Prevert**. The old quarter of Beloeil bustles with boutiques, art galleries, craft shops and interesting restaurants.

ⓘ 35 Boulevard Laurier (open June–Labor Day)

*Return to Montréal along **Highway 20**.*

Montréal – Chambly **49 (30)**
Chambly – Granby **44 (27)**
Granby – Magog **52 (33)**
Magog – Sherbrooke **37 (23)**
Sherbrooke – Melbourne **39 (24)**
Melbourne – Drummondville **39 (24)**
Drummondville – Saint-Hyacinthe **52 (32)**
Saint-Hyacinthe – Beloeil **25 (16)**
Beloeil – Montréal **33 (21)**

BACK TO NATURE

2 Recommended for nature lovers is the **Centre d'interpretation de la nature du Lac-Boivin** in Granby, which teems with swamp life. If you are fascinated by flora and fauna, take to one of the trails or just observe it all from the special viewing tower. The welcome center often shows related exhibits, and its shops sell items of interest to the amateur ecologist.

3/4 days – 623km (387 miles)

A PARADISE FOR PAINTERS

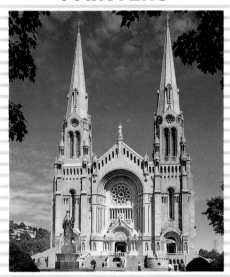

Québec City • Beaupré • Baie-Saint-Paul
La Malbaie • Baie-Saint Catherine/
Tadoussac • Chicoutimi • Jonquière
Hébertville • Québec City

This tour takes you through a good portion of the Charlevoix region, where a series of capes, headlands, bays and gorges through which torrents gush make up the dramatic – sometimes austere – scenery that has attracted so many artists. You will hear sailing stories and the sound of the sea; you will find hushed villages in fertile valleys; liquid silver lakes and flowering meadows. On route there are intimate inns and baronial manors in which to stay, and choice restaurants in which to sample the favorite smelt or lamb dishes and Québec's meat pie, the *tourtière*. In French-speaking Canada, the quality of the food is as high as you would expect.

SPECIAL TO . . .

Sainte-Anne-de-Beaupré has a number of annual religious events, the highlight of which is the **Feast of Sainte-Anne** on July 26, when there are long torch-lit processions (1). Seasonal art events and exhibitions frequently take place in the Baie-Saint-Paul (2) and La Malbaie (3) areas, and Baie-Sainte-Catherine holds a summer **Beluga Whale Festival** (4). Jonquière's celebrations include a summer fête with parades and dances and a winter festival which combines cultural and fresh-air activities (6).

FOR HISTORY BUFFS

7 Not far from Hébertville, on **Highway 169**, is the historic village of **Val-Jalbert**. When the pulpmill closed in 1927, company employees deserted it, though the site around a waterfall is an impressive one and can be seen at ground level or by cable car. The old houses and shops have all been restored.

Sainte-Anne-de-Beaupré, one of Canada's most famous shrines, attracts thousands of pilgrims from far and wide

ℹ️ 60 rue d'Auteuil, Québec City

*Take **Highway 138** to Beaupré (Sainte-Anne-de-Beaupré).*

Beaupré, Québec

1 Sainte-Anne-de-Beaupré is on the northern bank of the St Lawrence River, and its shrine is one of Canada's most famous. Pilgrims have been coming here since 1658, when the community only comprised 25 families and was called Petit-Cap. In 1872 the first **basilica** was constructed, replaced in 1926 with what you see today. 'Miraculous cures' were the reason for so much dedication, and a good number of the sick continue to claim that visits and water from the **Sainte Anne Falls** are beneficial. In any case, the neo-Romanesque **basilica** is magnificent, noted for its huge dimensions, stained glass windows and mosaics. One enormous piece of oak was used for the statue of the saint, crowned with gold and precious stones, and in the chapel behind, a silver reliquary contains a portion of the saint's forearm. Across from the basilica, the **Commemorative Chapel** was built in 1878 with materials from the old church, and also on site are the **Scala Santa** (Holy Stairs) and the **Way of the Cross** – a series of life-size statues. Guided tours of the complex are available all year round. **Cyclorama de Jerusalem**, on rue Regina, allows you to make a visual

Tadoussac's commanding position at the mouth of the Saguenay has ensured its continued existence

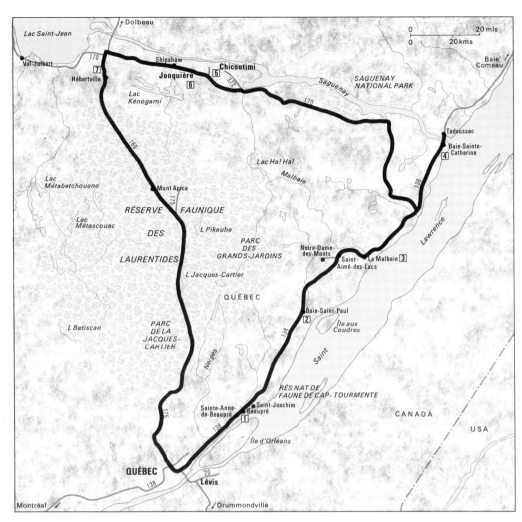

journey to the Holy Land by means of a huge mural (open April–November); and in the **Edison Museum**, on avenue Royal, more than 100 old gramophones and phonographs have been beautifully restored. In the **Alphonse Pare Workshop**, on the same avenue, you can see a mural depicting Canada's stories and legends, as well as local craftwork.

*Continue on **Highway 138** to Baie-Saint-Paul.*

Baie-Saint-Paul, Québec

2 This lovely little town was first settled in 1678, and became for a long time the only important settlement between Saint-Joachim and Tadoussac. Walk along its narrow streets, lined with houses over two centuries old. Near the disused wharf, a protected harbor is used by pleasure boats; at high tide you will see colorful windsurfers. Baie-Saint-Paul is also popular for gliding and for cycling. The local beauty spot is the **Bas-de-la-Baie Falls**, but there are many stunning views over the bay from lookout points in the surrounding mountains. The landscapes are enchanting enough to have been captured on canvas by countless artists, among them Clarence Gagnon, Marc-Aurele Fortin, René Richard and Jean-Paul Lemieux; the whole town is imbued with an infectious creative excitement.

i 4 rue Fafard

*Continue on **Highway 138** to La Malbaie.*

La Malbaie, Québec

3 Samuel de Champlain's ships ran aground here in 1608, so he called the place La Malbaie (The Bad Bay). It has since become the region's administration center. There are several historic properties in town, including the old **courthouse** and **prison** on chemin de Vallée (1860) and a century-old **blacksmith's**. The main museum is **Musée regional Laure-Conan**, on rue Patrick Morgan, specializing in popular art.

Southwest of the town is the pretty resort village of **Pointe-au-Pic**, whose grand hotel, **Manoir Richelieu**, is a superb place to stay if you like an old-fashioned style. Walk down **Boulevard des Falaises**: lovely homes have been built in the past against the mountainside; and along **avenue Richelieu**, where you will find art galleries and handicrafts. On **Boulevard de Comporte** there is a small 1867 **Protestant church**.

i 166 Boulevard de Comporte

*Continue north on **Highway 138** to Baie-Sainte-Catherine.*

Baie-Sainte-Catherine/Tadoussac, Québec

4 A village close to the estuary of the Saguenay River, with a sand beach along the bay. From July to winter several species of whale return to the Saguenay estuary, and cruises from the wharf at Baie-Sainte-Catherine offer a close look at these huge mammals. Regular sightseeing cruises on the Saguenay are also available.

FOR CHILDREN

Children who appreciate nature will be well rewarded on this circuit, where there are plenty of opportunities to spot whales. The **Pointe-Noire** rest area, overlooking Baie-Sainte-Catherine (4), is an ideal place to learn all about whales and see them from the observation tower. Cruises operate along this coast for a closer look. Deviate off route at Hébertville (7) and you can take the kids to the **St Felicien Zoo**, where a mini-train ride will take you through the natural habitat of North American wildlife and show you a 'jobber' camp, trading post, settler's farm and traditional Indian village (open June–September).

SCENIC ROUTES

Deviate from La Malbaie via **Highway 138**, through the municipalities of Saint-Aime-des-Lacs and Notre-Dame-des-Monts, to reach the **Hautes Gorges de la rivière Malbaie**, where an impressive network of valleys slices its way through a maze of high peaks. From La Malbaie to Baie-Sainte-Catherine is a particularly picturesque coastal stretch through small ports and villages. A circular tour of **Lac-Saint-Jean** from Hébertville is a pleasing drive, and the drive back to Québec through the 10,000sq km (3,860 square-mile) wildlife reserve of **Faunique des Laurentides** is also easy on the eye.

RECOMMENDED WALKS

Parc des Grands-Jardins' **Lac des Cygnes** (Swan Lake) ecological hiking trail rambles through changing scenery for 1.5km (1 mile) to a mountain summit for a view of the Charlesvoix region's main features. **Saguenay National Park** is certainly paradise for hikers; at the information center, naturalists will explain the evolution of the fjord and its wildlife. Energetic walkers climb up **Cap Trinité** in honor of Our Lady of Saguenay – views of the fiord all along the trail are breathtaking. At **Jonquière** (6) you can stroll alongside the Saguenay River on a 7km (4-mile) trail. A tour on foot of Tadoussac (4) is a must too.

BACK TO NATURE

This is a first-class tour for nature lovers. Among the highlights are the **Réserve nationale de faune du Cap-Tourmente** at Saint-Joachim, a natural habitat of the greater snow goose. A network of trails gives access to four habitat areas where 250 species of wild birds have been recorded. Guided tours are available (open mid-April to November). The **Interpretation Center** on rue de la Cale-Seche, at Tadoussac, has exhibits on the marine life in the area plus an aquarium (4), and **parc des Grands-Jardin**'s northern forests are filled with caribou.

For two centuries visitors have found the exhilarating air of La Malbaie attractive

An eight-minute ferry ride will take you to Tadoussac, one of North America's oldest settlements. Cartier himself sheltered here in 1535 and Champlain passed through in 1603. Its strategic position at the confluence of the Saguenay and St Lawrence rivers was the reason for the first 17th-century trading fort being established here. A replica of the first trading post is **Maison Chauvin** on rue Bord-de-l'Eau (open for inspection June–September). On the same street is the old wooden chapel (1747), which contains a number of religious treasures.

ℹ 120 rue de Bateau-Passeur, Tadoussac (open June–Labor Day)

*Return along **Highway 138** and take **Highway 170** to Chicoutimi.*

Chicoutimi, Québec

5 The Indian name of this major center of the Saguenay region means 'up to where the water runs deep'. The city has a full variety of shops, restaurants and hotels, and with three rivers running through it, no shortage of boating possibilities. A recommended lookout point is the **Jacques-Cartier**, at the end of Highway 175, where you can see Mont Valin rising 304m (1,000 feet) above sea level and the northern shore of the Saguenay River.

The best place to learn about the Saguenay is the **Saguenay-Lac Saint-Jean Museum**, on rue Jacques-Cartier Est, which also features Indian artifacts, Inuit art and Victorian furniture. Local painter Arthur Villeneuve's house has become a **museum** (open May–October), on rue Tache Ouest. He painted every wall with local and national historic scenes – a project he began in 1955. Chicoutimi's **cathedral** is also worth seeing: it has handsome rose windows and wood sculptures by Laureat Vallieres. The city's main street is rue Racine. A landmark is **Sainte Anne's Cross**, at the end of rue de la Croix, built as a

protective measure for those crossing the river by wooden rafts. Down at the old harbor is the **marketplace**, which is also the departure point for cruises on the fiord.

ℹ 2525 Boulevard Talbot

*Take **Highway 170** west to Jonquière.*

Jonquière, Québec

6 In this lively industrial center the sidewalk cafés and terraces well outnumber the factories and paper mills. Aluminum is one of the products made here; note the **Aluminum Bridge**, inaugurated in 1950, weighing a third of an identical steel bridge and seemingly maintenance-free. **Alcan** gives summer tours of its factory but you need sturdy low-heeled shoes, slacks and long-sleeved shirts. No one with a pacemaker, camera or magnetic card is admitted. (Reservations for industrial visits may be made at the tourist office.) The city's main street is rue Saint-Dominique, and the best lookout point is from Mount Jacob.

ℹ 2665 Boulevard du Royaume

*Continue on **Highway 170**, then **169** south to Hébertville.*

Hébertville, Québec

7 Hébertville is a base for touring blueberry country in an area dotted with lakes. Spring visitors should be sure to taste maple syrup at the local maple grove. The neighboring mountains are used as a setting for summer theater, and in winter for skiing.

ℹ 17 rue Commerciale (open June–Labor Day)

*Take **Highway 169** south through the Reserve fauniques des Laurentides to Québec.*

*Attractive stone-built Presbytere
Deschambault, near Trois-Rivières*

ℹ️ 60 rue d'Aeutuil, Québec City

*Take **Highway 138** to Champlain.*

Champlain, Québec

1 A former mail station on the King's Highway, Champlain has a neo-Romanesque **church** built in 1879 and is surrounded by buildings of similar architecture. A visit to the **Observatory** will help you become more familiar with astronomy (open summer only). In nearby Batiscan, there are good views of the river from the pier, and the **old presbytery** on rue Principale has become famous for its authentic period furnishings.

*Continue on **Highway 138** to Trois-Rivières.*

Trois-Rivières, Québec

2 This major administrative, industrial and cultural center has plenty of tourist facilities, and is set midway between Montréal and Québec. All types of shipping come through its inland seaport and there are many historic reminders of its past. (The city was founded in 1634 on the site where Champlain had earlier established a fur-trading post.) The lovely **cathedral** on rue Bonaventure is the only Westminster-style church in North America, built between 1854 and 1858. On the same street the **Manoir Boucher-de-Niverville** (1730) is a museum dedicated to one of its owners, Sieur Boucher de Niverville, who spoke the Indian language and was superintendent of the Abenakis. Beside the manor is a statue of former Premier Maurice Le Noblet Duplessis. Walk towards rue Notre-Dame and you will see the **Sacred Heart Monument** and the impressive post office located on **Le Platon** – land shaped like a small ball of wool (*peleton*). When the first settlers arrived, Le Platon proved a strategic point for a fur-trading post, followed by governors' residences and military barracks. A statue of founder Laviolette is another reminder of early colonization. (Summer guided walking tours of the old quarter of the city are organized by the local tourist office.)

One of the most important historic streets is **rue des Ursulines**, where

THE HEART OF THE PROVINCE

3 days – 450km (280 miles)

Québec City • Champlain • Trois-Rivières
Joliette • Sorel • Nicolet • Bécancour
Saint-Nicolas • Québec City

This tour takes you through the heart of the province where the majestic St Lawrence River flows and much of the population lives. Part of the route is along Chemin Du Roi (King's Highway), **Highway 138**, inaugurated in 1737 when it stimulated and developed commercial activity throughout New France. To travel it is to have a picture of both old and new Québec as it winds its way through historic villages and resort centers. Many of the first French settlers built their farms on this land, in long strips starting at the river bank, and much of it is used today for tobacco farming, while the river's south shore overflows with maple groves.

the rebuilt **Manoir de Tonnancour**'s unique architecture lends character to the events held here, and the **Maison Hertel-de-la-Fresniere** (1821) exhibits works of local and regional artists and contains the 'house of wines'. The **Ursuline Museum** is notable: the Ursuline Order greatly influenced Trois-Rivières' history, and the museum displays a collection of sculpture, plate, art, embroidery and furniture. There are several other worthwhile museums: **Musée Pierre Boucher**, whose exhibits include archaeological finds and home furnishings from bygone eras; the **Crypt Museum**, which presents

RECOMMENDED WALKS

The villages and heritage towns encountered on route are best seen on foot and the parks are perfect for easy walking, but this region is not of specialist interest to hikers.

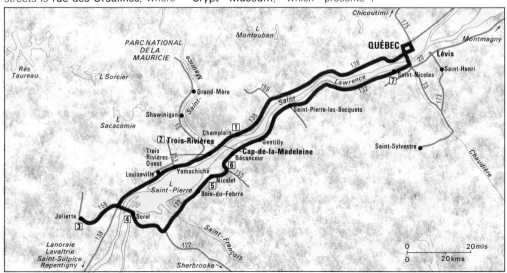

SPECIAL TO …

2 Trois-Rivières has several celebrations, most notably the **summer festival**, when there are shows for children, parades and music that goes on for 10 days. In early September, the **International Canoe Classic** features competitive events for North America's best canoeists. The most famous religious event is the **Novens of the Assumption** in August at Notre-Dame-du-Cap. Food festivals in the area include fish stews around Sorel and, in spring, plenty of maple syrup parties.

FOR HISTORY BUFFS

2 The **Shrine of Notre-Dame-du-Cap** is Québec's third most important pilgrimage site, dedicated to Our Lady of the Rosary. (The first pilgrimage took place in 1863.) The modern style basilica is noted for its stained glass windows and organ, but the old 1714 chapel is also on the site. Religious services are often held in both the chapel and the basilica. The Shrine is located in Cap-de-la-Madeleine, at the confluence of the Saint-Maurice and St Lawrence rivers.

FOR CHILDREN

Take the children to a sugaring-off party. Every spring, the sugar shacks in **Pays-de-l'Erable** (Maple Country) are the focus of traditional festivities, in small villages not far from Québec and this touring route. Once sunny days are following cold nights, the time has come to tap the maple trees, and as soon as the season starts, people flock to the sugar shacks to sample taffy and enjoy the lively atmosphere. Most shacks serve meals and sell products: you will find them in Saint-Henri, Saint-Sylvestre and surroundings.

SCENIC ROUTES

Chemin du Roi (King's Road, **Highway 138**) is an excellent scenic route. It winds through the ancient seigniories of Pointe-aux-Trembles, Repentigny, Saint-Sulpice, Lavaltrie and Lanoraie as it closely follows the north shore of the St Lawrence. There are many scenic side trips to beauty spots: from Louisville on **Highway 348** to Chutes-Sainte-Ursule (waterfalls), for instance, or from Yamachiche on **Highway 153** to Chutes a Magnan (waterfalls). Deviate off the route (**Highway 55**) and visit **Parc national de la Mauricie**, where a 60km (37 miles) paved tourist road leads you through delightful scenery.

Aerial view of one of Joliette's tobacco farms, a noted area of industry and agriculture

aspects of the life of Father Frederic Jansoone, who in 1888 purportedly saw the miraculous opening of the eyes of the statue of the Virgin at the Notre-Dame-du-Cap Shrine; and the **Archaeological Museum**, which focuses on evolution and French pre-history.

The iron industry has always been important to Canada; vestiges of the first foundry (1730) are to be found in **Les Forges du Saint-Maurice National Historic Park**, along with the remains of the Master's house, models, murals and an interpretative center. Paper continues to be a priority industry, and several paper mills are still dominant; the Saint Maurice River holds floating logs commonly referred to in the region as *pitounes*. Photos and models of industry-related equipment can be seen at the **Pulp and Paper Industry Exhibition Center**.

The city has several parks, including **parc Champlain** and **parc de l'Ile Saint-Quentin**, nice for a picnic, and cruises on the river are available.

ℹ 168 rue Bonaventure

*Take **Highway 138**, then **158** to Joliette.*

Joliette, Québec

3 This is the main center of the De Lanaudière region – an industrial, commercial and farming town, not far from Montréal. Established in 1841, it takes its name from founder Barthelemi Joliette, a descendant of that more famous Joliette who explored the Mississippi. Visit the **Musée de Joliette**, see **St Paul's Church**, sample spa water from the **Esplanade fountains** and browse for handicrafts. For sporting summer activities, you will find several resort areas close to town, including Rouge des Pins and Lake Cloutier.

ℹ 70 Place Bourger, bureau 301 (September–end June)

*Backtrack on **Highway 158** and cross the river to Sorel.*

Sorel, Québec

4 Sorel is a historic town, Canada's fourth oldest, dating to 1642 and centered by a handsome park, **Carre Royal**, designed in the shape of a Union Jack. A bustling port with a first-class marina, its most notable buildings include **St Peter's Church** on rue Georges, the Anglican **Christ Church** facing the port, and the **Governor's House** on chemin des Patriotes. There is a busy **marketplace** at the end of rue Roi and a wonderful view of the St Lawrence from the wharf. The nearby village of Sainte-Anne-de-Sorel is the departure point for a leisurely cruise of several small islands, associated with the author Germaine Guevremont.

ℹ 373 Boulevard Fiset

*Take **Highway 132** to Nicolet.*

A small rural community on the north shore of the St Lawrence

Nicolet, Québec

5 Nicolet is a religious center with many churches and convents, such as the richly decorated **cathedral**, known for its large stained glass window and modern style. All aspects of numerous religions are covered in **Musée des Religions** in rue Evariste Lecompte. Also see the birthplace of painter-engraver Rudolphe Duguay in its beautiful setting on **rang Saint-Alexis** with its impressive exhibition of furnishings and antiques.

ℹ Boulevar Louis-Fréchette

*Continue on **Highway 132** to Bécancour.*

Bécancour, Québec

6 A city formed by the merging of several villages, Bécancour today plays a major role in the region's economy, with the development of an industrial park and the Gentilly Nuclear Power Station. This is very much a 20th-century center, though the turn-of-the-century **Saint Gregory Church** (Eglise Saint-Grégoire) contains original furniture and decorative ornaments, and the **old mill** just off Highway 132 has recently been renovated to preserve some of the area's heritage.

*Continue on **Highway 132** to Saint-Nicolas.*

Saint-Nicolas, Québec

7 Stop for a photograph of the Pierre Laporte and Québec bridges. Saint-Nicolas, being so close to the city, provides the most unique view of them—the old cantilevered Québec Bridge supposedly has a longer span between its pillars than any other bridge. The **Saint-Nicolas Church** is unusual: it represents an enormous ship anchored in the St Lawrence, and its interior makes colorful use of marble and wood.

*Continue on **Highway 132** to Québec City.*

Québec City – Champlain **108 (67)**
Champlain – Trois-Rivières **17 (11)**
Trois-Rivières – Joliette **84 (52)**
Joliette – Sorel **33 (21)**
Sorel – Nicolet **57 (35)**
Nicolet – Bécancour **26 (16)**
Bécancour – Saint-Pierre-les-Becquets **30 (19)**
Saint-Pierre – Saint-Nicolas **68 (42)**
Saint-Nicolas – Québec **27 (17)**

BACK TO NATURE

Experience nature by staying at a farm or by fishing for tomcod, which in winter swim under the ice of the Sainte-Anne River. At the **Baie-du-Fêvre**, not far from Nicolet, every spring and fall thousands of wildfowl, including snow geese, pause in the surrounding fields for a quick rest. The **Parc des Chutes-de-Shawinigan** is a permanent home to white-tailed deer and, further on, **Parc national de la Mauricie** is a retreat for moose.

ONTARIO

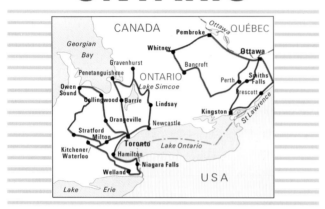

'**E**xpansive' is a good word to describe Ontario, a province justifiably called 'Shining Waters' by the Indians. There are 1 million sq km (400,000 square miles) of water shimmering in 250,000 lakes, rippling in rivers and canals, cascading at Niagara. Boating is more of a way of life than a pastime, and has been ever since the days when the Indians and the fur traders relied on canoes for transport. These days the choice is more varied: houseboats and cruise boats, sail boats and speed boats to take you into the nooks and crannies of waterways and islands.

A lot of the land is covered by forest, often set aside as a park, like the wild nature of Algonquin. This natural beauty is often accessible from lively, sophisticated cities, such as metropolitan Toronto, or Canada's legislative capital, Ottawa.

From the fertile farmland of the southwest to the rugged terrain in the far north, this province is truly one of contrasts, where wander-lust will be well rewarded. You might take to the route used by the first traders, or that of the Loyalist settlers; you might circle the Niagara Peninsula, home of acres of vineyards, or follow the shore of the world's largest freshwater lake, Lake Superior. You will pass through picturesque villages like Niagara-on-the-Lake, or perhaps take to a heritage canal like the Trent-Severn. The highways and byways will lead you to silver and lumber communities, to forts and battle sites and re-created pioneer villages.

After the British and French, waves of other immigrants came to Ontario, helping to characterize the small towns and bringing their festivals with them. That is why the world's second largest Oktoberfest takes place in this province, in Kitchener and Waterloo, and that is why Highland Games in Fergus and other towns acknowledge a Scottish heritage. Almost every community in Ontario boasts a pioneer museum.

Festivals are not always ethnic, and not always summertime affairs, for when the lakes freeze over in winter it is ice fishing time – especially in Georgina, during the annual Great Lake Simcoe Derby. This is skating time, too, even for civil servants, who go to work this way along the 8km (5-mile) Rideau Canal.

There is space and power in Ontario, a province that gives you the choice or combination of world-class museums, galleries and shops, with tranquil scenic splendor and adventurous outdoor activities to suit the keenest enthusiast. The Arts are taken as seriously as history; the preservation of beauty spots is as important as financial security.

Toronto:

Toronto, a dynamic, waterfronted cosmopolitan city, is Canada's commercial heart, film and communications center with a resort atmosphere. Situated on the shores of Lake Ontario, its dominating landmarks are the 553m (1,815-foot) free-standing **CN Tower**, and the massive **SkyDome**, whose field could hold eight Boeing 747s. The harbor is Canada's largest inland port, but the waterfront also has boutiques, restaurants and the antique market on Harborfront, as well as the rides and amusements of **Ontario Place**. You can take a ferry to the islands in the lake for summer sunning; take in the view from the **Leslie Street Spit**; visit **The Beaches**; or take a glass-topped boat tour.

Browse in Toronto's many shops: in elegant **Yorkville**, where Victorian buildings have been converted to cafés and specialty shops; along **Yonge Street** where the **Eaton Centre** is a famous shopping emporium; in the underground malls; in **Kensington Market**'s narrow streets, and in **Chinatown**, along Spadina Avenue. Don't miss the fruit and vegetable market in **St Lawrence Hall**.

There are treasures galore in the **Royal Ontario Museum**, including a Dinosaur Gallery; and you can enjoy more than 15,000 works of art in the **Art Gallery of Ontario** and hands-on exhibits in the **Ontario Science Centre**. Laser concerts are held in the **McLaughlin Planetarium**, and among the best places for cultural performances are the **O'Keefe Centre** and **Roy Thompson Hall**.

Ottawa:

Ottawa is a national capital on a bluff overlooking the Ottawa River, where the Changing of the Guard takes place, British fashion, on Parliament Hill, the heart of the city: tours take you through the Parliament Building, three Gothic stone buildings with copper roofs which form Canada's seat of government; and the Noon Day Gun is fired.

The city is notable for its arts and museums: Canada's cultural heritage is traced in the **Canadian Museum of Civilisation**; its battles in the **Canadian War Museum**. Not to be missed are the **National Museum of Natural Sciences** and the **National Museum of Science and Technology**. Among the historic residences, **Laurier House** (1878) has been the fine home of two prime ministers, and the **Mackenzie King Estate** has a beautiful setting. The best place to appreciate art is the **National Gallery of Canada**; best place for The Arts is the **National Arts Centre**, where performances range from puppet shows to symphony orchestras.

The dazzling splendor of Toronto's lakeshore skyline by night. The revolving CN Tower catches the eye

2 days – 453km (281 miles)

A TRIP TO THE FALLS

Toronto • Oakville • Hamilton • Stoney Creek • St Catharines • Niagara-on-the-Lake Niagara Falls • Fort Erie • Port Colborne Welland • Dundas • Kitchener/Waterloo Milton • Toronto

One of the most popular areas of the province, the Niagara Peninsula is also one of the most fertile. The dominant feature of this tour is Niagara Falls, but side roads will take you through vineyards and tobacco fields, through small villages to historic sites. There are plenty of inns *en route* and good places to eat – or sample Canada's wines in this prime grape-growing area. This is an ideal tour for those who like plenty to see at a leisurely pace.

SPECIAL TO...

There are many festivals concerned with fruit on this route. **The Niagara Grape and Wine Festival**, in late September in St Catharines (4), has 10 days of floats and sports events. The **Blossom Festival** takes place at the Falls (6) in April/May, when the parks are in full bloom. Unusual festivals include the June **Dundas Kite Fest** and the August **Dundas Cactus Festival** (10). **The Shaw Festival**, at Niagara-on-the-Lake (5), is where George Bernard Shaw plays are performed in Queen Street theaters between April and October. Kitchener/ Waterloo's **Oktoberfest** (11) is Canada's largest, with all the beer, bands and sausages worthy of German origins. Niagara Falls' **Festival of Lights** (6), between November and February, is an impressive occasion.

ⓘ 290 Yonge Street, Toronto

*Take **Highway 2** from Toronto to Oakville.*

Oakville, Ontario

1 A prosperous and attractive harbor-fronted community situated on Lake Ontario, only 34km (21 miles) from Toronto. It has graciously preserved its 19th-century charm, and you could perhaps visit the **Thomas House** (1829) and the old **Post Office** (1835) in Lakeside Park. A later-dated mansion at Lakeside has been converted into the **Gairloch Gallery** (1922). At **Bronte Creek Provincial Park** there is a working turn-of-the-century farm and children's farm. Wagon and tractor tours are given around the area. At the **Glen Abbey Golf Club** there is a championship course, and in the Golf House, the **Canadian Golf Hall of Fame and Museum**.

ⓘ 170 Country Squire Lane

*Continue on **Highway 2** to Hamilton.*

Hamilton, Ontario

2 This surprisingly smart, small city is Canada's steel capital. At the heart of downtown you can shop and eat well at **Jackson Square**, a mall that is linked to the **Sheraton Hotel**, the **Copps Coliseum**, the **Art Gallery of Hamilton** and **Hamilton Place**. Don't miss a look at **Farmers' Market**, beneath the library in this mall: farmers from all over southern

'The Owl and the Pussycat' – typical of the delightfully restored shopfronts in Niagara-on-the-Lake

Ontario converge here on Tuesdays, Thursdays, Fridays and Saturdays.

Hamilton boasts several interesting museums: the **Canadian Football Hall of Fame** at Civic Square traces the game's history, while the small **Children's Museum** on Main Street East is especially designed for the under-13s, with hands-on 'teaching' exhibits. The wonder of Victorian engineering can be explored in the **Museum of Steam and Technology**, housed in the old 1859 Waterworks on Woodward Avenue, but if you have a taste for military life, visit the **Military Museum**, in the grounds of Dundurn Castle, where memorabilia dates from 1700 to World War II.

Out at the airport the **Canadian Warplane Heritage Museum** keeps all its World War II aircraft in flying condition. The elegant Victorian mansion of **Whitehern**, at the corner of Jackson and McNab Streets, preserves the style of life of the prominent McQuestern family, who lived here from 1852 to 1968. At **Kartworld**, on Upper James, a 1,219m (4,000-foot) go-carting track has a double overpass and underpass; and there are bumper boats for the less daring souls. On the gentler side, Hamilton is often the base for scenic excursions to 22 surrounding conservation areas, such as **Christie**, just moments from downtown, with green hills and a sandy beach around the lake; or the **Spencer Gorge Wilderness Area**, where the Tew's Falls are only slightly smaller than Niagara. The **Royal Botanical Gardens** are 1,092 hectares (2,700 acres) filled with gardens where the highlights are May lilacs and summer roses.

ⓘ 1 James Street

*Take Queen Elizabeth Way (**QEW**) to Stoney Creek.*

Stoney Creek, Ontario

3 In 1812 Stoney Creek was a mere village, and it was here that one of the most significant battles took place between the Canadians and the Americans. To commemorate the Battle of Stoney Creek, **Battlefield House** (a 1795 settler's home) is now a museum, where costumed guides take you on a tour of its rooms. Another historic site is the **Erland Lee Home**, on Ridge Road, which used to be the residence of the co-founder of the Women's Institute, Janet Lee, in 1897. Now a museum, it houses some of the original furniture built by James Lee.

Conservation areas in the surrounds include **Devil's Punch Bowl** (noted by geologists for its exposed rock strata), with a dramatic waterfall and engaging view. **Felker's Falls** is another viewpoint within easy distance.

ⓘ 6 King Street East

***QEW** continues to St Catharines.*

St Catharines, Ontario

4 This is 'the Garden City', thanks to the bounty of fruit grown in the surrounding belt of land, in the heart of wine country. Originally, St

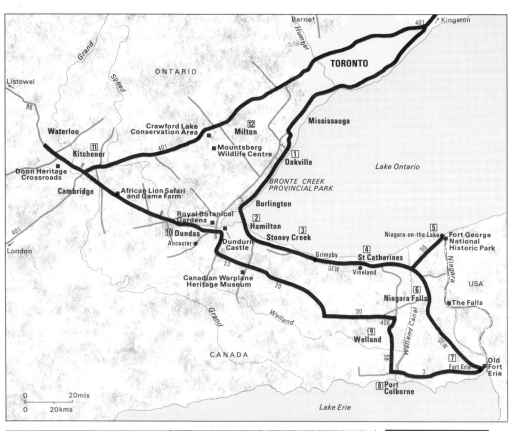

This deceptively pleasant spot in Stoney Creek in fact commemorates an important battle in 1812 between America and Canada

Catharines was settled by the Loyalists. It had been a depot of the Underground Railway and the site of the first Welland Canal. Remnants of the first three canals can be seen throughout the city. At **Port Dalhousie**, where the Loyalists entered Lake Ontario, you will see locks, weirs and lighthouses, and at **Mountain Locks Park**, where the second canal climbed the Niagara Escarpment, there are locks and early industrial mills. At **Lock III**, a new visitor center enables you to watch ships passing between Lakes Erie and Ontario. In the **museum** next

door there is a working model of one of the first wooden locks.

At **Tivoli Miniature World**, near Vineland, the world's favorite landmark buildings can be seen in scaled-down detail.

ℹ️ 11 King Street

*Take **Highway 55** north to Niagara-on-the-Lake.*

Niagara-on-the-Lake, Ontario

5 Although the population is too great for this to be considered a village, Niagara-on-the-Lake has village appeal. Carefully and lovingly preserved, it is a pretty 19th-century town in a delightful Lake Ontario setting at the mouth of the Ontario River. It was also the first capital of Upper Canada (Ontario) between 1791 and 1796. Few visitors can

FOR HISTORY BUFFS

5 **Fort George National Historic Park**, just outside Niagara-on-the-Lake, gives interpretive tours of the officers' quarters, barracks, guard room and ramparts.

7 **Old Fort Erie**, south of the Peace Bridge, was first built in 1794. Now restored, it contains relics and equipment used by both the British and American armies. The best time for a visit is in summer, when the guard, appropriately dressed in period uniform, perform their military drills.

FOR CHILDREN

2 The **African Lion Safari and Game Reserve**, not far from Hamilton (west off **Highway 8**), is a drive-through park covering six animal reserves, where you will see lions, tigers, bison, giraffes and many more.

3 **Wild Waterworks**, in Confederation Park at Stoney Creek, is one of the best of many water theme parks. Small children will find **Little Squirt Works**, with its computerised sprays, mists and fountains and big wading pool, ideal.

6 Amusements in Niagara Falls include **Marineland**, where killer whales, sea-lions and dolphins perform, and the **Dragon Mountain** roller coaster, a real stomach-churner.

SCENIC ROUTES

From Mississauga to Burlington and Niagara-on-the-Lake to Fort Erie there is a marked **Heritage Highway** scenic route, and from Fort Erie to Port Colborne the **Talbot Trail** is marked. The drive along Niagara Parkway from Hamilton to the falls meanders through Queenston Heights, past impressive estates, as it follows the Niagara Gorge. However, it was the stretch of green belt along the Niagara River between Niagara-on-the-Lake and Fort Erie that Sir Winston Churchill described as 'the prettiest Sunday afternoon drive in the world'.

RECOMMENDED WALKS

The Trail Center in **Dundas Valley Conservation Area** is a focal point for a 20km (12-mile) trail system through 1,011 hectares (2,500 acres) of wilderness and parkland. This area is part of **The Bruce Trail** – a 437km (271-mile) footpath that winds along the rocky cliffs of the Niagara Escarpment from Niagara to Tobermory, passing through Hamilton, Burlington and Dundas. From Hamilton, drive up Hamilton Mountain to Mountain Brow Boulevard, then take the scenic trek down the wooded Albion Valley to see the **Albion Falls**. The **Mountsberg Wildlife Center** and the **Spencer Gorge Wilderness Area** both have hiking trails, and a guided hike starts from the **Nature Interpretive Center** at the Arboretum in Dundas. **Felker's Falls Conservation Area** offers trails that are easy for children and the disabled.

resist a stroll down the main street: **Queen Street**, where an old apothecary shop (1866) has been restored, and where McClellands Store has been operating since 1835. In **The Fudge Shop** you can buy the product after seeing it made on the marble slab. Make sure you have lunch in the **Prince of Wales Hotel**, a Victorian-style inn (one of several), but book first.

McFarland House, 1.6km (1 mile) south on **Niagara Parkway**, is furnished in early 1800s style (open mid-May to Thanksgiving). Local history is covered by 20,000 items at the **Niagara Historical Museum**, on Castlereagh Street; and, at the **Niagara Fire Museum**, on King Street, fire equipment, including hand pumpers and water wagons, dates from 1760.

There are many accessible wineries, and cruising on the lower Niagara River in an Edwardian-style vessel is a relaxing possibility. In the **French Perfume Museum and Factory (Highway 55)**, 19th-century equipment and techniques are explained and a tour shows how today's fragrances are created.

ⓘ Masonic Lodge, King and Prideaux Streets

*Return to **QEW** and continue to Niagara Falls.*

Niagara Falls, Ontario

6 No matter how popular Niagara Falls has become, the Falls themselves are undeniably impressive. The roar, the spray and the vast sweep of cascading water are spectacular, and are illuminated every night of the year. If you don't mind getting wet, take a ride on the famous *Maid of the Mist*, the little boat that plies its way in front of the American Falls and upriver into the horseshoe of the main Falls (mid-May to mid-October; hooded plastic raincoats are provided). Just as spine-tingling is the aerial view: helicopter flights depart from near Whirlpool Rapids (February to December, weather permitting). For the cautious, there is a 45-minute film on the Falls shown at the **Imax Theater** at Pyramid Place.

Honeymooners have been in love with Niagara ever since Napoleon's brother purportedly came with his bride to stay here. Most of the motels and hotels offer honeymoon packages, and there is a wide choice of accommodation. There are several man-made attractions: **Louis Tussaud's Waxworks** and **Ripley's Believe It or Not Museum**, for instance.

One of the better complexes is **Maple Leaf Village**, a three-floor entertainment complex with restaurants, shops, museums, an amusement park and the 109 m (359 feet) **Kodak Tower**. At the **Minolta Tower Center**, high-speed elevators whisk you to a panoramic restaurant 202m (665 feet) up. From **River Road**, an elevator takes you down to the Niagara Gorge below the Falls, where a walkway follows the river edge to the **Whirlpool Rapids**. A high-speed glass elevator on the outside zooms you up to the revolving restaurant of **Skylon Tower**, 236m (775 feet) up.

The **Falls Art Gallery**, on QEW and McLeod Road, houses much of William Kurelek's work, including *The Passion of Christ* series of panels and the **Niagara Falls Museum**, on River Road, North America's oldest museum, contains over 700,000 exhibits, including the Daredevil Hall of Fame.

ⓘ 4673 Ontario Avenue

*The **QEW** continues south to Fort Erie.*

Fort Erie, Ontario

7 A major port of entry to Canada, opposite Buffalo, New York, Fort Erie is situated at the junction of Lake Erie and the Niagara River and linked to the US by the Peace Bridge. As well as the old fort, the **Historical Railroad Museum** will delight all railroad buffs with its steam-era memorabilia, and the **Mildred M Mahoney Doll's House Gallery**, in Bertie Hall, charms adults as well as children.

ⓘ 200 Jarvis Street

*Continue on **QEW** to the junction with **Highway 3**, then head west to Port Colborne.*

Port Colborne, Ontario

8 You may be surprised by the clean and sandy beaches in this port on Lake Erie and the Welland Canal. It is, however, better known as a flour-milling center, and the site of one of the world's largest single locks, which can be seen from **Fountain View Park**. The port's maritime heritage is a major feature at the **Port Colborne Historical and Marine Museum**.

ⓘ 76 Main Street West

*Take **Highway 58** to Welland.*

Welland, Ontario

9 Welland takes the title of Rose City of Ontario (a June festival celebrates the Flowers), but in truth it is a large industrial center specializing in steel. It is most famous for its canals: the fourth canal built cuts through the city center, so that all types of shipping pass close by. Canal history is the prime reason for the **Welland Historical Museum**, but there is also a Discovery Gallery for children. The **Festival of Arts Murals** is an outdoor gallery with 24 giant murals, some three storys high.

ⓘ 32 East Main Street

*Take **Highway 406** north to the junction with **Highway 20**, then north to Hamilton and **Highway 8** west to Dundas.*

Dundas, Ontario

10 The route now takes you back into the Hamilton vicinity. Here attractions include the **Ben Veldbuis Greenhouses**, full of cacti, downtown, and the **Historical Society Museum**, with its varied collections of costumes, toys, china and glass. The **Dundas Valley Conservation Area** is the nearest for wildlife and vegetation.

ⓘ 10 Market Street South

*Take **Highway 8** to Kitchener/Waterloo.*

Kitchener/Waterloo, Ontario

11 Amish and Mennonite farmers were the early German settlers who have given these sister cities their character, at its most evident during the annual Oktoberfest. An example of a pioneer home is the **Joseph Schneider Haus**, on Queen Street South, lived in during the 1850s by a Pennsylvania German Mennonite. Mennonite paintings are featured at **Peter Etril Snyder Studio**, on Erb Street East, and Mennonite artifacts are among those on display at **Doon Heritage Cross-roads**, a 24-hectare (60-acre) complex comprising a museum, church, school, store, railroad station and other buildings (north off **Highway 401**). The cities' farmers' markets are particularly well known – the larger in Kitchener, the smaller Waterloo – selling local produce and handicrafts. Heritage properties include the **Homer Watson House and Gallery**, on Old Mill Road, dedicated to the landscape artist, and the **Woodside National Historic Site**, where Canada's 10th Prime Minister, William Lyon MacKenzie King, lived as a boy, in Kitchener. Family attractions may be found in **Bingeman Park**, with its wave pool, water slides and summer activities, and at **Sportsworld**, a theme park with go-carts, golf and the Canadian Country Music Hall of Fame.

ⓘ 67 King Street East, Kitchener; also 5 Bridgeport Road West, Waterloo

*Take **Highway 401** to Milton.*

To most visitors, Niagara means only one thing – the Falls

Milton, Ontario

12 Bristling with activity, this former mill town is right on **Highway 401**. You won't even have to leave the highway to visit the **Ontario Agricultural Museum**, where demonstrations of the changes in rural life are given. Travel 17km (11 miles) west (south of **Highway 401**) to visit the **Mountsberg Wildlife Center**, which gives its own country demonstrations and hosts several seasonal events, or take Steeles Avenue, 5km (3 miles) south of 401, to **Crawford Lake Conservation Area**. The latter is an old Indian village site where longhouses have been reconstructed, and scenic trails follow the shores of a glacier-formed lake. There are also special activities and audiovisual displays.

ⓘ Steeles Avenue and Highway 25

*Return via **Highway 401** to Toronto.*

Toronto – Oakville **35 (22)**
Oakville – Hamilton **28 (17)**
Hamilton – Stoney Creek **7 (4)**
Stoney Creek – St Catharines **31 (19)**
St Catharines – Niagara-on-the-Lake **18 (11)**
Niagara-on-the-Lake – Niagara Falls **25 (16)**
Niagara Falls – Fort Erie **31 (19)**
Fort Erie – Port Colborne **29 (18)**
Port Colborne – Welland **11 (7)**
Welland – Dundas **87 (54)**
Dundas – Kitchener/Waterloo **53 (33)**
Kitchener/Waterloo – Milton **56 (35)**
Milton – Toronto **42 (26)**

BACK TO NATURE

Christie is a haven for wildlife, as is the man-made lake of **Valens**, off **Highway 6**. Ducks and geese gather at **Cootes Paradise**, at the tip of Lake Ontario, where there are miles of nature trails. **Mountsberg Wildlife Center** features a wildlife walkway, as well as elk and buffalo compounds. Visit **Tiffany Falls**, off **Highway 2** in Ancaster, where a nature trail gives access to The Bruce Trail, and **Borer's Falls**, off York Road in Dundas.

3 days – 481km (298 miles)

TAKING TO THE WATERS

Toronto ● Barrie ● Penetanguishene
Midland ● Gravenhurst ● Fenelon Falls
Lindsay ● Newcastle ● Toronto

This tour is for everyone who loves water sports, for it introduces you to the Georgian Lakelands, where cruising, sailing and fishing are the most popular pastimes. For winter visitors, there's a wealth of snow sports. The Muskokas are a string of pleasure lakes that stretch from Georgian Bay to Algonquin Park; the Kawarthas have Fenelon Falls as their jewel; and the Trent–Severn Waterway is the old water route followed by the frontiersmen between Georgian Bay and Lake Ontario.

Seventeenth-century Mission life is relived daily for the benefit of visitors to Sainte-Marie Among the Hurons

ℹ 290 Yonge Street, Toronto

*Take **Highway 400** to Barrie.*

Barrie, Ontario

1 A lively resort city situated on Lake Simcoe's Kempenfelt Bay, with plenty of accommodations and entertainment, including summer theater and year-round harness racing at the Fairgrounds. At the western tip of the bay, **Centennial Beach Park** has a sandy beach and is a recommended picnic spot. Annual festivities often take place here or in Molson Park. If you are in search of museums, visit **Simcoe County Museum and Archives** (north on **Highway 26**), a large complex that traces the history of the area's inhabitants. There are several pioneer buildings, and the display center includes an 1840s shopping street. Also visit the **Base Borden Military Museum**, at the Canadian Forces base (west on **Highway 90**), which displays an excellent array of firearms and military memorabilia.

ℹ 80 Bradford Street

*Take **Highway 93** north to Penetanguishene.*

Penetanguishene, Ontario

2 After the war of 1812, the British established naval and military bases in preparation for a war which never happened. The French settled around these bases on the bay, giving today's attractive town its bicultural heritage. The most important visitor sites are historic naval and military establishments, unusually combined,

SPECIAL TO ...

In this area there are several summer festivals that revolve around theater or music, such as **Muskoka Festival** in Gravenhurst and the summer Sunday evening band concerts given from a stage in Gull Lake (4). Muskoka Festival theater also takes place in the picturesque holiday village of **Port Carling**.

FOR HISTORY BUFFS

3 Sainte-Marie Among the Hurons, near Midland on **Highway 12**, is a fascinating re-creation of the 17th-century Jesuit mission founded in 1639. Inter-tribal warfare between the Hurons and Iroquois, disease and famine led to the mission's destruction and massacre of the missionaries. The **Martyrs' Shrine** opposite Sainte-Marie, is a memorial to eight of those missionaries. The Indian Longhouse is particularly impressive, in the nearby full-scale replica of a Huron Indian village as it would have been in the 16th century.

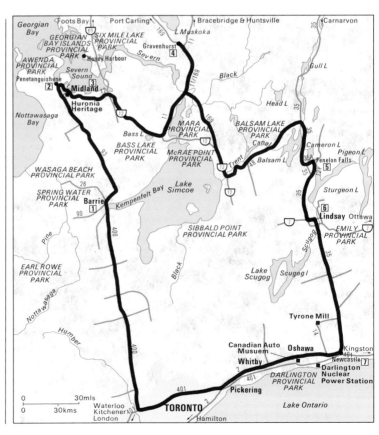

north of the **Georgian Bay** shore, on **Highway 93**. Costumed interpreters relive the period (1812–1856) in a tour of 15 reconstructed buildings and on board the replica schooner HMS *Bee* docked at the wharf. Another Penetanguishene favorite is a three-hour cruise through the islands in the bay on the MS *Georgian Queen*.

Highway 81 *leads to nearby Midland.*

Midland, Ontario

3 This popular center, also on Georgian Bay, is the gateway to thousands of islands and an access point for watersports in the bay. Midland is in the middle of a region called Huronia, where French Jesuits arrived in 1633 to convert the Huron Indians. Displays that show the Indian and early pioneer lifestyle are included at the **Huronia Museum and Gallery of Historic Huronia**, in Little Lake Park. Children with a ghoulish streak will probably drag you off to **Castle Village** and **Dracula's Museum of Horrors**, where 13 dungeons of terror await you on Balm Beach Road. Although wheels are your primary way of getting around, Midland is a great base for sightseeing flights over the 30,000 islands, and for cruises that follow the route taken by early explorers such as Champlain, through the inside passage to Georgian Bay.

ⓘ 208 King Street

Take **Highway 12** *east, then* **11** *and* **169** *north to Gravenhurst.*

Pope John Paul II has been among the pilgrims to this shrine at Midland where North America's martyred missionaries are remembered

Gravenhurst, Ontario

4 Gravenhurst is a pretty resort, whose prime position at the gateway to the Muskoka region meant it catered to tourists before the turn of the century – although, like many Ontario towns, it owed its original fortunes to lumber and shipping. Typical of the Victorian houses on the tree-lined streets is **Bethune Memorial House**, on John Street, where Dr Henry Norman Bethune was born. It commemorates this Canadian doctor for his heroic work in China, and contains family memorabilia.

A cruise on the lakes is the top attraction, particularly on the SS *Segwun* (Indian for 'springtime'), a restored steamship that departs regularly from the town wharf on a variety of cruises. Many of the handsome, well-to-do homes seen as you sail by have been converted into resort hotels. Other summer attractions are the free concerts – 'Music of the Barge' – on a stage in Gull Lake, north of Fenelon Falls.

ⓘ 150 Second Street

Return south on **Highway 11/169** *and continue on* **Highway 12** *to the junction with* **48**. *Go east, then south on* **35** *and* **35A** *to Fenelon Falls.*

FOR CHILDREN

7 In Newcastle, the **Bowmanville Zoo**, on King Street East, allows children to pet and feed a number of the animals and take a ride on an elephant. Not far from town (north of Orono at **Highway 35** and Taunton Road), **Jungle Cat World**'s main feature is the exotic cats, but there are other, gentler animals in the petting zoo.

SCENIC ROUTES

You will find the **Bluewater Route** specifically signed as a scenic route from Penetanguishene to Foots Bay, and the **Algonquin Route** signed from Carnarvon to Newcastle. If you take to a boat you can travel the whole of the Trent–Severn Waterway for 346km (215 miles) through central Ontario, passing through lush farmland, marshes, chains of lakes and Canadian Shield landscape.

RECOMMENDED WALKS

Although this tour is better for boating than walking, there are parks *en route* where hiking is pleasant. Arrowhead Park, for example, a few miles north of Huntsville, has both nature and hiking trails that range from less than 1.6km (1 mile) to around 9.6km (6 miles). At **Six Mile Lake Provincial Park**, on **Highway 69** in the Georgian Bay area, there are interpretive trails. The **Resource Management Park**, on **Highway 11** north of Bracebridge, is an equally good walking area.

BACK TO NATURE

Georgian Bay Islands National Park is composed of 59 unspoiled islands which may only be reached by boat. Water taxis to the largest, Beausoleil, can be taken from **Honey Harbor**, a small Georgian Bay resort. One organized way of viewing the marsh wildlife of these parts is to take in the **Wye Marsh Wildlife Center** at Midland (next to Sainte-Marie) where there are boardwalks, trails, an observation tower and an underwater window.

Fenelon Falls, Ontario

5 Two lakes meet at this small town. There is a difference of 7m (23 feet) in the levels of Cameron and Sturgeon lakes, resulting in the falls, rapids and limestone gorge below. Nicknamed 'the Jewel of the Kawarthas', the place took its name from an early Canadian missionary. For a touch of local history, visit the town's earliest house (1830s), now the **Fenelon Falls Museum**.

ⓘ 103 Lindsay Street (Train Station)

Highways 121 and 35 lead south to Lindsay.

Lindsay, Ontario

6 The gateway to the Kawartha Lakes recreational region, Lindsay is situated on the Scugog River and is part of the Trent Canal system. It is a year-round tourist center, with summer theater and good facilities. At the **Lindsay Gallery**, on Victoria Avenue North, the permanent collection emphasizes Canadian art; and at the **Victoria County Historical Museum**, varied displays include 19th-century Canadian glass. Like many towns on this tour, the main

---

White-water canoeists are among other enthusiasts who can find opportunities to practise their sport at Fenelon Falls – a thrilling background for many activities

appeal is the water: you have a choice of several scenic cruises on the Kawartha Lakes or on the Trent–Severn.

ⓘ 200 Kent Street West

Highway 35 continues to Newcastle.

Newcastle, Ontario

7 Newcastle spreads from Lake Ontario to the hills of the Great Pine Ridge, and incorporates apple orchards and farmland. You may watch apples being pressed at Tyrone Mill in the village of Tyrone, 13km (8 miles) north on **Highway 14**. The mill (1846) is water-driven, and originally produced flour. Later, it was converted to a sawmill, which is still in operation. In town, the **Bowmanville Museum**, on Silver Street, an 1860s house, features period rooms and a doll collection. Bus tours and a film show of the **Darlington Generating Station** site or, with advance notice, walking tours of the plant are available.

*Return to Toronto on **Highway 2**.*

Toronto – Barrie **78 (48)**
Barrie – Penetanguishene **55 (34)**
Penetanguishene – Midland **7 (4)**
Midland – Gravenhurst **79 (49)**
Gravenhurst – Fenelon Falls **117 (73)**
Fenelon Falls – Lindsay **24 (15)**
Lindsay – Newcastle **53 (33)**
Newcastle – Toronto **68 (42)**

Canada offers the visitor sport and leisure all the year round – some of the best skiing in the world is to be found here, in Georgian lakeland country

ⓘ 290 Yonge Street, Toronto

*Take **Highway 10** to Orangeville.*

Orangeville, Ontario

1 You will have passed through the flower-filled city of **Brampton** with its abundant nurseries to reach this scenic town, the county seat of Dufferin County, which is especially beautiful in the fall, when the valleys of Pine River and Hockley are ablaze with rich hues. The views around here at this time of year are said to be among the most breathtaking in Ontario. Walkers might note that **The Bruce Trail** passes through the Hockley Hills. The **Dufferin County Museum**, on Zena Street, illustrates local history, and the area is very good for craft shops.

ⓘ 87 Broadway

*Take **Highway 10**, then **24** north to Collingwood.*

Collingwood, Ontario

2 At the highest part of the Niagara Escarpment, Collingwood is best known as a ski center. Located at the base of Blue Mountain, the town became prosperous as a Great Lakes port: its Victorian Main Street and fine Victorian homes are an indication of that wealth. The **Collingwood Museum**, on St Paul Street, is located in an old railroad station and deals mainly with pioneer life and shipbuilding, but includes a full courtroom display. West on **Highway 26**, **Kaufman House** displays this well-known craftsman's furniture, from period to modern, in 18 well-appointed rooms. Also on **Highway 26**, the sweet-toothed can view the making of old-fashioned sweet at **The Candy**

3 days – 527km (328 miles)

LAKELAND, CAVES AND COLORS

Toronto ● Orangeville ● Collingwood ● Meaford
Owen Sound ● Flesherton ● Stratford ● Guelph
Toronto

This tour offers a scenic mix that should suit most tastes. Some of it encompasses Georgian Lakeland country, with water views and activities. Some of the route traverses fine apple orchards around Thornbury and Meaford, while around Elora, there are limestone canyons and caves. There will be opportunities to admire early Canadian architecture, go 'antiquing', and visit museums and farmers' markets. Pick the appropriate time of year and you will find great festivals, beautiful autumn colors or terrific skiing.

Factory, which hands out free samples.

The best summer view is from the **Blue Mountain** chair lift, which transports you 914m (3,000 feet) up. You can descend the same way or sled down through the woods. Both slopes of the mountain offer ski runs and slide rides of varying degrees of

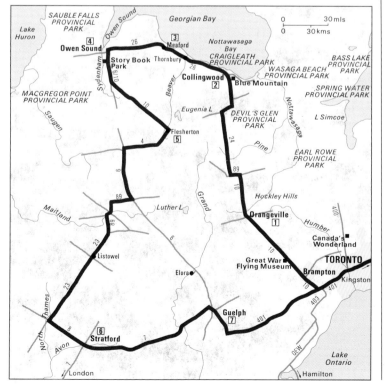

SPECIAL TO . . .

6 In Stratford is the **Stratford Festival**, based on a Shakespearean theater season and involving three theaters. In addition to world-class theater of that ilk, musicals and contemporary drama are also featured during the May to October season.

7 In Guelph, the **Spring Festival** in May and June brings in top names in the classical music world. Recitals, concerts, song and dance programs are all part of the occasion.

FOR HISTORY BUFFS

1 The **Peel Heritage Complex** in Brampton may well be worth stopping for. It comprises a restored 19th-century jail, adjacent Register Office, museum, archives and art gallery. Museum displays cover aspects of local life from prehistoric times, and archive records date from 1805. Also, 15km (9 miles) north of Brampton on **Highway 10**, is the **Great War Flying Museum**, which will appeal to some for its World War I memorabilia.

FOR CHILDREN

4 **Story Book Park**, just south of Owen Sound off **Highways 6** and **10**, is magic for small children. It features reproductions of characters and scenes from popular story books, rides and an animal farm.

7 Children with a sweet tooth can be taken on a tour of **Schneider's Reliable Sweets** in Guelph (off **Highway 7**), makers of old-fashioned treats such as humbugs, Turkish delight and sponge toffee.

Canada's Wonderland is a must for everyone who is young at heart. The Disney-style theme park, located in Maple, about 30km (19 miles) from Toronto, covers 150 hectares (370 acres) and is excellent for all the family, with plenty of rides, activities, live shows and special events.

difficulty, and cross-country facilities. Near the top of the escarpment, natural scenic caves give visitors good views to the north and the east.

ⓘ 97 Hurontario Street

*Take **Highway 26** west via Thornbury to Meaford.*

Meaford, Ontario

3 This small town is the center of an extensive apple-growing region, located on the Georgian Bay. In spring, it's a perfumed wonderland of blossom. It has a busy harbor and active marina. Learn how the community developed by visiting the local museum on Bayfield Street.

ⓘ Sykes Street

*Continue west on **Highway 26** to Owen Sound.*

Owen Sound, Ontario

4 A flourishing, attractive city that overlooks Owen Sound towards Georgian Bay, and is surrounded by

The Indians believed their spirits lived between the limestone walls of the spectacular Elora Gorge

the limestone cliffs of the Niagara Escarpment. It is a natural for sailing enthusiasts, and the fishing is good too. Photographers will appreciate local beauty spots: **Inglis, Jones** and **Indian Falls**, close to the city; and right in Owen Sound, **Harrison Park** is a pleasant spot for picnickers with its trees and waterfalls.

The former railroad station has become **The Marine and Rail Heritage Museum**, on the west harborfront, where you can see how the area's shipbuilding and transportation industries developed. A collection of cultural material relating to city and county in the 1815–1920 period is displayed at the **County of Grey-Owen Sound Museum** on Sixth Street East. Interpretive displays are shown in three galleries and five restored period buildings. Owen Sound was the birthplace of Tom Thomson, one of the Group of Seven and a noted landscape artist; some of his work, along with others', can be seen in a **gallery** dedicated to him, located on First Avenue West.

ⓘ 832 Second Avenue East

*Take **Highway 10** to Flesherton.*

Flesherton, Ontario

5 Stop here if you want to look for antiques and also to visit the **South Grey Museum**, commemorating the pioneers of the area. If you are here in the fall, you will find the surrounds of Beaver Valley a colorful spectacle.

*Take **Highway 4** west, then **6** south, **89** west and south, continuing on **23** via Listowel, to the junction with **8**, then southeast to Stratford.*

Stratford, Ontario

6 This city brings Shakespeare to mind – and not only because of its name. It has all the facilities you would expect of a place with a population of some 26,000, plus its own Avon River with swans, as well as excellent theaters where Shakespearean plays are a major event. Stratford is a highly regarded cultural center in Ontario: one of the most attractive art galleries is the one on Romeo Street North, which also features sculpture, films and concerts.

38 Albert Street

*Take **Highway 7** east to Guelph.*

Guelph, Ontario

7 A large manufacturing center set out on several hills, Guelph is a handsome town, whose wide avenues are shaded by maples and whose fine old limestone houses are

To many Canadians, the wild, rugged seascape of Georgian Bay represents the essence of their country

perfect examples of early Canadian architecture. On the highest hill, the **Church of Our Lady**, modeled on Cologne's famous cathedral, is the dominant feature. Guelph's history is best seen in the **Civic Museum**, on Dublin Street South, while the most important art collection (emphasizing Canadian and Inuit work) is to be found in the **Macdonald Stewart Art Center**, seven galleries on three floors in Gordon Street. John McCrae, the author of the celebrated poem *In Flanders Fields*, written in 1915 about the Battle of Ypres, was born here, and his **birthplace** on Gordon Street may be visited. Guelph's novelty is its mechanical floral clock in Riverside Park, which has a diameter of 13m (44 feet) and is comprised of 6,000 to 7,000 flowers.

485 Silvercreek Parkway North

*Return to Toronto south on **6** and east on **401** via Milton.*

Toronto – Orangeville	55 (34)
Orangeville – Collingwood	77 (48)
Collingwood – Meaford	35 (22)
Meaford – Owen Sound	28 (17)
Owen Sound – Flesherton	48 (30)
Flesherton – Stratford	146 (91)
Stratford – Guelph	71 (44)
Guelph – Toronto	67 (42)

SCENIC ROUTES

You will find the **Bluewater Route** specifically signed between Collingwood and Owen Sound. Much of the route is especially beautiful in the fall – such as **Hockley Valley** around Orangeville and the **Beaver Valley** around Flesherton. You will be well rewarded if you take the offshoot from **Highway 6** to Elora.

RECOMMENDED WALKS

Some of the best hiking is along **The Bruce Trail**, which runs along the top of the Niagara Escarpment at Owen Sound (4). Walking may also be enjoyed in the provincial parks along route: **Devil's Glen** and **Craigleith**.

BACK TO NATURE

7 **Kortright Waterfowl Park**, close to Guelph, is one of the best places to observe wild birds in their natural surroundings. Both a wildlife park and research center, it is home to over 90 species. Located 1.6km (1 mile) west of the **Hanlon Expressway**, on the Speed River.

2/3 days – 399km (249 miles)

THROUGH A THOUSAND ISLANDS

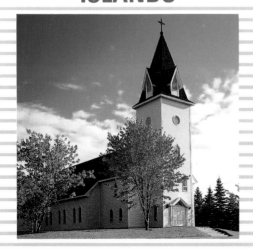

Ottawa • Manotick • Merrickville • Smiths
Falls • Kingston • Gananoque • Prescott
Iroquois • Morrisburg • Ottawa

This tour follows the Rideau–Trent–Severn waterway heritage route, which winds around lakes and granite cliffs and passes craft shops and cheese factories, visiting towns unchanged for years. This is the route of the St Lawrence Parks system and the Thousand Island Parkway, with its heart at Gananoque; a resort area of great beauty that, thanks to a hotel owner called Boldt, has given its name to a salad dressing—Thousand Island Dressing.

ⓘ National Arts Center,
65 Elgin Street, Ottawa

*Take **Highway 16** from Ottawa to Manotick.*

Manotick, Ontario

1 This pretty little town was christened 'Island in the River' by the Indians because of its location. The main reason to stop here is to visit the **Dickinson Square Con-**

Canada's finest on parade at the Royal Military College, Kingston – formerly the nation's capital

---

The colors of Canada displayed in all their beauty at Manotick

---

servation Area. Here, restored **Watson's Mill** is an operating water-powered gristmill, built in about 1860; **Dickinson House** dates from 1868, and the **Union Bank** building about 1900; the 1870 **Howard E Henry** building has become a restaurant.

*Take **Highway 16**, then **43** west to Merrickville.*

Merrickville, Ontario

2 This used to be a mill village; it was named for William Merrick, the first settler who was a millwright, before it became a port on the Rideau Canal. Today it is a small, unspoiled spot which hardly seems to have changed in appearance since the 1800s. The **Blockhouse Museum**, at the lock station on St Lawrence Street, was originally built in 1826 as a fort to protect the canal, complete with moat and drawbridge. Today it is devoted to artifacts from those earlier days.

ⓘ Blockhouse Museum

*Continue west on **Highway 43** to Smiths Falls.*

Smiths Falls, Ontario

3 Smiths Falls is the halfway point along the Rideau Canal and is a central holiday base for those wishing to explore the Rideau waterway and the Rideau lakes region. All kinds of pleasure craft use its docks and marina. Its strategic position made it an early trading center and a junction for the railroad system. Railroad artifacts and rolling stock are now displayed in a former CNOR (Canadian National Overland Railway) station on William Street West: the **Smith Falls Railway Museum**. See also the historic home of former mill owner Truman Ward, who lived in what is now **Heritage House Museum** from 1867 to 1893. It contains furnished period rooms and local history displays.

ⓘ 77 Beckwith Street North

*Take **Highway 15** south, then **2** west to Kingston.*

You might like to take a cruise on a paddlewheeler on the St Lawrence River through the **Thousand Islands**. A French explorer called the region Thousand Islands (there are, in fact, more than 1,700) and the name has stuck. Some are mere rocks, others are village size. There are numerous old stone mansions and colonial houses on the islands and markers commemorating the French and Indian War and the War of 1812.

FOR HISTORY BUFFS

4 **Old Fort Henry**, at the junctions of **Highways 2** and **15**, was the principal stronghold of Upper Canada, as can be seen from its massive Martello towers bristling with cannon, its walls and powder magazines, its barracks and workshops. Built between 1832 and 1834 for a war that never happened, it has become a living military museum, as musket fire echoes around its limestone battlements, the drums rattle and scarlet jackets flash during the summer infantry drills and the Ceremonial Retreats.

6 **Fort Wellington**, on **Highway 2** at Prescott, was one old military post that did see action during the War of 1812. You are able to visit the restored barracks, subterranean passage, armory, guardhouse and officers' quarters, but the fort is at its most impressive when a military pageant is performed in period dress.

FOR CHILDREN

4 **Polliwog Castle** in Kingston will appeal to small children: it features several hundred antique dolls among other children's toys.

5 **House of Haunts**, built in Gananoque in 1883, gives you a 'ghost' host to take you through the automated displays – recommended for family fun.

8 **Prehistoric World**, 10km (6 miles) east of Morrisburg, portrays full-size replicas of dinosaurs and other prehistoric creatures along a nature trail.

Kingston, Ontario

4 An impressive historic city, Kingston is set at the southern end of the Rideau Canal, where Lake Ontario flows into the St Lawrence River, and is a choice place to stay overnight. There is plenty to see and do, including good theater, an Olympic sailing course and a twice-weekly open-air market. Kingston developed from a fur-trading post into a military stronghold, and at one time was even the national capital. Today it is a thriving industrial, agricultural and tourist center. Its numerous limestone buildings give the city its distinctive appearance. One of the most classical structures is City Hall, built in 1833 when Kingston was the capital of Canada's Upper Provinces, and handsomely domed. Tours are given in summer. **Bellevue House** (about 1840) was a former home of Canada's first prime minister, Sir John Macdonald; now it is a museum filled with Macdonald memorabilia.

There is no lack of museums in town: **Murney Tower Museum** is a remnant of the 1846 defenses, a huge Martello tower that today houses historic material. The largest Martello tower, however, is to be seen in the grounds of the Royal Military College. The **College Museum** houses Fort Frederick, which depicts College and Royal Dockyard history and contains a small-arms collection, located east of the city, off **Highway 2**. Also of military note is the **Kingston Mills Blockhouse**, at the southern entrance to the canal. The history of Canadian military communications is traced at the **Canadian Forces Communications and Electronic Museum** with the aid of heliographs, Verey pistols and a large collection of telephones (east on **Highway 2**).

Among other interesting museums are the **Kingston Penitentiary Museum** which shows what life was like in the past inside Canadian prisons; and the **Marine Museum**, which covers Great Lakes shipping from 1678, including items discovered by scuba divers and the icebreaker *Alexander Henry*.

Kingston is a university town, and in the **Miller Hall** of Queen's University you can visit the **Miller Museum of Geology and**

SCENIC ROUTES

The route from Ottawa to Kingston is specifically marked the **Rideau Route** and is noted for its photogenic scenery. Between Kingston and Morrisburg the **Heritage Highway** is signed. You are spoiled for scenic choice, whether you stick to the main Rideau Route or take to the backwater roads.

RECOMMENDED WALKS

4 **Frontenac Provincial Park** is the perfect place for wilderness hiking, since there are 159km (99 miles) of trails for both this form of exercise and for canoers. Located 11km (7 miles) north of Sydenham, close to Kingston, it is the southernmost tip of the Canadian Shield. If you want expert advice on wilderness skills, drop in at the Trail Center.

BACK TO NATURE

5 **1000 Islands Wild Kingdom** at Gananoque shows off exotic and native wildlife in 10 hectares (25 acres) of natural setting.

8 A superb refuge for migratory birds can be found 14km (9 miles) east of Morrisburg, off **Highway 2**. The **Upper Canada Migratory Bird Sanctuary** covers 1,416 hectares (3,500 acres) and, for the widest variety, is best visited in spring or fall, though the summer months are not without numerous species on view.

Mineralogy. The International Hockey Hall of Fame is notable because Kingston saw the first organized hockey game, in 1885.

As a change from car or foot, you might care to take advantage of the trackless train tour that travels a 16km (10-mile) circuit through the city, departing opposite City Hall. If you cannot afford the time to take a mini cruise along the St Lawrence River on the replica steamship, the MV *Canadian Empress* (it takes four or six days), at least take a harbor cruise on the replica sidewheeler' *Island Princess*, for a great view of the historic waterfront.

ℹ️ 209 Ontario Street

*Take **Highway 2** to Gananoque.*

Gananoque, Ontario

5 A favorite tourist center for excursions through the Thousand Islands, Gananoque (pronounced gannon-ock-way) is in the center of that region. It is a charming resort, only a few miles from the American border. A boat tour is really a must: some offer an optional stop at **Boldt Castle**, a local millionaire's previous home. The old Victoria Hotel (1863), beside the town park, is these days the **Gananoque Museum**, furnished in Victorian style and featuring military items. Another historic building, the Canoe Club, is now the **1000 Islands Playhouse**, where summer theater is staged.

ℹ️ 2 King Street East

*Continue on **Highway 2** to Prescott.*

Prescott, Ontario

6 Prescott is a transshipping point on the St Lawrence River, with a deep water port, and is connected to Ogdensburg, New York, by the International Bridge. It is noted for its commanding position and for **The Blue Church**, an 1845 clapboard church which is the burial place of Barbara Heck, a founder of Methodism in Upper Canada.

ℹ️ Rotary Lighthouse, Water Street

*Continue on **Highway 2** to Iroquois.*

Ottawa, center of Canada's political and economic life, is a city of parks

Iroquois, Ontario

7 When the St Lawrence Seaway flooded the area, this was the largest town to be entirely relocated. Stop for a quick look at the **Iroquois Seaway locks** – the only ones in eastern Ontario. From the lookout, ships can be seen *en route* to distant ports-of-call.

ℹ️ Carman Road

*Continue on **Highway 2** to Morrisburg.*

Morrisburg, Ontario

8 This was one of the earliest settled parts of Canada. **Upper Canada Village**, at Crystal Farm Battlefield Park, 11km (7 miles) east of Morrisburg, re-creates the town as it was in 1820 to 1860; when the St Lawrence waters rose, the best of the town was moved to its new location. This is an excellent pioneer park comprising 35 buildings, corduroy roads (made of treetrunks laid across swamps) and canals which you can see on foot, by horse-drawn carriage or *bâteau*. The details have been authentically reproduced and everything works in the sawmill, the blacksmith's shop, the gristmill, the cabinet-maker's *et al*, and the guides are suitably attired to show you around. There is also an operational 1860s farm. To appreciate this park fully, you need several hours. This and other attractions, including professional summer theater and a bird sanctuary, make Morrisburg a popular excursion from Ottawa.

ℹ️ Upper Canada Village entrance

*Return to Ottawa via **Highway 31**.*

Ottawa – Manotick **22 (14)**
Manotick – Merrickville **46 (29)**
Merrickville – Smiths Falls **19 (12)**
Smiths Falls – Kingston **98 (61)**
Kingston – Gananoque **33 (21)**
Gananoque – Prescott **71 (44)**
Prescott – Iroquois **23 (14)**
Iroquois – Morrisburg **13 (8)**
Morrisburg – Ottawa **74 (46)**

The National Gallery at Ottawa is a marvel in glass and pink granite, designed by Moshe Safdie

ⓘ National Arts Center, 65 Elgin Street, Ottawa

*Take **Highway 17** to Pembroke.*

Pembroke, Ontario

1 A large town in the Ottawa Valley, roughly halfway between Ottawa and North Bay, Pembroke has always been associated with timber, due to the forests which surround it. Among its claims to fame is that it was Canada's first town to use electric street lighting. One of the most thrilling activities on the Ottawa River is whitewater rafting through the rapids: bookings may be made in Pembroke. History buffs will want to visit **Champlain Train Museum**, on Pembroke Street, whose displays cover a variety of local and general history during the 19th and 20th centuries, but whose prime feature is a log house from the late 1800s.

ⓘ 169 William Street

*Take **Highway 62** west to Whitney.*

Whitney, Ontario

2 This town at the east gate of Algonquin Park is really an access point. From here you can take off by canoe or on foot to explore the park's interior. The semi-wild area around Whitney is good for hunting, fishing and canoeing and in winter for cross-country skiing.

ⓘ East Gate, Algonquin Park

*Take **Highway 60** into the Park*

Algonquin Provincial Park, Ontario

3 Algonquin is Ontario's oldest provincial park and one of its largest, covering 7,770sq km (3,000 square miles). Located on the southern edge of the Canadian Shield between Georgian Bay and the Ottawa River, it is a region of lakes,

ROUTE OF THE VOYAGEURS

Ottawa ● Pembroke ● Whitney ● Algonquin Provincial Park ● Bancroft ● Bon Echo Provincial Park ● Perth ● Almonte ● Ottawa

From the capital's spires in Ontario East, this route takes you northwards towards the timberlands on the Route of the Voyageurs. By way of contrast to city lights, the Near North is full of the forests and lakes of the Almaguin Highlands. The highlight is Algonquin Provincial Park, 7,770sq km (3,000 square miles) of wilderness and natural peace. You will delve into central Ontario, which has something of everything, before returning to the Ottawa Valley. For those who like a change of scenery with the miles and a mixture of lively centers and quiet retreats, this diversified circular tour is ideal.

forests and rivers. There are several access points around the perimeter but only one through road (**Highway 60**). There are lodges, campsites and picnic areas but it is its relative inaccessibility which is its charm, with unpopulated areas for canoeing, quiet places to fish, getaways to understand nature better, or simply

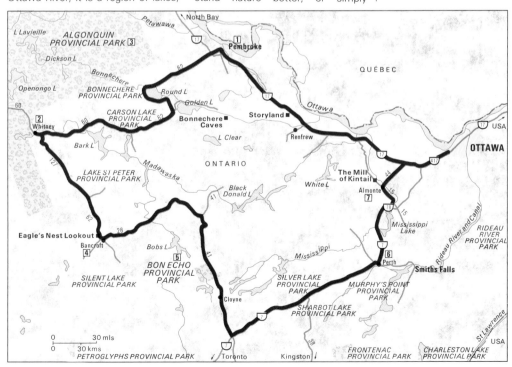

SPECIAL TO . . .

4 At Bancroft there is the **Bancroft Rockhound Gemboree** in early August, when thousands of rockhounds descend on the town bringing their collections with them. They sell, swap, learn and take field trips during the five-day fête.

FOR HISTORY BUFFS

By the time Wellington had defeated Napoleon, he was considered such a good military tactician that no one batted an eye when he suggested that a canal system should be built in Canada, linking and deepening the natural waterway between Ottawa and Kingston, to allow British gunboats to avoid enemy fire. It was done, and is today the **Rideau waterway**, a system that extends 201km (125 miles), and includes 49 locks and 19km (12 miles) of excavated channels.

meditate. Exhibits and audiovisual presentations tell the park's story at the **Park Museum**, and at the **Pioneer Logging Exhibit** just inside the East Gate.

Return to Whitney, then take ***Highway 127*** *southeast to join* ***Highway 62*** *to Bancroft.*

Bancroft, Ontario

4 Thanks to its location on the edge of the Precambrian Shield, this area yields 80 per cent of Canada's minerals – the result of billions of years pressure build-up in the rock. Zircons, beryl and rose quartz are among the more familiar finds. A fine display of minerals from around the world may be seen in the **Mineral Museum** (resembling a mine interior) in the Old Station. An extensive mineral collection is also displayed at the **Bancroft Historical Museum**, in a log house. Also see the **Bancroft Art Gallery**, in a renovated train station, which shows year-round exhibits of local artists' work.

Bancroft is a major center for the highlands of Hastings, studded with lakes that are good fishing grounds and waterways for canoeing. A particularly pleasant picnic site is **Eagle's**

Nest Lookout (take Highway 62 north), on a 182m (600-foot) hill overlooking the town and countryside.

ⓘ The Old Station, Station Street

*Take **Highway 28** east, then **41** south to Bon Echo Provincial Park.*

Bon Echo Provincial Park, Ontario

5 Eastern Ontario's largest park, covering 6,643 hectares (16,417 acres), is reached from **Cloyne**, a small village in the heart of lake country. Its major feature is **Mazinaw Rock**, a chunk of pre-Cambrian granite formed millions of years ago, sometimes nicknamed the Canadian Rock of Gibraltar. It was renamed Bon Echo for its acoustic properties, which you can try out when you take the spectacular walkway to the summit. The park is good for hiking, swimming and canoeing: take to a canoe and you will discover Indian pictographs on the rock at eye level.

*Continue on **Highway 41** south to the junction with **Highway 7**, then east to Perth.*

Smoke Lake in Algonquin Provincial Park: the meaning of wilderness

FOR CHILDREN

1 **Storyland**, 13km (8 miles) north of Renfrew, on the route to Pembroke (off **Highway 17**) will delight the very young: over 200 storybook characters, many of them animated, are displayed in fairy story settings in woodland. There is also a **wildlife museum** here and other themed areas such as **Astro Playground** and **Frontierland**, as well as paddle boats, miniature golf and picnic areas.
   Logos Land, 22km (14 miles) west of Renfrew (on **Highway 17**), is a biblical theme park in the meadows of the Ottawa Valley. In addition to a replica Noah's Ark and other religious favorites, the park has water slides and paddle boats.

BACK TO NATURE

3 **Algonquin** is a vast wilderness area and is home to a wide range of birds and mammals. In the fall, when the leaves have started to change color, the park's timber wolves can be seen and heard. White-tailed deer are a common sight and beaver dams are a feature of the river systems. In the spring, a colorful array of wildflowers can be seen and the woods come alive with the sound of migrant and resident birds singing to advertize their territories; woodpeckers, flycatchers, chickadees and over a dozen species of warblers are among the highlights.

Perth, Ontario

6 Both this town and the River Tay, on which it sits, are named after Scottish counterparts. Perth's 19th-century **Main Street** has been handsomely restored, and one of the Georgian houses on Gore Street East has become the **Perth Museum**, with period-furnished rooms and displays of historical artifacts. You can also see a model of the **Mammoth Cheese**, made in 1893 by eastern Ontario dairy farmers for the Chicago World Fair. It weighed 9,979kg (22,000lbs) and after the exhibition was exported to England for consumption. One pleasant recreational spot is **Murphys Point Provincial Park**, a few miles out of town, where you can boat along the Rideau waterway, take a self-guided trail or explore an abandoned mine.

ℹ 80 Gore Street East

   Take **Highways 7, 7B** and **15** to Almonte.

Almonte, Ontario

7 A picturesque village, Almonte was one of the first to be settled in the Ottawa Valley, beside the Mississippi

A picture of tranquillity at the Mill of Kintail, Almonte

River with its own waterfall (no relation to the *other* Mississippi!). The textile industry contributed to its development, as you will see if you visit the **Mississippi Valley Textile Museum** in town. A more photogenic museum a few miles north (off **Highway 15**) is **The Mill of Kintail** – an 1830s water-powered gristmill converted into a summer home by famous surgeon Robert Tait McKenzie a century later. He was also a sculptor, and many of his pieces are displayed inside. Open mid-May to mid-October.

ℹ 70–72 Mill Street

   Take **Highway 44**, then **17** and **417** to Ottawa.

RECOMMENDED WALKS

3 **Algonquin Park** is a walkers' paradise. **The Highland Trail** with 19 and 35km (9-and 22-mile) loops, and the **Western Uplands Trail** with 32, 55 and 71km (20-, 34- and 44-mile) loops both start from **Highway 60**. Nine interpretive trails along the highway are each designed to explore different aspects of the park's environment, but during summer, visitors may take a leisurely conducted walk with a park naturalist.

Ottawa – Pembroke **149** (93)
Pembroke – Whitney **143** (89)
Whitney – Algonquin **5** (3)
Algonquin – Bancroft **70** (43)
Bancroft – Bon Echo **87** (54)
Bon Echo – Perth **112** (70)
Perth – Almonte **46** (29)
Almonte – Ottawa **51** (32)

SCENIC ROUTES

Much of this route takes you through some of Canada's best provincial parks, with fine scenic views along much of the way.

MANITOBA

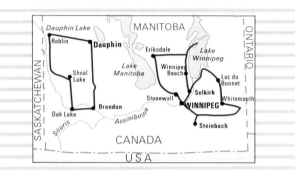

Canada's heartland is as big as its welcome, a province that covers 650,000 sq km (251,000 square miles) – big enough to embrace several American states. They call it the Prairie Province for its grain-rich plains – wheat and more wheat – yet it boasts thousands of lakes, among them Lake Winnipeg, larger even than Lake Ontario. There are forests, too, in the north, and wooded parkland in the middle; so as golden as its image may be, Manitoba also has its green belt; massive glaciers carved out the fertile valleys and rolling grasslands, as well as the plains.

The early Scottish and Mennonite settlers who came to farm here in the mid-1800s, along with the Ukrainians, have stamped a very definite mark on Manitoba: the province prides itself on its pioneer museums and ethnic festivals. (The biggest multicultural festival of all is Folklorama, one of the largest in North America.)

There is history here, and adventure: you will be able to discover the sites of the old fur trading forts, relax on a lakeside beach, photograph polar bears or take to the whitewater rapids in a kayak. If you thought this central province was just about agriculture, you are in for a surprise: a holiday here can be as rugged or as civilized as you care to make it. There are challenges for fishermen, exciting winter skiing, untouched wild beauty spots, world class culture and fine dining.

Manitoba's 12 provincial parks and one national park are big attractions, covering 1 million lake-studded hectares (2.5 million acres) and ranging from the desert-like sand dunes at Spruce Woods to the pre-Cambrian shield forests in the Whiteshell. There are also fine rural resorts, offering the carefree atmosphere of a hotel, plus the soothing influence of natural surroundings.

Basically, there are eight geographically defined tourist regions: Winnipeg itself; the south-central Pembina Valley, through which the Red River runs – a mixture of rich farmland and industrial wealth; the central plains, noted for hunting and wildlife management areas; the southwest corner, a combination of rolling prairie, desert, wooded hills and oilfields, traversed by several major highways; parkland territory, with its fish-filled streams, abundant game and one of Canada's finest golf courses; the northern region with thousands of evergreen square miles; the interlake region between huge Lake Winnipeg and Lakes Manitoba and Winnipegosis; and the eastern region, with its luxury fishing lodges and picturesque towns.

Manitoba's name is derived from the Indian for 'great spirit' – but you will find out for yourself.

Winnipeg:
Winnipeg is a capital city which is bright, bustling fun and home to 40 cultures. With excellent hotels, over 700 restaurants (including dinner theaters) and a multitude of shops, in underground and surface malls, Portage Place complex and Osborne Village, this city is Manitoba's most cosmopolitan center, with world-acclaimed Performing Arts.

Prominent landmarks include the **Holy Trinity Ukrainian Orthodox Cathedral**, which contains the **Ukrainian Museum of Canada** (arts and crafts) and the neoclassical limestone **Legislative Building**. Of the many fine museums, the **Museum of Man and Nature** has to top the list, ranking three Michelin stars for the way it shows man's relation to the environment through dioramas, reconstructions, specimens and audiovisual displays. The city's French heritage is best explored in **Museum St Boniface**, the oldest structure in Winnipeg, built as a convent in 1846, and **St Boniface Basilica**, whose churchyard contains the grave of Louis Riel, famous participant in the North West Rebellion. His birthplace, **Riel**

House, is an historic park.

Red River cruises are a major attraction on replica paddle-wheelers: many take the route to Lower Fort Garry. Rickshaw tours of downtown, Osborne Village and Chinatown or the steam train run to Grosse Isle are other ways of getting around. A walking tour of the old Exchange District/Old Market Square is another idea: tours start at the Museum of Man and Nature. Children should enjoy **Assiniboine Zoo**, in the city's oldest park, and nature lovers can head for **Assiniboine Forest**, a preserve containing wildlife and rare flowers; to **Bluestem Nature Park**, a 2-hectare (6-acre) natural prairie with 160 species of native plants and 71 species of bird; and to the **Fort Whyte Centre for Environmental Education**, whose Aquarium of the Prairies showcases native fish. It is also worth seeing **Grant's Old Mill**, **Imax Theatre** and the **Royal Canadian Mint and Planetarium**. The **Winnipeg Art Gallery** contains one of the world's largest collections of Inuit art and makes an absorbing visit. The city's two major festivals are the Folk Festival in mid-July, a four-day music event in Birds Hill Provincial Park; and Folklorama, during the first fortnight in August.

Dauphin:

Dauphin, in the heart of the parkland region, has plenty of accommodation, restaurants and shops. Located beside the Vermillion River, the town is also only minutes away from Lake Dauphin for golf and watersports. A self-guided walking tour of the town is recommended, with the aid of a booklet from the information center. See the **Fort Dauphin Museum**, a replica of a North West Company trading post, with fur trade and pioneer artifacts and several pioneer structures within the palisade walls. In mid-September, **Trader's Rendezvous** is a festive event taking place here. The **Trembowla Cross of Freedom Museum**, 8 km (5 miles) northwest of Valley River, comprises a pioneer home and rural school. A colorful sight in season are the sunflower harvests, grown in this area for their seeds and oil.

Panorama of Winnipeg by night, with the Parliament Buildings to the fore

2 days – 477km (297 miles)

SOMETHING FOR EVERYONE

Winnipeg • Ste Anne • Steinbach • Falcon Lake • Whitemouth • Lac du Bonnet • Pine Falls • Grand Marais • Lockport • Winnipeg

You can expect plenty of variety on this tour, which takes you around part of the Eastern Region, where the Precambrian rock is jeweled by crystal lakes and lush forests. It takes you to small southeastern towns, proud of their heritage, and to lakeside resorts delighted to welcome tourists who love sailing and sunning. You have the choice of the easy-to-reach resort centers and those slightly less accessible, but more natural. This tour is recommended for those who like a little of everything in a short, circular sweep.

🛈 750–167 Lombard Avenue, Winnipeg

*Take **Highway 1** southeast, then **Highway 12** south to Ste Anne.*

The pacific heritage of the persecuted Mennonite Christians is lovingly preserved in Steinbach

Ste Anne, Manitoba

1 This small southeastern town was founded by the French on the old Dawson Trail, a land and water route between Winnipeg and Thunder Bay that was trodden by Colonel Garnet Wolseley's soldiers during the Riel rebellion. Louis Riel led the rebels of the Red River settlements in 1869 to 1870 and headed their provisional government, but the rebellion collapsed when Wolseley's Canadian and imperial troops were despatched to meet the insurgents at Fort Garry. In the 121-hectare (300-acre) **Sandilands Forest Center**, you can learn a great deal about forestry. The site contains several different forest environments, including a black spruce bog and jackpine forests as well as eastern deciduous trees—self-guiding tours will take you through most of the more interesting sections. Visit the **museum** which displays local plants and animals and demonstrates how logging operations were handled in the past, as well as in the present.

*Take **Highway 12** to Steinbach.*

Steinbach, Manitoba

2 As its name might suggest, this township has German foundations. These days, it looks more full of car dealers than of anything else, but its Mennonite heritage is recalled by the **Mennonite Heritage Village**, just north of town, which is laid out traditionally with farmhouses along one side of the street and shops and other commercial enterprises, including a blacksmith's along the other—all overlooked by a windmill with 18m (60-foot) sails. The best time of all for

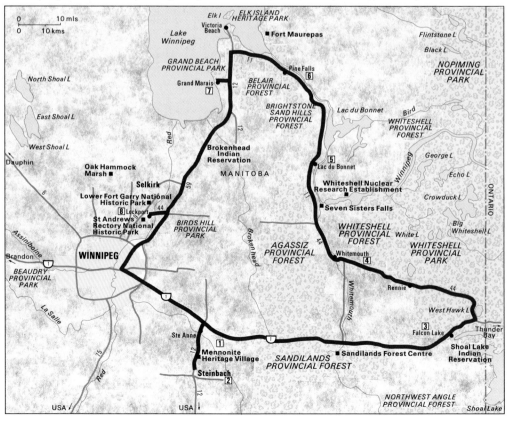

a visit is during the Pioneer Days celebration in the summer.

*Return to **Highway 1** via **Highway 12** and head east to Falcon Lake.*

Falcon Lake, Manitoba

3 You will find accommodations, a shopping center, Manitoba's largest sailing club and one of the region's best golf courses in this resort township, just inside one of the province's largest parks: the 2,590sq km (1,000 square mile) **Whiteshell Provincial Park**. The park contains some 200 lakes full of pike, perch and trout. Nearby **West Hawk Lake** is popular for scuba diving and, at 111m (365 feet), is the province's deepest. Geology enthusiasts will discover much to interest them when

The Golden Boy statue atop the Legislative Building in Winnipeg – a great example of the neo-classical style – is 72km (240 feet) high and sheathed in 23½ carat gold

they explore this park—such as the cliffs, billions of years old, that surround the waterlily lake known simply as the **Lily Pond** (west of Caddy Lake), or the strange petro-forms, north of Betula Lake—small stones laid on the bedrock in the shape of animals and birds, probably made centuries ago by the Indians. **Beaver Days**, in February, features a cross-country ski derby, downhill ski races, sleigh rides and a sponge hockey tournament.

*Take **Highway 44** to Whitemouth.*

SPECIAL TO . . .

In this area are festivals much concerned with heritage and pioneer days. **Steinbach Pioneer Days** (2), during late July and early August, for example, celebrates with threshing and baking demonstrations, serves Mennonite foods and features a horse show and barbecue, while **Whitemouth Heritage Days** (4), in early September, has similar events, including entertainment for children.

FOR HISTORY BUFFS

8 There are plenty of pioneer museums along this route, though few are as impressive as **Lower Fort Garry National Historic Park**, 32km (20 miles) north of Winnipeg on **Highway 9**. Here, at North America's oldest intact stone fur-trading post, you can experience life of the era, aided and abetted by costumed actors playing their Hudson's Bay Company parts, including those of the 'governor', his wife and household, with whom you can talk up at the 'Big House'. Fur-trading operations are realistically carried on in the fur loft, as the players describe their long journeys by boat and their daily tasks. There are several buildings to be visited at the fort, including the men's house, Ross Cottage, blacksmith's and farm cottage. During the August long weekend the Red River Rendezvous takes place.

FOR CHILDREN

City children will probably find the heritage fêtes a novelty, and most of those occasions include special events for young visitors. They should also enjoy **Fort Garry**, for its animated presentation. In the vicinity of Lockport (8), on **Highway 44**, **Skinner's Wet'n'Wild** waterslide park seems just the thing for a hot day—with giant slides and small children's slides and pool.

SCENIC ROUTES

Thanks to the lakes and parks that are so much a part of this tour, almost the whole journey has scenic value. Particular mention might be made of the park interior stretch from Falcon Lake to Rennie on **Highway 44**; **Highway 11** between Lac du Bonnet and Pine Falls; and the River Road Heritage Parkway as it follows the Red River.

RECOMMENDED WALKS

A long, renowned hike (but very strenuous) is the 59km (37-mile) **Mantario Hiking Trail**, which starts at Caddy Lake in Whiteshell Park and winds its way through meadows and forests and across rivers to end up at Big Whiteshell Lake. There are, however, plenty of other trails in this park, notably **Pine Point, Hunt Lake, Assinika, White Pine** and **Beaver Creek**. Far less tiring is the 3km (2-mile) self-guided trail at **Grand Beach**.

Whitemouth, Manitoba

4 On the edge of Whiteshell Provincial Forest, this could be a base for visiting the more northerly extremities of Whiteshell, or canoeing on the river of the same name. The park contains 200 lakes and all kinds of outdoor activities are available throughout the year. Places to visit include the **Seven Sisters Falls**—cascades which together create a hydroelectric station with an 18m (61-foot) dam. Tours of the **Whiteshell Nuclear Research Establishment** at Pinawa, where they do research into reactor safety storage, among other research, may also be taken.

*Take **Highways 44**, then **11** north to Lac du Bonnet.*

Lac du Bonnet, Manitoba

5 A hospitable resort base within easy reach of both Whiteshell and Nopiming Provincial Parks, Lac du Bonnet is only 98km (61 miles) north-west of Winnipeg. Supposedly, a Vérendrye named the place after seeing the Winnipeg River at a point where it swells to form a picturesque lake. The whole area is one of unspoiled natural beauty. The truly sporty will take themselves to Bird Lake where there is a drive-in fishing camp. Follow in the footsteps of the early trappers and gold seekers as you pass by black spruce and granite outcrops, and watch for the woodland caribou.

*Continue on **Highway 11** to Pine Falls.*

Pine Falls, Manitoba

6 Stop here for a tour of the **Abitibi-Price paper mill**—anyone over 12 is welcome year round. There are many waterfalls and other beauty spots in the area. On Labor Day weekend, the **Paper, Power, Pea and Pickerel Festival** holds a fishing derby and ladles out a lot of pea soup!

*Continue north on **Highway 11**, then take **Highway 12** south to Grand Marais.*

Grain elevators in a flowerfield: a reminder of Manitoba's agricultural wealth

Grand Marais, Manitoba

7 This excellent resort center on Lake Winnipeg has a full range of visitor services, including hotels, restaurants and snack bars. The lake is one of the continent's largest freshwater bodies and is ideal for boating. Its eastern shore is fringed with sandy beaches, among them **Grand Beach**, a mass of white sand and grassy dunes which can rise to 9m (30 feet). Behind them, a host of birds flocks to the lagoon, around which is a self-guided nature trail. Farther north is the more secluded **Victoria Beach**.

*Take **Highways 12 and 59** south, then **44** west to Lockport.*

Lockport, Manitoba

8 Lockport's **Heritage Park** is part of the Red River Corridor. In the **Kenosewun Center**, you will find interesting exhibits, an audio-visual presentation and a working archae-ological lab unlocking the doors to 3,000 years of prehistory. Kenosewun is a Cree word meaning 'many fishes' and, indeed, the Red River is full of

Manitoba is a rich cultural and ethnic mix. Here, a Ukrainian Church stands testament to this

fish, especially catfish, though it is from its opposite neighbor, Selkirk, that most are hauled out. The park offers picnic facilities and footpaths which overlook **St Andrews Lock and Dam**. **St Andrews Church**, on the Red River Heritage Parkway, is western Canada's oldest Anglican stone church still in use, with buffalo-hide kneelers. Opposite, in **St Andrews Rectory National Historic Park**, exhibits illustrate its founding, and north up river, the **Captain Kennedy House** is furnished in 1860s style.

*Return to Winnipeg via **Highway 59**.*

BACK TO NATURE

1 Nature is truly omnipotent at the **Sandilands Forest Center** where there are various forest environments, self-guided nature trails, logging operations and wildlife displays (located just south of the junction of **Highways 1** and **11**).

4 Near Rennie, in Whiteshell Provincial Park, the **Alf Hole Goose Sanctuary** lets you observe Canada geese at close range; in summer some 200 birds rest here. In addition to the observation gallery at the visitor center, which overlooks a small lake, there is a self-guided trail.

3 days – 467km (289 miles)

WILDLIFE WANDERINGS

Winnipeg ● Selkirk ● Winnipeg Beach ● Gimli
Hecla Provincial Park ● Eriksdale ● Lundar
St Laurent ● Stonewall ● Winnipeg

You will have the chance to enjoy the lakeside beaches of Lake Winnipeg's western bank on this tour, on your way north to one of the province's finest parks for wildlife viewing. The route takes you to the Interlake region (with Lake Manitoba on the west), containing a great diversity of attractions which range from first-class catfish angling and hunting to historic stone structures and archaeological digs; and your choice of where to stay is equally good, from simple campsites to well-equipped resorts.

In July, Selkirk goes West with the Triple S Fair and Rodeo – one of many lively annual festivals

ⓘ 750–167 Lombard Avenue, Winnipeg

*Take **Highway 9** to Selkirk.*

Selkirk, Manitoba

1 If you have a penchant for catfish – or have never sampled it – Selkirk is the place to visit. They call it 'the catfish capital of the world', and the specimens angled out of the Red River are often as large as 9kg (20lbs): this is why a 7m (25-foot) fiberglass statue of Chuck the Channel Cat, on the town's main street, is an unofficial mascot. It is difficult to get away from marine life here, especially in **Selkirk Park**, where you can swim, boat and fish. At the entrance to the park is the **Marine Museum**, a major attraction where Manitoba's oldest steamship, the SS *Keenora* is moored; catwalks lead to the 1915 former icebreaker, CGS *Bradbury* and the river tug boat *Peguis II*, as well as the elderly passenger and freight ship, the *Chickama II*, and the fish freighter *Lady Canadian*. On board the ships are interesting artifacts and pictures of their heyday.

*Take **Highway 9** to Winnipeg Beach.*

Winnipeg Beach, Manitoba

2 As you travel the highway you will be passing some of the province's most popular beaches to reach this lively summer town, where there are

SPECIAL TO ...

1 Selkirk has a good few festivals, from the July **Manitoba Highland Gathering** – a grand old ceilidh in the true Scottish tradition – to the **Triple S Fair and Rodeo**. The **February Festival** on the Red River, is a novel winter event with motorcycles on ice, snowmobile drags and talent contests.

2 At Winnipeg Beach in July, **Boardwalk Days** features a parade and street dancing, while the **Wonderful Winter Weekend** in February includes a demolition derby on ice.

3 One of the biggest festivals in this area is the **Islendingadagurinn** (Icelandic Festival) in Gimli, when typical Icelandic food is served and the Fjallkona (Maid of the Mountain) presides over musical and other festivities.

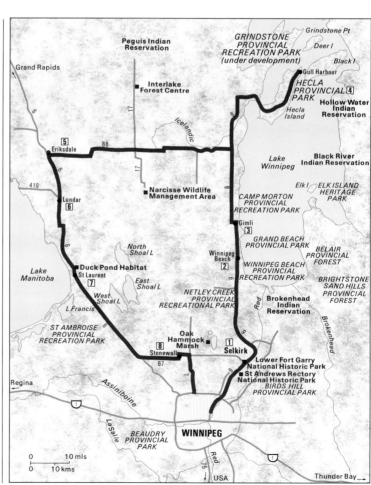

The shores of Canada's fifth largest Lake, Winnipeg, offer sport, bird-watching – or just the peace and quiet to relax and enjoy its magnificent natural splendor

plenty of motels, restaurants and stores. The place to go is **Winnipeg Beach Provincial Recreation Park**, which offers one of the best windsurfing bays on the lake, as well as wide beach and park areas.

*Continue north on **Highway 9** to Gimli.*

Gimli, Manitoba

3 Gimli is the largest Icelandic community outside Iceland, and is heralded by a giant Viking statue, it should come as no surprise that this is a commercial fishing center whose focal point is the harbor. Besides boating and sailing, the small sandy beach allows for swimming and windsurfing. If you wonder why there is a mounted jet trainer on Center Street, it is because there was a Royal Canadian Air Force base at Gimli. It has now become **Gimli Industrial Park**, whose jet runways are used to offer fly-in service to the northern lakes, and whose administrative center provides parachuting and gliding instruction. Also here is the **Gimli Motorsport Park**, whose 2km (1.5-mile) track is used for professional and amateur racing events. **Gimli Historical Museum** preserves Icelandic and Ukrainian heritage, along with Lake Winnipeg's commercial fishing history.

*Go west on **Highway 231** to join 8, north to Hecla Provincial Park.*

Hecla Provincial Park, Manitoba

4 This park comprises a number of wooded islands tucked along the western shore of Lake Winnipeg, which are superb for wildlife viewing. The largest island, Hecla, was originally settled by the Icelandic fishermen who had immigrated in their thousands to Manitoba after the 1876 eruption of Mount Hecla. In their quest for prime fishing areas, they happened upon this island and made it their home. Part of their original village has been restored to preserve the heritage, and the much newer **Gull Harbor Resort and Conference Center** has been built in Scandinavian design. This is a plush resort with its own marina and 18-hole golf course, and it is suited to all-seasons, for in winter, hiking and cross-country ski trails lead through the woods, snowmobiling is also available. Recommended for those who want comfort to go with their peace and quiet.

*Retrace the route on **Highway 8** to the junction with **68**, then head west to Eriksdale.*

Eriksdale, Manitoba

5 You might want to stop here for a coffee and a quick look at the local **museum** in the former St John's Anglican Church. To the west of Eriksdale lie the narrows of **Lake Manitoba** from which the province took its name, for the Cree word for 'Voice of the Great Spirit'. The sound of water crashing on the rocks led the Indians to believe it was the Great Spirit's drum.

*Take **Highway 6** south to Lundar.*

The drama of the 19th-century fur trade is recreated daily for visitors to Lower Fort Garry

Lundar, Manitoba

6 This town is at the heart of Canada geese country, as you will see by the giant statue of that bird. Each Thanksgiving, the **All-Canada Goose Shoot** takes place here, when competing teams try to bag the most geese with a restricted number of shells. For those who prefer gentler activities, there are beaches 16km (10 miles) west on **Highway 419**. Lundar's **museum** comprises the former CNR (Canadian National Railways) station, the Mary Hill School, the former Notre Dame Church, farm machinery and two historic log houses.

> *Continue south on **Highway 6** to St Laurent.*

St Laurent, Manitoba

7 This small town is close to one of the best duck wetlands and to the sandy beaches of Lake Manitoba. The duck pond habitat, just north of St Laurent (off **Highway 6**), is where all types of ducks are raised. Throughout the summer you can see a variety of migratory waterfowl here.

> *Continue south on **Highway 6** to the junction with **Highway 67**, east to Stonewall.*

Stonewall, Manitoba

8 The main feature at Stonewall is **Quarry Park**. There are early 1900s lime kilns here, a museum, interpretative trails and a man-made lake and beach. The area's human and natural history is explained at the interpretive center. A big occasion is **Quarry Days**, an exuberant August celebration. A few miles east of Stonewall, **Oak Hammock Marsh** is an excellent wildlife area. This reclaimed wetland covers 3,500 hectares (8,650 acres) and is home to 250 species of birds and 25 species of mammals. During the spring and autumn migratory periods, thousands of ducks, geese and shorebirds swell the numbers.

A system of boardwalks and dykes make it easy for visitors to get around and, in summer, interpretive programs are offered.

> *Continue on **67** to the junction with **7** and return south to Winnipeg.*

3 days – 519km (323 miles)

The green and scenic charm of Minnedosa valley

ⓘ 107 Main Street North, Dauphin

*Take **Highway 10** south to Riding Mountain National Park.*

Riding Mountain National Park, Manitoba

1 This aspen-laden park straddles the rocky western uplands, covering 3,000sq km (1,150 square miles). There are great tracts of forest, open grassland and flower filled meadows, sparkling lakes and abundant wildlife. You don't have to rough it if you don't want to, since there is a luxurious resort, **Elkhorn**, just outside the park and a good choice of accommodations in Wasagaming, as an alternative to camping. Wasagaming is a resort town situated on the south shore of Clear Lake, a deep spring-fed lake well-stocked with trout and pike, where you can go swimming, boating and windsurfing. All the assistance and advice you need is available from the Interpretive Center. The golf course at the eastern end of the lake is considered to be one of Canada's most beautiful. At Wasagaming there are shops, a movie theater, marina and tennis courts and its summer arts program includes exhibitions of provincial artists' work, craft classes and sales. Should you prefer more rustic

---

Clear Lake, Riding Mountain National Park offers forest, mountain, meadow – and fine fishing!

PICTURESQUE PARKS

Dauphin • Riding Mountain National Park Minnedosa • Brandon • Oak Lake • Shoal Lake • Russell • Roblin • Dauphin

Great parkland is the focus of this tour. The national and provincial parks are right on route for the spirited open-air life of fishing, camping, hiking and horseback riding, and for the golfer, a spectacular course. Many summer fairs take place in the area and there are old fur forts and a resort town along the way. The route also takes you into the western part of the province with a stop at Manitoba's second largest city, a flourishing tourist center and you can visit the 'desert' and drive through fertile farmland.

RECOMMENDED WALKS

1 **Riding Mountain National Park** is paradise for hikers, since there are 32 trails, from easy day-use boardwalks to hardier, long, overnight treks. There are detailed guides and maps at the Interpretive Center in Wasagaming.

7 In **Duck Mountain Provincial Park**, south of Wellman Lake, is a 1.6km (mile-long) forest trail, or you can hike to the top of Baldy Mountain—the view is superb. **Asessippi Provincial Heritage Park**, with its self-guiding trails, is also loved by keen walkers.

3 Self-guiding walking trails are a big attraction, too, in **Spruce Woods Provincial Heritage Park**, off **Highway 5**, south of the Assiniboine River—in the Spirit Sands, Manitoba's 'desert'. One of them leads through the 25sq km (10-square-mile) tract of sand dunes to the Devil's Punchbowl, a sunken pit created by an underground stream.

BACK TO NATURE

Wildlife is legion in the parks in this part of the province. In **Riding Mountain National Park** (1) you could well see elk and certainly bison—a herd of them live in an enclosure near Lake Audy. In **Spruce Woods Park** (3) there are lizards, snakes and cacti unique to Manitoba. **Duck Mountain Park** (7) is another good place.

SPECIAL TO . . .

In the Dauphin area is one of the biggest festivals which takes place on the long August weekend at the **Selo Ukraina** (Ukrainian Village), about 13km (8 miles) south of Dauphin, west of **Highway 10**. This is Canada's National Ukrainian Festival, which thousands of people attend to watch ethnic folk song and dance performances.

3 Manitoba's largest livestock show, the **Ag-Ex**, takes place at the end of October in Brandon, in conjunction with the **Manitoba Rodeo Championship**. Western Canada's largest agricultural fair also takes place in this city in March, while summer rodeos, horse shows and general family fun take place in June at the **Provincial Ex**.

FOR HISTORY BUFFS

3 One important archaeological site in Brandon is the **Stott Site**. It used to be a bison kill area: bones and artifacts discovered here date back 1,200 years. A bison enclosure and prehistoric encampment have been reconstructed for visitor viewing. Much of what is of historical interest on this route can be seen in the pioneer museums in the towns and along the highways.

FOR CHILDREN

Near Dauphin, the **Wild Kingdom Game Farm** is a small zoo that houses Siberian tigers, cougars and hippos, as well as more gentle varieties.

3 Perfect for cooling off is **Thunder Mountain Water Slide**, 8km (5 miles) west of Brandon on the Trans-Canada Highway. Here there are slides for small children, a huge hot tub, the province's longest twisting slides, a speed river run and The Bullet—a slide which gives you the impression of being in a car: speeds reach 72kph (45mph).

accommodations, you will find campgrounds at many of the other lakes in the park, including Audy, Grayling, Katherine, Moon and Whirlpool.

Should you be planning a winter visit, head for the **Mount Agassiz ski resort** at the park's eastern border.

Continue south on Highway 10 to Minnedosa.

Minnedosa, Manitoba

2 This picturesque agricultural community sited in a scenic valley has a love of summer country fairs— including the **Agricultural Fair** in July and the **Minnedosa Rodeo** in August which features traditional chuckwagon as well as chariot and Ben-Hur races.

Continue south on Highway 10 to Brandon.

Brandon, Manitoba

3 Tourism flourishes in the province's second largest city, so there is no shortage of places to stay or eat. You might well use it as a base for a visit to **Spruce Woods Provincial Heritage Park**, but the city itself offers many attractions of its own. Among the heritage sites are: **Brandon Court House** (1884), the **Paterson Matheson House** (1895), the 1912 former **Brandon School** and the 1913 **Display Building 11** on the Exhibition Grounds. The Admin-

istrative Building at the University (1901) is also a historic site.

The performing arts are strong in Brandon: some of the special events take place at the **Centennial Auditorium**, some at the **Allied Arts Council**. There are a number of museums in the city, notably **Daly House** on 18th Street, furnished as an 1880s wealthy home; **B J Hales Museum** in the University's Arts and Library Building, featuring mounted birds and animal specimens and geological displays; the **Commonwealth Air Training Plan Museum** at the airport, relating to World War II; and the **26th Field Artillery Regiment Museum** at Brandon Armories, filled with military memorabilia.

This is an agricultural area—much of western Canada's barley acreage is seeded with varieties developed at the **Agriculture Canada Research Station** (off Highway 10), which offers interested visitors drive-through and guided tours. Well-known agriculturists are remembered in portraiture at the **Agricultural Hall of Fame** on Queen's Avenue.

Take Highway 1A, then 1 west to Oak Lake.

Oak Lake, Manitoba

4 This is where early settlers stopped to repair their ox carts, thanks to the availability of wood. Today's visitors

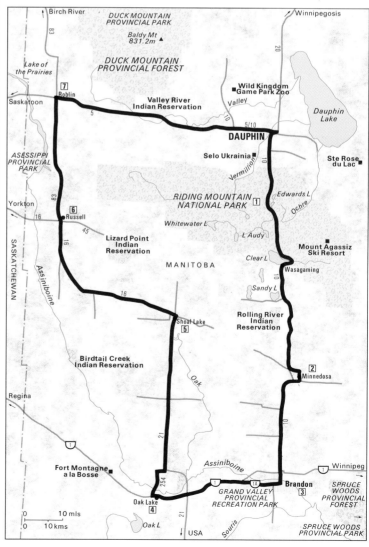

A tapestry of trees in Riding Mountain National Park

stop for the **Oak Lake Goose Refuge**. The sanctuary covers thousands of hectares and has a variety of wildlife including geese, swans, ducks and cranes. A restored **fire and curfew bell**, one of the very few in Western Canada, can be found on Main Street.

*Take **Highway 254**, then **21** north to Shoal Lake.*

Shoal Lake, Manitoba

5 One of the first posts of the North West Mounted Police, this town's history is recalled in the **Police and Pioneer Museum** (open summer only) which contains archival material and pioneer artifacts.

*Take **Highway 16** west, then north to Russell.*

Russell, Manitoba

6 Situated not far from **Asessippi Provincial Park**, at the southern end of the prairies, this town's artificial lake yields some of the best walleye in the province, and is therefore highly regarded by fishermen. If you are daring enough, try hang gliding— the view of the Assiniboine Valley is worth the effort. Russell itself is the site of **Boulton Manor**, home of the Boulton scouts, who fought in the North West Rebellion.

*Continue north on **Highway 83** to Roblin.*

Roblin, Manitoba

7 This is a possible base for visiting **Duck Mountain Provincial Park** where the fishing is superb. The park is part of a series of highlands known as the Manitoba Escarpment, thickly wooded and embedded with countless deep clear lakes that seem to overflow with trout and walleye. The town celebrates Museum Days in early July and a Fun Fair in October.

*Take **Highway 5** east to Dauphin.*

Dauphin – Riding Mountain National Park **16 (10)**
Riding Mountain National Park – Minnedosa **104 (65)**
Minnedosa – Brandon **45 (28)**
Brandon – Oak Lake **55 (34)**
Oak Lake – Shoal Lake **78 (48)**
Shoal Lake – Russell **75 (47)**
Russell – Roblin **53 (33)**
Roblin – Dauphin **93 (58)**

SCENIC ROUTES

The **Yellowhead Highway, Highway 16**, which traverses the western portion of this tour route, is one of the most scenic ways of crossing Manitoba. There is also a scenic drive along the Assiniboine River valley, north of Oak Lake, which reveals the effects of glaciation in the area.

SASKATCHEWAN

A young province (1905) but a large one (more than 647,500 sq km, 250,000 square miles) half of which is forest, Saskatchewan is known as Canada's Breadbasket, because it produces so much wheat. It was the Cree Indians, centuries ago, who called the province's greatest body of water Kisiskatchewan – 'the river that flows swiftly' – but it was European immigrants, many from Russia and Scandinavia, who swelled the population early this century.

Although much of the province is flat prairie, there are mountains: Cypress Hills in the southwest, at 1,392m (4,567 feet), is higher than Banff, and Duck and Moose Mountains also add relief in the south. Some of the time you may think you are in a desert, for there are great areas of sand dunes; but then there is the gigantic Qu'Appelle Valley, with a string of eight lakes and resort communities. Saskatchewan boasts 100,000 freshwater lakes, but most of them are in the rugged north.

It was across Saskatchewan prairies that the first North West Mounted Police trudged to bring law and order to scattered settlements – some of their original posts, including force headquarters, Fort Walsh, revive the life and times of those 'riders of the plains'.

Farming has given Saskatchewan its wholesome reputation and a number of friendly country farms offer accommodation. There are perhaps a dozen cities, but it is rural peace that is this destination's trademark. In addition to the national parks, thousands of acres have been designated provincial parks.

Crafts and country fairs are a way of life here, as are rodeos and Indian pow-wows. Wild west celebrations, such as Buffalo Days in Regina, are much loved events, while the Metis people celebrate their cultural heritage during Back to Batoche Days. Pow-wows, with traditional food, costumes and dancing, are to be found at many reserves, including Sakimay, Poundmaker, Piapot and Standing Buffalo. And you can go wagon trekking the old fashioned way in the Cypress Hills: rides can be as short as an hour or several days long.

Saskatchewan lacks a coastline, but has plenty of watersport possibilities. Large Lake Diefenbaker is perfect for boating; Waskesiu Lake has a popular beach; the Valley lakes are well suited to waterskiing and windsurfing; Little Manitou Lake is so salty that you can lie back and read a paper in it.

Saskatoon:
Saskatoon, the largest city in the province, sits on the banks of the South Saskatchewan River. On the eastern side, the **Diefenbaker Centre**, on the campus of the University of Saskatchewan, showcases memorabilia of Canada's 13th Prime Minister, John Diefenbaker. On the western side the **Mendel Art Gallery** is the city's biggest.

A major attraction is the **Western Development Museum**, which features a typical Boomtown 1910 street and an interesting collection of vintage cars. The **Ukrainian Museum of Canada** pays tribute to those settlers who helped shape the province as it is today. (In mid-May there is an annual traditional Ukrainian celebration in the city, one of several ethnic events.)

Large enough to offer a full range of restaurants and hotels, including the majestic **Hotel Bessborough**, Saskatoon is also small enough to stay hospitable and friendly. It has its own symphony orchestra and theaters, plus summer river-side Shakespeare performances. Shopping areas include Broadway Avenue, and children will enjoy

Kinsmen Park, with its play village, mini train and ferris wheel, and the **Forestry Farm Park** and **zoo** which features a wide range of prairie animals. For a scenic walk or cycle, the 14km (9-mile) **Meewasin Valley Trail** follows the riverbank through parks, natural areas and parts of downtown. (Walking tours are available from the Meewasin Valley Interpretive Center.)

Regina:

Regina, a cosmopolitan capital with small city appeal, grew from a settlement called Pile o'Bones (so named because of the buffalo bones left by Indian hunters). The creek *Oskana* (meaning bones) has become Wascana, an enormous urban park of 930 hectares (2,230 acres) in the heart of town, whose focal point is Wascana Lake. The **Legislative Building** dominates Wascana Centre (summer tours available). The Centre is also the setting for the **Museum of Natural History**, among whose displays is a moving mechanical dinosaur; the **Science Centre** with hands-on exhibits; and **Diefenbaker's Homestead**, a modest wooden dwelling containing family memorabilia. Take a summer

Old and new co-exist in peaceful order in welcoming Saskatoon, Saskatchewan's second city

carriage ride through the park or a horse-drawn sleigh ride in winter.

Regina's long association with the Royal Canadian Mounted Police has resulted in the **RCMP Museum**, which includes accounts of Indian Chief Sitting Bull, the Klondike Gold Rush and the North West Rebellion. The city also boasts Canada's only Mountie training academy: RCMP sunset retreat ceremonies take place in July and August, and performances of the Musical Ride take place at the **Agridome**.

The city has its own symphony orchestra, over 500 restaurants, a choice of hotels and plenty of shops. Summer festivals include Buffalo Days in July – a week of parades, thrill rides, craft exhibits and entertainment. In winter, there is an international snowmobile race in early February. For children there is a **Wildslides** waterslide park; for sports fans, racing on **Queensbury Downs**; and for history buffs, tours of **Government House**.

3/4 days – 630km (391 miles)

THE GREAT OUTDOORS

Saskatoon • Wakaw • Melfort • Tisdale
Greenwater Lake Provincial Park • Foam Lake
Wynyard • Saskatoon

This east central part of the province is a region of great parks and outdoor opportunities. Though you would have to deviate to visit the jewel of the parks, Prince Albert, there are many other natural and recreational areas close to the route you will follow. European settlers were the first to farm the fields, clearing the land for homesteads, building towns with onion-domed churches, and preserving their traditions, now enjoyed in many a summer festival. Watch out for the symbol of a barn along highways and secondary roads if you are looking for a vacation farm, and linger at the lakes for a change of pace.

The official flower of Saskatchewan, the western red lily, now protected by law

ℹ 102–310 Idylwyld Drive North, Saskatoon

*Take **Highway 41** to Wakaw.*

Wakaw, Saskatchewan

1 Stop for coffee in this town with its tranquil lake setting. The local **Heritage Museum** on First Street will show you a restored school with memorabilia of the 1900–1940 period; and near by, in Lion's Park, the **John Diefenbaker Law Office** features a replica of the first office used by Canada's former prime minister in 1918.

ℹ 122 Main Street

***Highway 41** continues to Melfort.*

Melfort, Saskatchewan

2 This is a good base in the province's parkland belt. The fertility of the surrounding Carrot River Valley underlines the prime importance of agriculture to the region. Admission is free to the **Canada Agriculture Research Station** just south of town (**Highway 6**), where methods of harvesting, storing and feeding are researched, and guided tours may be arranged on request. During the big July agricultural exhibition on the fairgrounds you can also watch championship

An aerial view of the South Saskatchewan River at Saskatoon, a city divided in two by the river

chariot and chuckwagon races. The **Pioneer Village Museum** is located on those fairgrounds, next to a replica pioneer farm, and contains artifacts from the early days of Melfort and its district.

ℹ Saskatchewan Avenue (summer only); 213 Main Street

*Take **Highway 3** to Tisdale.*

Tisdale, Saskatchewan

3 The fairgrounds of this reasonably serviced town, which is also in the agricultural belt, are the scene for several livestock exhibitions and

Sport and spectacle in Saskatchewan reflect the province's farming heritage and tradition

horse shows, especially during the **July Fair Days**. A big April event is the **Rambler Indoor Rodeo and Trade Fair**, featuring all the standard rodeo events, such as bronco and steer riding, which takes place at the **Recplex**, near the town center. Small country fairs often take place in the surrounding communities.

ℹ 100 Street and 99th Avenue

SPECIAL TO ...

In Saskatchewan there are various festivities, though in this region they are limited in size, as none of the towns is large. Summer, however, is generally the time for craft fairs and what are often called **Heritage Days**. Baked goods, art sales and livestock shows are on offer—but on a small scale. In June, there is the **Earth, Wind and Sky Kite Festival**, something every child and adult will enjoy.

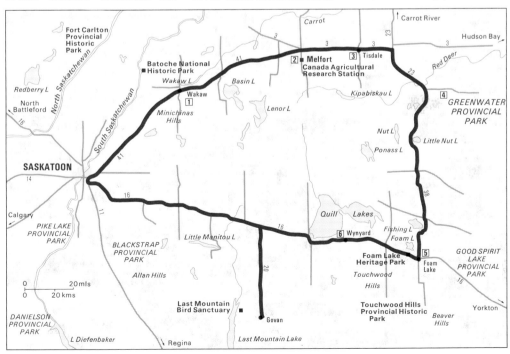

FOR HISTORY BUFFS

Wanuskewin Heritage Park, near Saskatoon, is being opened to visitors in 1992. On this site archaeologists have discovered native Indian artifacts that predate Egypt's pyramids, and these are being incorporated into a major tourist attraction for Canada with a visitor center, tours, audiovisual programs and interpretive trails. Among the finds have been a 5th-century medicine wheel, several buffalo jumps and early habitation sites.

SCENIC ROUTES

A circular tour around any of the lakes *en route* including Foam Lake and Quill Lakes, promises pleasurable driving since both these areas are good for birdspotting. Best access for these wetlands is in good (dry) weather.

FOR CHILDREN

If the children are not sporty, this tour is not ideal for them. The parks and lakes, however, do provide outdoor amusements. Close to Saskatoon, **Blackstrap Provincial Park** has a lakeside beach, boating facilities and a manmade mountain, built to accommodate the 1971 Winter Olympics. If you stay at a farm the children will be able to help feed the cows, go berry picking and maybe have a go at maneuvering a tractor.

RECOMMENDED WALKS

Within the region of this route, gentle walking is encouraged in two 'natural environment' provincial parks—**Greenwater Lake** and **Good Spirit Lake**, near Yorkton. Both are large areas, representative of natural landscapes with a range of attractions. At Good Spirit, the best trail access is from the lake's south shore, where you can see sand dune succession and vegetation that includes willows and juniper.

BACK TO NATURE

6 In common with many lakes in Saskatchewan, the freshwater and surrounding wetlands of **Quill Lakes** are home to numerous wildfowl and waders. Look for spotted sandpipers around the shorelines and other species such as solitary sandpiper and lesser yellowlegs in variable numbers during spring and autumn migration. Wildfowl of the area include Canada goose, bluewinged teal, green-winged teal, American wigeon and pintail.

Top: There are so many lakes in Saskatchewan you could fish every day for a year in a different one! Above: With 24 national and provincial parks to choose from, Saskatchewan is one of the last great solitudes on earth

*Continue on **Highway 3**, then south on **Highway 23**, and continue on **Highway 38** to Greenwater Lake Provincial Park.*

Greenwater Lake Provincial Park, Saskatchewan

4 Spruce and aspen grow on the 18,333 hectares (45,300 acres) of Greenwater Lake's rolling hills, where you can camp or rent a log cabin for an overnight stay, or simply stop for a picnic. There are facilities for paddleboats and canoes, fishing, horse riding and tennis, and during the summer interpretive programs are given.

***Highways 38** then **310** continue to Foam Lake.*

Foam Lake, Saskatchewan

5 Nature lovers taking advantage of the area's lakes and wetlands will appreciate the service center here, with its small **museum** of local history, including pioneer artifacts. The major attraction is **Foam Lake Heritage Marsh**, which is open year round. These 1,618 hectares (4,000 acres) of wetlands are home to waterfowl such as great blue and green herons, sora rail, spotted sandpipers and American bitterns.

ℹ️ 402 Cameron Street

***Highway 16** leads to Wynyard.*

Wynyard, Saskatchewan

6 This small town is a useful base for outdoor pursuits around the **Quill Lakes**, where ducks and geese congregate. The **Frank Cameron Museum**, housed in an old school, features a mixture of agricultural, medical, education and sports items.

ℹ️ Main Street

***Highway 16** leads back to Saskatoon.*

Saskatoon – Wakaw **89 (55)**
Wakaw – Melfort **86 (53)**
Melfort – Tisdale **40 (25)**
Tisdale – Greenwater Lake **64 (40)**
Greenwater Lake – Foam Lake **114 (71)**
Foam Lake – Wynyard **49 (30)**
Wynyard – Saskatoon **188 (117)**

Batoche: steeped in a history of conflict and bloodshed

ⓘ 102–310 Idylwyld Drive North, Saskatoon

*Take **Highway 11** to Rosthern.*

Rosthern, Saskatchewan

1 Stop here to see the brick-built former junior college, which has now become the **Mennonite Heritage Museum**. The items it houses illustrate how the district was settled and developed and how the Mennonite School of Protestants was founded and flourished.

ⓘ corner of Main Street and Railway Avenue

*Take **Highway 312** east to Batoche.*

Batoche, Saskatchewan

2 It was here that the mixed-blood Metis people settled after leaving Red River in Manitoba, hoping to continue their traditional way of life. It was not to be so and in 1885 the North West Rebellion, following land rights arguments and declining fortunes, brought clashes between the Canadian militia, under General Frederick Middleton, and the Indians and Metis, led by Louis Riel and Gabriel Dumont. The first of the battles took place on the site which is now the small town of **Duck Lake**. The regional historical museum here has displays on Indian and Metis communities and the Rebellion. West of Duck Lake is the old fur-trading post of **Fort Carlton**, and to the east is **Batoche National Historic Park (Highway 225)**, which tells how the little Batoche settlement grew into a thriving Metis community, whose way of life was threatened by the Canadian government. A short walk away is the **Church of St Antoine de**

REBEL COUNTRY

Saskatoon ● Rosthern ● Batoche ● Prince Albert ● Waskesiu Lake/Prince Albert National Park ● Shellbrook ● Blaine Lake ● North Battleford ● Saskatoon

Take a tour through west central Saskatchewan and you will discover the heart of Canada's old northwest. After the explorers and the fur traders came the pioneers, transforming the prairie into workable land. Here, too, the last armed conflict on Canadian soil took place: the North West Rebellion in 1885, whose story and that of its Metis leader, Louis Riel, have become legendary. A section of the route is along the Yellow-head Highway (Route 16) named after yellow-headed Iroquois trapper and guide Pierre Hatsinaton; while other roads take you to beautiful unspoilt parks and lakes.

Padoue and the **rectory** (restored to 1896). Look for the bullet holes near the top window, another reminder of the past conflict. The cemetery con-

SPECIAL TO ...

In late July, **Back to Batoche Days** is a reminder of old times in Batoche with Metis dancing, fiddling and jigging contests and cultural events (2). North Battleford's **Western Development Museum** (7) has special demonstration days at the end of May and in August, but around mid-July **North West Territorial Days** (on the exhibition grounds) is even livelier with chuckwagon races, fiddling contests and a parade. Rodeos are frequently held in this part of the province; notable are **North Battleford's Kinsmen Indoor Rodeo**, late April, and Shellbrook's outdoor July competitive event (3).

FOR HISTORY BUFFS

2 Fort Carlton Provincial Historic Park, 25km (16 miles) west of Duck Lake on **Highway 212**, was built by Hudson's Bay Company in 1810 as a fur trading post. Guides will explain how trading was done and show you a store stocked with items useful to fur-traders. Outside the reconstructed stockade you can follow a trail to the river.

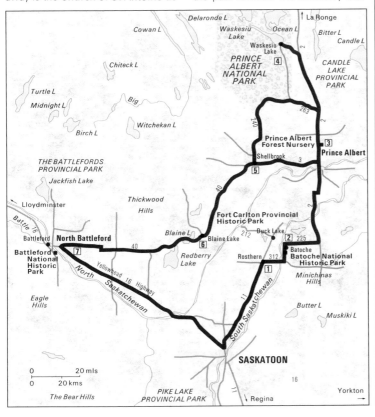

BACK TO NATURE

The best place, once again, is Prince Albert National Park, where, for instance, **Lavallee Lake** is home to Canada's second largest white pelican colony, and herds of bison roam freely. The park protects a variety of wildlife, from moose and red fox to a healthy population of black bears, which should not be considered as cuddly pets. Watch the beavers, otters, ducks and loons on the lakes; catching a glimpse of the coyotes and badgers who live in the park is more difficult. Canoeing is a good way to spot wildlife. Routes vary from the easy **Bagwa Route** to the challenging **Grey Owl Wilderness** or **Bladebone** canoe route.

FOR CHILDREN

Children who are intrigued by battle sites and/or appreciate nature can be well occupied on this tour. The country fairs and rodeo events will probably appeal, too. Water slides, however, are the main purpose-designed amusement for youngsters. **Battlefords Superslide**, on King Hill at North Battleford (7), is one prime example, with 11 waterslides offering various degrees of challenge. **Kinsmen Water Park**, in Prince Albert (3), features two 91m (300-foot) slides and a 10m (35-foot) vertical 'river ride', much loved by young visitors.

tains the graves of Gabriel Dumont, Batoche founder Xavier Letendre and those Metis killed in the final assault. On the site are the remains of the original Batoche village and the trenches used by Middleton's army.

*Take **Highway 225** east then join **Highway 2** heading north to Prince Albert.*

Prince Albert, Saskatchewan

3 Gateway to the north, this bustling city on the banks of the Saskatchewan River is a recommended overnight base; the surrounding area is among the best for year-round recreation, especially for hiking and fishing. This is a scenic city, bordered by forests and grain fields, and has long been an important center for the forest industry. You can visit the **Prince Albert Forest Nursery**, 17km (11 miles) north next to Highway 2, at no charge. Millions of trees are grown here as part of a reforestation program and for restocking parks.

Of historic interest is **Diefenbaker House**, on 19th Street West, which commemorates Canada's past Prime Minister John Diefenbaker's close links with the town, and contains some original furnishings; and **Nisbet Church**, in Kinsmen Park, built in 1866. The **Prince Albert Historical Museum** is located in an old fire hall on River Street, documenting the area; in summer one-hour walking tours leave from here. In what was a North West Military Police guardroom on Marquis Road is the **Rotary Museum of Police and Corrections**, where there are displays on the law and correction in Northern Saskatchewan. Next to it, the **Evolution of Education Museum** was a 1920s school and now displays educational items from 1900 to the 1940s. Art lovers will find a variety of local and provincial works at the **Grace Campbell Gallery** in John M Cuelenaere Library and **The Little**

Gallery in Prince Albert Art Center. A particularly good private collection of wildlife specimens may be seen at the **Lund Wildlife Exhibit**, River Street West, on a riverbank in the downtown area.

ⓘ Marquis Road and **Highway 2** (open May–September); also 3700 Second Avenue West

*Continue north on **Highway 2** to Waskesiu Lake and the entrance to Prince Albert National Park.*

Waskesiu Lake and Prince Albert National Park, Saskatchewan

4 This service center for the park's visitors is a hub of activity, where you can use the lakeside beach, take a scenic boat tour, buy native handicrafts or stock up on groceries. Guided walks depart from the **Prince Albert National Park Nature Center**, where you should drop in anyway before exploring the park, one of the finest in the West. Its woods and wildlife inspired woodsman-turned-orator and author, Grey Owl, who lived for several years at **Beaver Lodge**, on Ajawaan Lake. His cabin, accessible by boat or by overnight hike, is one of the park's attractions. For many years, Grey Owl was thought to be an authentic Canadian Indian and was widely acclaimed for his written work and speeches on tour in Europe on behalf of the native peoples and the need for conservation. When he died, it was discovered that he was actually an Englishman. Though this killed the myth, his memory and his writings live on.

ⓘ Waskesiu Drive

*Retrace your route until the sign for **263** and **240**, leading to Shellbrook; alternatively, return to Prince Albert and take **Highway 3** west.*

The Prince Albert National Park is home to herds of bison, and is one of the West's finest parks

Open country near North Battleford. Saskatchewan is called 'Canada's Breadbasket' and produces over 60 per cent of Canadian wheat

Shellbrook, Saskatchewan

5 Stop for coffee here, and visit the small town's old railroad station, now a Heritage Building and a **local history museum**, whose rodeo grounds are the setting for a three-day July event that promises fun for anyone who loves cowboy activities.

ⓘ 54 Main Street

*Take **Highway 40** south to Blaine Lake.*

Blaine Lake, Saskatchewan

6 Picturesque countryside surrounds this small lakeside community, not far from **Martins Lake Regional Park**. Its old railroad station is being developed into a **local history museum**, and will concentrate on the history of the area.

ⓘ Main Street

*   **Highway 40** *continues to North Battleford.*

North Battleford, Saskatchewan

7 Near the spot where the North Saskatchewan and Battle rivers meet, the city of North Battleford is linked by the province's longest bridge to its historic sister town of Battleford, first seat of government for the North West Territories, an important Mounted Police post, and a center of conflict during the North West Rebellion. Together, the two communities form an interesting and popular tourist area; it is well worth spending some time here. North Battleford offers all the usual city facilities, including several excellent art galleries, and hosts many seasonal events and activities. Make an appointment and you can visit the **George Hooey Wildlife Exhibit (Highway 16)**, a wildlife museum of taxidermy, with more than 400 specimens. No appointment is necessary to see North Battleford's most famous museum: **Western Development Heritage Farm and Village (Highways 16 and 40)**, which recreates the streets of a small 1925 Saskatchewan town, demonstrates early farming techniques and has special summer programs.

In neighboring Battleford, you will find a first-class collection of firearms in the **Fred Light Museum**, but the 'must' is **Battleford National Historic Park**, just southeast of North Battleford. This was the original post for the Canadian Mounties, and costumed guides will show you the 1886 barracks and four period furnished buildings.

A half-hour's drive north will bring you to **The Battlefords Provincial Park**, on the shores of Jackfish Lake (a favorite with anglers). There is an 18-hole golf course here along with a sandy beach, picnic spots and a nature trail.

ⓘ junction of **Highways 16 and 40**

*Take **Highway 16** back to Saskatoon.*

Saskatoon – Rosthern **66 (41)**
Rosthern – Batoche **24 (15)**
Batoche – Prince Albert **76 (47)**
Prince Albert – Waskesiu Lake **84 (52)**
Waskesiu Lake – Shellbrook **128 (80)**
Shellbrook – Blaine Lake **60 (37)**
Blaine Lake – North Battleford **100 (62)**
North Battleford – Saskatoon **138 (86)**

SCENIC ROUTES

Scenically you can't beat **Prince Albert National Park**—almost 405,000 hectares (a million acres) of forested wilderness and wonderful waterways (off **Highway 2**) which preserve three types of the province's landscape: tracts of grasslands, gentle wooded parkland, and northern boreal forest. Admittedly much of the park's beauty is best enjoyed on foot or by canoe, not by car, but you can drive past several of the park's lovely lakes and stop at vantage points *en route.*

RECOMMENDED WALKS

Prince Albert National Park has several well-established trails that don't need too much stamina. The self-guiding **Mud Creek Trail** is a loop under 3km (2 miles) long, as is the **Boundary Bog Trail**; neither should take you more than an hour. Even shorter, and just as popular, is the **Tree Beard Trail**, near the Narrows Campground. Along the Waskesiu River, a short boardwalk trail is accessible to the disabled. Longer hikes include the 9.6km (6-mile) **Kingfisher Trail** and the 24km (15-mile) **Freight Trail**, part of an original track used by the fur traders.

4/5 days – 932km (578 miles)

ON THE COWBOY TRAIL

Regina ● Moose Jaw ● Swift Current ● Maple Creek ● Cypress Hills Provincial Park Eastend ● Shaunavon ● Assiniboia Avonlea ● Regina

You will travel on this tour through the sprawling southwest, a mixture of ranchland, badlands and prairie. In the wide open spaces where the cattle graze you will probably see mule deer and antelope from the highway, and you will certainly find a rodeo or two in Saskatchewan's cowboy country. One of the highest parts of the province is at Cypress Hills, and sand dunes can be found just north of Maple Creek. Accommodations range from country farms scattered through prairie country to the facilities of two of Saskatchewan's best-known cities.

ⓘ Highway No 1 East, Regina

Take Highway 1 to Moose Jaw.

Moose Jaw, Saskatchewan

1 A large but friendly city smack in the middle of wheat lands, Moose Jaw has enough restaurants and accommodations to suit a short or longer stay. Canadian forces based just south keep its airport busy and make it home for their famous aerobatics team, the Snowbirds. Ask how the city got its name and you will be given all kinds of answers, including one theory that the river bend here resembles a moose's jawbone.

Home to rare animals and wild flowers, the Cypress Hills Provincial Park welcomes visitors too

However, the most likely reason is that the word is derived from the Cree Indian word *moosegaw*, meaning 'warm breezes'.

The locals may say Al Capone once stayed here, but that is doubtful. Nevertheless, there is a sense of history along Main Street and you can take yourself on a walking tour of the city's most historic sites; a booklet is available from the **Moose Jaw Art Museum** at Crescent Park, where some of the most interesting artifacts are the Sioux and Cree beadwork.

If you permit yourself museum time, visit the **Western Development Museum** on Diefenbaker Drive, which traces the history of transportation on the prairies. A few miles out of town on **Highway 2, Sukanen Ship, Pioneer Village and Museum** contains 13 old buildings and many pioneer artifacts, including veteran tractors. The *Sukanen*, an ocean-going vessel, was built on the prairies and the museum hosts several summer events.

If you plan to relax, you will find the recently developed **Wakamow Valley** a pleasant spot. A short trail leads to **Plaxton's Lake**, which, along with **Kiwanis River Park** and **Kinsmen Park**, is a place for a summer picnic. The Valley's parks and arenas, along with the exhibition grounds and Civic Center, are settings for a variety of shows and fairs in season.

ⓘ 88 Saskatchewan Street East

The Trans Canada Highway (1) continues to Swift Current.

Swift Current, Saskatchewan

2 Not only concerned with the trade of livestock and grain, this city is the base for all the provincial oil exploration and can feed and water you well. Bison no longer wallow in the creek that flows through town, past parks and a golf course, but the depressions they made around the latter's 17th hole are still visible. These days it is two-legged animals which take to the creekside **Chinook Pathway**. There is an **agricultural research station** just east of town,

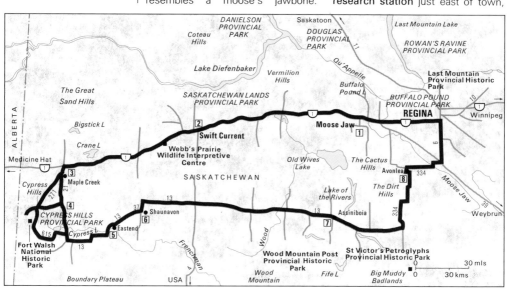

The Legislation Building in Regina, the province's capital named in honor of Queen Victoria

which interested parties may visit, and the **local museum** naturally contains a pioneer room and Indian items. **Kinetic Park** is the location of a number of shows and fairs.

The sports-minded might take a side trip to **Saskatchewan Landing Provincial Park** (north of the city), one of three on the shores of Lake Diefenbaker, a reservoir on the South Saskatchewan River both favored by fishermen and watersport enthusiasts. The region around Swift Current is also a mecca for goose hunting.

ℹ junction of **Highways 1** and **4**

Highway 1 *continues to Maple Creek.*

Maple Creek, Saskatchewan

3 Now you are in the heart of the ranchlands, on the brink of Cypress Hills, in a 'cow town' which still has that frontier-days feeling. The town acts as a service center for the surrounding ranching and farming communities and for visitors, and is a base for touring the high country and its provincial park.

Maple Creek's old-time heritage is quite obvious in a quick walk down

Main Street and a look at the store fronts, but **The Old Timer's Museum** on Jasper Street has a very good collection of old-time pictures and early ranching memorabilia, while an old two-story brick school has been converted into the **Jasper Cultural and Historical Center** with art gallery and general store, and where you can take afternoon tea in a Victorian parlor.

ℹ 205 Jasper Street

*Take **Highway 21** south to Cypress Hills Provincial Park.*

Cypress Hills Provincial Park, Saskatchewan

4 In this park you will find acres of peaceful pine forests and rare wild flowers. The highest point east of the Rockies, it is a delightful contrast to the rest of the province, and may tempt naturalists to stay overnight; there is first-class accommodation as well as campsites.

Cypress Hills is a hideaway, too, for many native animals such as the wapiti, moose and endangered trumpeter swans. Active visitors may take horse rides, play golf or tennis and use the park's outdoor pool and beach.

*Leave the park via **Highway 21** or **615** south, to join **Highway 13** east to Eastend.*

SPECIAL TO . . .

In this region are rodeos whose events include ladies' barrel races, bull riding and calf roping, steer wrestling and bareback bronco riding. Moose Jaw's **Hometown Rodeo** (indoors) takes place in April (1). Swift Current's **Frontier City Stampede** is in late May and standard rodeo events are very much a part of **Frontier Days**, in late June (2). Chuckwagon and chariot races are part of Maple Creek's late May **Cowtown Rodeo**; arts and crafts have their role in the annual late June **Ranch Rodeo** (3). Almost every small town holds similar summer festivities, including Eastend, Shaunavon and Assiniboia.

FOR HISTORY BUFFS

4 Fort Walsh National Historic Park is accessible from Cypress Hills Park in dry weather or otherwise via **Highway 271** from Maple Creek. It was a major Mountie post in the 1880s and has been reconstructed with interpretive displays.

FOR CHILDREN

City children who have never ridden in a wagon or watched a bucking bronco should enjoy some novel experiences on this tour and will probably be delighted that denim is *de rigueur* and pancake breakfasts common. The scarlet-coated Mounties and the history that surrounds them are generally an attraction, too. For small children, there is a petting zoo section at the **Moose Jaw Wild Animal Park** in Moose Jaw River Valley (1) which also features wildlife exhibits of creatures native to the province.

SCENIC ROUTES

Deviate from the tour slightly and you will discover the **Great Sand Hills**, north of Maple Creek, where there are active sand dunes (4), or travel south of Regina, where the **Big Muddy Badlands** (once a haven for outlaws) is scenically intriguing. Providing it is not wet, the less developed western segment of Cypress Hills Provincial Park may be reached via the scenic **Gap Road**, which leads to Fort Walsh (5). From the road there are trails to the conglomerate cliffs — hills made up of sand, gravel and pebbles.

RECOMMENDED WALKS

A short paved trail follows the river to **Plaxton's Lake**, in the Wakamow Valley at Moose Jaw (1), and is recommended for an easy summer stroll. The nature trails within **Cypress Hills Park** (4) are a definite must for hikes that are not too exhausting. The area has an alpine atmosphere and there are many country guest farms, as well as working ranches, some of which accept guests.

BACK TO NATURE

The southwest is a good area for viewing wildlife: it is not difficult to spot a prairie-loving pronghorn antelope without leaving the highway. In **Cypress Hills Provincial Park** (4), prairie falcons and a multitude of songbirds can be seen and heard.

The view from Conglomerate Cliffs, Cypress Hills Provincial Park

Eastend, Saskatchewan

5 The local museum of this small, agriculturally minded community is housed in a former downtown theater and features paleontological specimens collected in the area: plant and animal fossils. Just east of town the **Beef City Feed Mill** invites you to look around its commercial operation. In summer, Eastend holds rodeos in its rodeo grounds.

ⓘ Red Coat Drive

Highway 13 continues to Shaunavon.

Shaunavon, Saskatchewan

6 This slightly larger town on the Red Coat Trail has fossil exhibits, Indian artifacts and pioneer tools displayed in its **Grand Coteau Heritage and Cultural Centre**, and it also hosts country fairs and rodeos. Highway 13 is known as the Red Coat Trail because of the famous 1,300km (800-mile) march west by the first 300 recruits of the North West Mounted Police in the mid-1870s. This march was to bring law and order to the unruly North West.

ⓘ 401 3rd Street West

Highway 13 continues to Assiniboia.

Assiniboia, Saskatchewan

7 Named after the district formed in the North West Territories in 1882, this town is used as a base for hunting ducks, upland game birds and deer. Four regional parks are within close proximity, and the downtown

District Historical Museum on Main and Dominion is worth a quick stop, featuring several turn-of-the-century displays.

A short drive from this town takes you to **Willow Bunch**, whose local museum (in an old convent) commemorates Jean Louis Legare, a respected Metis who founded the community, and Edouard Beaupre, the 'Willow Giant' who was over 2m (8-feet) tall and wore size 22 shoes. A little way west, at **St Victor's Petroglyphs Provincial Historic Park**, rock carvings illustrate the ancient Indian way of life.

ⓘ 131 3rd Avenue West

Take Highway 13 east, then 334 north to Avonlea.

Avonlea, Saskatchewan

8 This small community is situated in an area once called Sunshine Valley, but it now takes its name from Lucy Maud Montgomery's book *Anne of Avonlea*; during homesteading days, relatives of the authoress lived in the district. The local museum on Main Street features displays that illustrate pioneer life.

ⓘ 203 Main Street

Take Highway 334 east, then 6 north to Regina.

Regina – Moose Jaw	71 (44)
Moose Jaw – Swift Current	174 (108)
Swift Current – Maple Creek	138 (86)
Maple Creek – Cypress Hills Provincial Park	27 (17)
Cypress Hills Provincial Park – Eastend	89 (55)
Eastend – Shaunavon	33 (20)
Shaunavon – Assiniboia	189 (117)
Assininboia – Avonlea	132 (82)
Avonlea – Regina	79 (49)

Grain elevators at sunset near Saskatoon, in a province where 'agriculture is king'

ⓘ Highway No 1 East, Regina

> Take **Highway 33** southeast to the junction with **35** and continue south to Weyburn.

Weyburn, Saskatchewan

1 The only real city on this route and the main urban center along the Red Coat Trail is able to provide a range of visitor services. W O Mitchell, who wrote the novel *Who Has Seen the Wind*, immortalized the city as Crocus, Saskatchewan—the reason all points of interest are signmarked with a crocus.

You could well find an unusual memento in Weyburn's shops, and in summer you can expect to find a country music jamboree or old-fashioned fair taking place in the exhibition grounds or in **Nickle Lake Regional Park**. This may be a growing city, but it still has a small-town air. The fine **Soo Line Historical Museum** concentrates on pioneer articles used in the district, and **Turner's Museum** contains curling memorabilia gathered from a variety of sources and ice rinks.

ⓘ Soo Line Historical Museum

> Continue east on **Highway 13** to Carlyle.

The Qu'Appelle Valley reaches two-thirds of the way across Saskatchewan. Among other sports, it is a paradise for hang-gliders

A PRAIRIE EXPERIENCE

Regina ● Weyburn ● Carlyle ● Whitewood
Grenfell ● Melville ● Abernethy ● Fort
Qu'Appelle ● Regina

Expect stunning scenery on this tour of the southeast—a true prairie experience, with miles of golden wheat under an endless sky and brilliant sunsets silhouetting the grain silos. There are also some surprises: the cavernous 'garden' of the Qu'Appelle Valley, carved by ancient glaciers and now a recreational playground, and Moose Mountain highland, an improbable contrast to the flat stretch of plains. This is a rural route of crafts and crops, farms and small towns: do not expect city thrills. It is a discovery of the quiet open space.

SPECIAL TO . . .

In this part of the province there are country fairs in the summer season, many of them revolving around agricultural events, like that in early July in Weyburn (1), when pony chariot and chuckwagon races are extras to a light and heavy horse show, or that in Melville (5) in late June, when firework displays and craft exhibits add to the cattle and horse shows.

FOR HISTORY BUFFS

2 Cannington Manor Historic Park, 29km (18 miles) northeast of Carlyle on grid roads, portrays a pre-1896 prairie settlement of the type that attracted the English gentry. For a short time those early settlers lived the lives of country gentlemen, with fox hunts and cricket matches, until they were forced to give up British traditions and adapt to a New World existence.

FOR CHILDREN

Sophisticated teenagers may grow bored on a tour like this, but those who are happy to be outdoors will enjoy the rural pursuits. Few of the regional attractions are totally geared to children, but the **Kenosee Superslide** on Highway 9, near the entrance to **Moose Mountain Provincial Park** (2), is worth a try for the waterslides.

BACK TO NATURE

From the prairies, away from city lights, you may well catch sight of the *aurora borealis* (Northern Lights)—natural fireworks which glow and dart high above the earth—from 130 to over 965km (81 to 600 miles), their beams sometimes flaring red or green. They are formed by fast-moving electrons hitting rarefied gases and causing natural 'neon'.

SCENIC ROUTES

The most scenic route is through the Qu'Appelle Valley, which contains eight lakes surrounded by parks, among them **Crooked Lake** in the east and **Echo** and **Pasqua Lakes** in the middle. According to legend, while an Indian brave was out canoeing through this valley, his love became ill and began to call his name. Though miles away, he heard her cries and called out *Qu'Appelle?* (who calls?), but by the time he reached home she had died.

Carlyle, Saskatchewan

2 Carlyle, named after the Scottish author, is not very large and, as a town, is quite new (incorporated in 1905), but it is an important tourist center for the southeast because of its location close to **Moose Mountain Provincial Park**. Its **Rusty Relic Museum**, on Third Street West, is housed in a 1910 Canadian National Railways Station. Displays are featured in room settings and include a dentistry collection which is enough to give you toothache!

ⓘ 210 Main Street

*Take **Highway 9** north to Whitewood.*

Whitewood, Saskatchewan

3 In this typical small country town of the southeast, homesteader days are annually revived and the **Chopping Museum and Old George Collectibles** manages to be both museum and antique shop (on Highway 1). The handsome 19th-century, 22-room mansion houses an eclectic collection, from coal oil lamps to rifles. Pioneer history, much of it personal, unfolds at the **Historical Museum** in town.

ⓘ corner of Lalonde and 4th Avenue

*Take **Highway 1** west to Grenfell.*

Grenfell, Saskatchewan

4 Local handicrafts are on sale here in summer at the **Grenfell Regional Park Craft Shop**. Drop into the **local museum** on Wolseley Avenue, a large turreted 1904 house containing turn-of-the-century pieces, with an annex of pioneer and military artifacts, one of the region's best. A good picnic spot is **Crooked Lake Provincial Park**, not far away on the north shore of Crooked Lake in the Qu'Appelle Valley.

ⓘ 800 Desmond Street

*Take **Highway 47** north to Melville.*

Melville, Saskatchewan

5 This Saskatchewan rail center is a stop on the main line to Churchill, and gained importance when it was chosen as a major service center for the Grand Trunk Railway. It was named in honor of one of the railway's presidents, Charles Melville Hays, who died in the *Titanic* disaster. Naturally enough there is a **Railway Museum** in Melville Regional Park, featuring a CN steam engine, Grand Trunk Pacific flat car and CN old-style caboose. What was the first Lutheran Academy, then the province's first old people's home, is now a **Heritage Museum**, but you need an appointment to visit. Recreation areas in the vicinity of Melville include the **Crooked Lake Park** to the south and the **Thomas Battersby Wildlife Protection Area** to the north.

ⓘ 430 Main Street

*Take **Highway 10** to Abernethy.*

Abernethy, Saskatchewan

6 Only a tiny hamlet like this one would include a 'diaper derby' in its summer agricultural fair, but though it has a miniscule resident population, the **Motherwell Homestead National Historic Park** attracts visitors. Here you can catch a glimpse of life as it was for farmer and politician W R Motherwell. Costumed guides take you through the handsome 1912 homestead and explain its innovative farming techniques. At the **Abernethy Community Museum** on Main Street there is a film presentation on local folklore and special events during the year, but the focal point is the collection of mounted animals and birds and memorabilia belonging to naturalist R P Stueck, who died in 1979.

*Return to **Highway 10** and continue to Fort Qu'Appelle.*

Fort Qu'Appelle, Saskatchewan

7 This town, in scenic Qu'Appelle Valley, has its roots in the fur-trading era, as will become evident

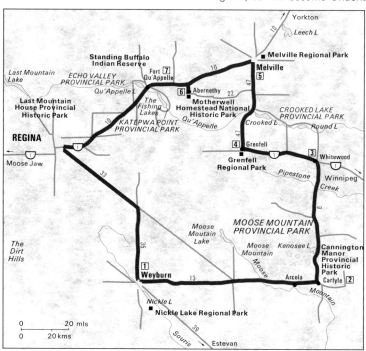

Harvest at Gray, on the Great Regina Plain. Saskatchewan's official flag is green and gold – green for her many forests, but gold for the wheat

when you visit the **local museum** on Bay Avenue. It is linked to an original 1864 Hudson's Bay Company trading post, and houses some of the items that would have been here at that time, along with Indian artifacts and pioneer photos. If there is a pow-wow on, do visit **Standing Buffalo Indian Reserve**, just over 8km (5 miles) west of town. On **Highway 210** (east of nearby Echo Valley

Provincial Park), **Saskatchewan Fish Culture Station** raises cold and warm water species and freely welcomes tourists to its hatchery and information center.

⊡ 160 Company Street South

Highway 10 continues to Regina.

Regina – Weyburn	**115 (71)**
Weyburn – Carlyle	**117 (73)**
Carlyle – Whitewood	**80 (50)**
Whitewood – Grenfell	**49 (30)**
Grenfell – Melville	**64 (40)**
Melville – Abernethy	**51 (32)**
Abernethy – Fort Qu'Appelle	**26 (16)**
Fort Qu'Appelle – Regina	**72 (45)**

RECOMMENDED WALKS

Moose Mountain Provincial Park (2), situated on the highest plateau in the southeast, has good hiking trails, and there are many scenic trails throughout the Qu'Appelle Valley. The provincial parks offer several outdoor programs that combine hiking with other outdoor pursuits. To find out more about back-country adventures, contact the **Saskatchewan Parks and Renewable Resources** on Albert Street in Regina.

ALBERTA

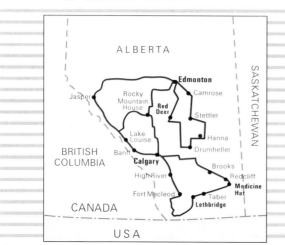

No province could be more dramatic or more majestic than Alberta, where eastern prairies meet western rugged Rockies. Canada's fourth largest province covers 661,185 sq km (225,285 square miles) of contrasting scenery and fresh outdoor living.

Settlers did not come to this land where Indians hunted until the late 1800s, and then they came from around the world, bringing their cultural heritage with them. Some came to rope cattle, which is why even today the province is real cowboy country where there are many working ranches and rodeo riders are serious about winning the purse; there is no finer rodeo event than the annual Calgary Stampede. Some came to seek gold, and the Klondike Days spirit is revived every year in Edmonton. More recently they came for oil – the reason for flourishing urban centers and sophisticated facilities.

For the active, Alberta is a four-season paradise. The mountains are a natural mecca for experienced climbers and adventurous skiers. Those not up to ice climbing or conquering lofty peaks will find more manageable hiking routes and well-maintained trails, numerous alpine campgrounds and novice winter slopes backed by comfortable ski resorts. The swirling rivers – Saskatchewan, Peace, Mackenzie and Athabasca – are ideal for whitewater rafting and kayaking and battling the rapids, but there are quieter stretches for peaceful canoeing or fishing. Visitors can stay in any one of over 1,000 campgrounds and dine around a campfire. As it so happens, 16,796 sq km (10,500 square miles) of this land is water, much of it brimming with fish: the Bow River is one of North America's finest fly-fishing rivers.

Alberta can be split into three main geographical regions: the south, for notable scenic beauty; central, where hoodoos (rock formations) and badlands reveal their past; and the north, where nature is less tamed. The Albertans are renowned for their 'downhome' hospitality, the helping hand and the community spirit. The food is as hearty as the people: giant barbecued steaks, fresh grilled fish and ethnic cuisine – hardly any touched by a nouvelle cuisine brush. The luxury treatment is available too – in château-hotels like Banff Springs and Lake Louise.

This province seems purpose-made for a combination of feet and wheels – just what the doctor ordered!

Edmonton:
Edmonton, provincial capital, festival city and gateway to the unspoilt north, is surprisingly full of skyscrapers. Many celebrations take place in central Sir Winston Churchill Square, overlooked by the **Citadel Theatre**, **Centennial Library** and **Edmonton Art Gallery**. Of the seven major summer festivals, Klondike Days in late July is a favorite, with parades, costume parties, raft races and gold-panning events.

Situated on the banks of the North Saskatchewan River (best view from the revolving restaurant of **Château Lacombe**), the dome of the **Alberta Legislature Building** is an important feature of the skyline. Parks throughout the river valley offer recreational facilities year round. In the valley, wildlife walks are possible at the **John Janzen Nature Centre**. Adjacent is a key city attraction – **Fort Edmonton Park**, a living history museum portraying life between 1846 and 1920. In season, costumed guides tour around the trading fort, prairie farms, saloon and old hotel. Across the river is the **Valley Zoo**.

Among the museums, the **Edmonton Space Sciences Centre**, with its IMAX theater, planetarium and laser light show arena, takes priority. Others include the **Provincial Museum of Alberta**,

The capital, Edmonton – a combination of natural beauty and modern architecture

Canada's **Aviation Hall of Fame**, **Edmonton Police Museum** and the **Ukrainian Canadian Archives and Museum**. The **Edmonton Art Gallery**, **Beaver House Gallery** and several private galleries please art lovers, and **Muttart Conservatory's** four glass pyramids of 'themed' flowers are worth seeing. An overall city view is possible from **Vista 33**, atop the Telephone Tower, the home of the **Telecommunications Museum**.

Don't miss a visit to **West Edmonton Mall** (15 minutes from downtown). Not only are there 800 shops, 110 restaurants and 34 cinemas, but also an ice rink, a water park with a wave pool, a marine theater with performing dolphins, submarine rides and – most amazingly – a giant indoor roller coaster.

Calgary:

Calgary, also known as Stampede City and Olympic City, was originally a mountie fort; now it is a vibrant but friendly metropolis. The best overall view is from the revolving restaurant of the **Calgary Tower**, in Palliser Square. Shop in indoor **Toronto Dominion Square**; be entertained at the **Calgary Center for Performing Arts'** concert hall and theaters; sit in the cafés of pedestrianized **St Stephen's Mall** or in the trendy area of **Kensington**.

Among the museums, the **Glenbow** rates highly, displaying a large collection of Canadiana, but the **Energeum**, a hands-on way of teaching all about oil and gas, including computer games, is fun. Other major museums are the **Calgary Centennial Planetarium and Science Centre**, with its special-effect star shows, observatory and hands-on exhibits; the **Alberta College of Art Gallery**; the **Muttart Gallery**; and the **Museum of Movie Art**. The **Nickle Arts Museum** offers contemporary and historical arts and coin collections, while the **Canadian Forces Base** houses two military museums.

A key attraction is **Heritage Park Historical Village** where costumed staff help re-create the old days of Calgary with the help of a frontier fur fort, turn-of-the-century town buildings, vintage vehicles and restored sternwheeler. Children will appreciate the **Calgary Zoo**, especially its Prehistoric Park display of life-sized dinosaur replicas. Below the zoo, the **Inglewood Bird Sanctuary**, noted for its warbler migration in autumn, is pleasant for a summer stroll. The **Devonian Gardens** are lush indoor sub-tropical gardens, with an ice-skating rink.

3/4 days – 900km (561 miles)

JOURNEY ON ICE

Edmonton • Hinton • Jasper • Icefields Parkway • Rocky Mountain House Edmonton

This tour takes you to the mountains and glaciers, formed aeons ago, which are highlights of any visit to Alberta. The Icefields Parkway, along which you will travel for part of the route, is one of the most scenic stretches of road found in any province, but the essential ingredient is magnificent Jasper National Park. Even if you made no other stops at all, the natural beauty, wildlife and outdoor activities available here should tempt you to linger and explore, not only by car, but on foot. Thanks to dramatic landscapes and seasonal color changes, this tour may be enjoyed any time of year.

SPECIAL TO ...

2 Many festivals and events take place during the year in Jasper National Park: in January, the annual **Ice Sculpturing Contest** is novel, followed by February's **Winter Carnival**. Throughout the winter there are ski racing events in the Marmot Basin area.

ℹ️ 9797 Jasper Avenue, Edmonton

*Take **Highway 16** to Hinton.*

Hinton, Alberta

1 Forests mean a great deal to this province, which is why here on the campus of the Forest Technology School, the **Alberta Forest Service Museum** keeps a record of the history of forestry. About 53km (33 miles) northeast of town on Emerson

Along the Icefields Parkway at Jasper National Park, Alberta, truly one of Canada's most unforgettable sights

Creek Road, a short Sculpture Trail will show you some of the curious sandstone formations called hoodoos, which are a feature of central Alberta. The area around Hinton used to be an active coal-mining region, and though most of the towns once reliant upon mining have long since been abandoned, the **Luscar Coal Mine** (on **Highway 40**) 40km (25 miles) south, continues and can be toured.

ℹ️ 308 Gree Avenue

***Highway 16** continues to Jasper.*

Jasper, Alberta

2 The little gem-like town of Jasper and the park of the same name (Canada's largest mountain park) are the highlights of this tour. To appreciate just what this mountain retreat can offer, you should stay for at least one night, if not two. There is a good choice of accommodation, from sufficiency units or park lodges aimed at families to **Jasper Park Lodge**, more like a resort in itself. One of the community's main streets, **Connaught Drive**, is where you will find a number of boutiques, restaurants and places to stay. Nor is there a shortage of spots to while away the evening hours. What is more, Jasper welcomes visitors year round, with festivals, special events, interpretive programs and seasonal sport activities.

Natural beauty and wildlife are obvious assets. One very easy thing to do is to take the **Jasper Tramway**, 7km (4½ miles) from town, to the top of **The Whistler's Mountain**, 2,464m (8,084-feet). The view is stunning, and there is a restaurant and interpretive display, and a hiking trail to the summit. A winding road leads to **Patricia** and **Pyramid Lakes**, 8km (5 miles) away—a lovely setting for a picnic, summer water sports or winter skating. Many park lakes are within easy access of town, including

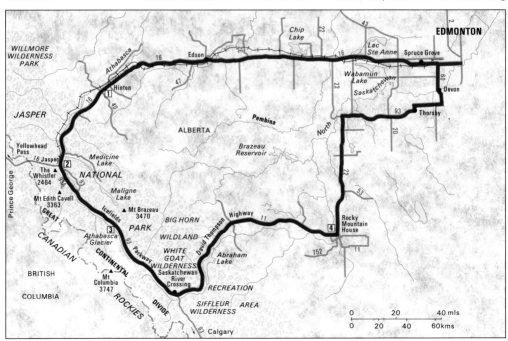

Lake Edith, Lake Annette and Lac Beauvert, all under 8km (5 miles). In winter, when the mountains are clad in snow, waterfalls are frozen and elk move through the lowlands, you can try out ice fishing, snowshoeing or sleigh riding. Skiing, too, of course— Marmot Basin's 228 hectares (565 acres) of ski terrain is a downhill skier's dream. In spring, you may still cross-country ski at Maligne Lake, hike and horseback ride. Summer is the season for wind surfing, river rafting and golfing; many activities last till October. In autumn, the days are

Visitors leaving their snowcoach at Athabasca Glacier, Jasper National Park. The snowcoach excursions take sightseers on a spectacular ride across the glacier

still warm and the wildlife returns to the valley. You can buy or rent a self-guided taped tour to see the best of the park at your own pace.

ⓘ 632 Connaught Drive

*Take **Highway 93** to the Icefields Parkway.*

FOR HISTORY BUFFS

4 Alberta's only **National Historic Park** is situated just southwest of Rocky Mountain House on **Highway 11A**, telling the story of four fur-trading posts built in the area between 1799 and 1875. In July and August interpretive demonstrations show what life would have been like in the era, but at any time (May to September) you can follow the nature trails.

FOR CHILDREN

4 From July to mid-August (if you make a reservation) you can visit the **Sleepy Valley Game Farm**, about 13km (8 miles) east of Rocky Mountain House on **Highway 598**. This game farm offers trails and children's rides, and features elk, moose and buffalo.

SCENIC ROUTES

Highway 93 (Icefields Parkway) is a dramatic scenic route off which are side roads to Jasper National Park. Goat Lookout, 37km (23 miles) south, is a panoramic viewpoint up and down the Athabasca Valley where you will probably glimpse mountain goats and bighorn sheep. **Sunwapta Falls**, about 54km (34 miles) south, plunges into a deep canyon producing a magnificent cascade.

RECOMMENDED WALKS

2 An easy paved walking trail leads around **Lake Annette**, a short distance from Jasper on **Highway 16**, and a three-hour scenic walk loops around five small lakes at the foot of the **Maligne Mountains**, 10km (6 miles) south of Jasper on **Highway 93**. Not to be missed is the trail from **Mount Edith Cavell's** north wall to lovely **Angel Glacier**, a major park attraction. Another longer trail leads to **Cavell Meadows**. The mountain, 29km (18 miles) south of Jasper off access road **93A**, was named after the British nurse executed in 1915 for helping Allied forces.

BACK TO NATURE

2 Jasper is home to a variety of native wildlife including black and grizzly bears, elk, moose and caribou. The best viewing times are spring and fall. Beauty spots are abundant, especially lakes, glaciers and waterfalls. **Medicine Lake**, 30km (19 miles) southeast of Jasper, is unusual for its water level varies and sometimes the lake 'disappears', due to an underground drainage system, not, as the Indians thought, the work of spirits.

Icefields Parkway, Alberta

3 This is probably the scenic route to beat all other scenic routes, with a number of 'must sees' along the way. This 230km (143-mile) route offers spectacular vistas of snow-capped mountains interspersed with waterfalls, lakes and a succession of rivers. Flanking the parkway are magnificent giant icefields and glaciers; and don't be surprised to see caribou or a grizzly bear in May or early June. Novel coach rides in special snow coaches on ice tour the **Athabasca Glacier** daily from May to September. They leave from the ticket office on the Icefields Parkway, 101km (63 miles) south of Jasper, every 15 minutes and take about one and a half hours. The glacier is part of the Columbia Icefield, a large and impressive area of glacial ice and snow; a scale model can be seen in the **Mount Athabasca** information center.

ⓘ on Highway 93 (summer only)

*Leave the Parkway at the Saskatchewan River Crossing, 154km (96 miles) south of Jasper. Take **Highway 11** to Rocky Mountain House.*

The breathtaking beauty of autumn foliage in the Rocky Mountain foothills, near Hinton

Rocky Mountain House, Alberta

4 A pleasant, small town on the brink of the plains, Rocky Mountain House grew from a fur-trading post. An old furnished homestead (now the **Rocky Mountain House National Historic Park**) commemorates the first pioneers. A few miles east (**Highway 598**) visitors are invited to view one of the area's oldest studio potteries—**Beaver Flats**—and buy if they like, while just southwest (**Highway 752**), the **Mandelin Antique Museum** houses, among other things, an unusual wire and barbed wire collection.

ⓘ Highway 11 at main intersection

*Take **Highway 22**, then **39** back to Edmonton.*

Edmonton – Hinton **283 (176)**
Hinton – Jasper **75 (47)**
Jasper – Icefields Parkway **75 (47)**
Icefields Parkway – Rocky Mountain House **252 (157)**
Rocky Mountain House – Edmonton **215 (134)**

IN THE DINOSAURS' FOOTSTEPS

The Creatures that time forgot— drop in on a dinosaur at the Tyrrell Museum in Drumheller where visitors are transported back 70 million years in time

ⓘ 9797 Jasper Avenue, Edmonton

*Take **Highway 2**, then **2A** to Wetaskiwin.*

Wetaskiwin, Alberta

1 Big enough and well enough equipped to be a city, Wetaskiwin's ambience is nevertheless that of a rural community, in keeping with its Indian name, meaning 'Hills of Peace'. You might stop off to tour the **Courthouse** on 50th Avenue, which used to be the main one in central Alberta. Or you might stop in at the **Reynolds Museum** on 57th Street, which houses one of North America's largest collections of vintage vehicles.

ⓘ 55A Street – 49 Avenue

***Highway 2A** continues to Ponoka.*

Ponoka, Alberta

2 This is a reasonably sized town for a coffee stop and a visit to **Fort Ostell Museum** in Centennial Park, which was established by Captain Ostell in 1885 to protect settlers from rebellious Indians. The exhibits show pictures and artifacts of pioneer and Indian days.

Built on the site of a fort, the beautiful Legislative Building in Edmonton dates from 1912

Edmonton ● Wetaskiwin ● Ponoka ● Red Deer ● Trochu ● Drumheller ● Hanna Stettler ● Camrose ● Edmonton

A circular tour through central Alberta leads you through dinosaur country – the Badlands which line the Red Deer Valley, where many important finds have been made. You will see hoodoos created by erosion by the elements over millions of years, and when you take the Dinosaur Trail you will have some insight into the land's geographic history. The region is rich in minerals, particularly coal and oil, and *en route* you will see the spires of drilling derricks and pass abandoned coal mines. This is a good tour for discovering the province's prairies as well as its past.

SPECIAL TO . . .

3 Red Deer hosts a variety of festivals, among them the **Silver Buckle Rodeo** in April and the **Highland Games** in June. July sees the **International Folk Festival**, held in the Cronquist House Municipal Centre, and in the same month, the **Westerner Exhibition. Heritage Days** and the **International Air Show** both occur in August.

FOR HISTORY BUFFS

5 The most interesting Badlands history dates back to prehistoric times. At the **Drumheller Dinosaur and Fossil Museum**, which doubles as a tourist information center, on the Dinosaur Trail, you can see displays relating to the prehistory of the Valley of the Dinosaurs. Exhibits explain why there is an inland sea and petrified forests, and show how coal is formed and how it is processed, as well as the many varieties of dinosaur remains found in the region. On the northern section of the trail, the **Homestead Antique Museum** displays over 4,000 items, including Indian relics and pioneer clothing and household items.

FOR CHILDREN

5 The Tyrell Museum of Palaeontology, along the Dinosaur Trail (**Highway 838**), traces the evolution of life. Its extensive number of preserved dinosaur skeletons is bound to fascinate the younger family members as much as the life-size reproductions. This facility, concerned as it is with research, features computers and videos to bring prehistory to life, but also takes interested visitors to excavation sites and on fossil hunts. It is one of Canada's top museums. On the subject of dinosaurs, the **Prehistoric Park** (on the south section of the trail) also features life-size models in typical Badland canyon scenery. The shop here sells fossils and rockhound supplies. South of town, **Dinosaur Provincial Park** is one of the world's most extensive dinosaur fields.

SCENIC ROUTES

The **Dinosaur Trail** is a 48km (30-mile) circular route that ends in Drumheller. In addition to the points of interest along the way, there are many viewpoints such as **Horsethief Canyon**, whose multi-layered walls and scenery live up to the Badlands name. At the top of Orkney Hill, you will be able to see the whole of Red Deer River Valley and imagine vast numbers of buffalo being herded over the edge. On **Highway 10, East Coulee Drive** passes all kinds of hoodoos, the curious sandstone rock formations created by time and the elements.

RECOMMENDED WALKS

In **Midland Provincial Park** (off the Dinosaur Trail), self-guided walking trails lead to the old site of a coal mine, where now a small collection of mining equipment is housed and outdoor displays depict the coal-mining history of the Red Deer River Valley. In the middle of the park, **McMullen Island's** pathways along the river offer shade from summer temperatures as they pass willows and cottonwood trees.

ℹ️ South side of Ponoka, next to stampede ground (summer only)

Highway 2A continues to Red Deer.

Red Deer, Alberta

3 This is a major city with plenty of accommodation, restaurants and shops. The Cree Indians called the site Waskasioo, meaning elk, but what they saw were the abundant red deer. Its community museum in Recreation Park depicts its history and often features art shows and agricultural exhibits. In the Red Deer River Valley, the **Waskasioo Park** is natural open space for recreation that includes a golf course and cycle routes. Horseback riding is available at **Heritage Ranch**, off Longquist Drive, and water-orientated activities are possible at Bower Ponds. Every August the Airshow is 'The Greatest Show Off Earth'. **Lacomb**, to the north, is the site of the Canadian Agriculture Department's experimental farm.

ℹ️ Old Court House, 4836 Ross Street

*Leave Red Deer on Highway 2, joining **Highway 42**, then on to **Highway 21** and follow south to meet **Highway 585** and the town of Trochu.*

Trochu, Alberta

4 At this stop *en route* between Red Deer and Drumheller, you might visit the **Trochu Valley Historical Museum** on the town's main street. Exhibits concentrate on finds in the immediate area, such as dinosaur bones and Indian artifacts. There are also displays from **St Mary's Hospital** (still in operation), founded in 1909 by three sisters from the order of Notre Dame and d'Evron in France. At the northern end of town, the former country retreat of Dr Stewart Hay is being developed as the **Troalta Arboretum Botanical Gardens**, where you may take a stroll along tree-flanked pathways.

ℹ️ Kneehill Historical Museum, Main Street (summer only)

*Continue south on **Highway 21** to the intersection with **Highway 9**, which leads east to Drumheller.*

Drumheller, Alberta

5 The highlight of this tour and recommended for an overnight stay, this small city which terms itself 'Alberta's Dinosaur Capital' is situated in an oddly rugged valley created by the elements over thousands of years. Until the late 1940s, this thriv-

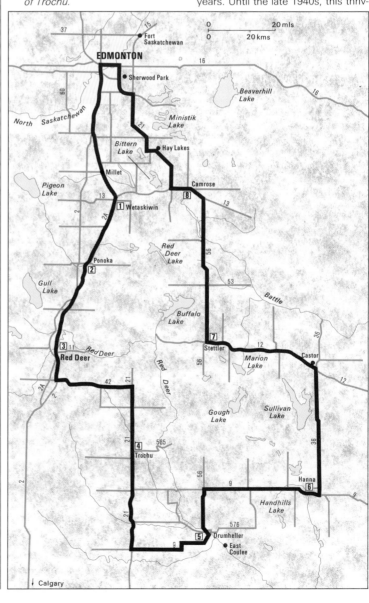

Drumheller's Badlands, graveyard of dinosaurs and site of these hoodoo formations, created in the last glacial period by wind and water erosion. Visitors can follow the Dinosaur Trail through the valley

ing community relied on coal, but these days it is the oil and gas fields in the vicinity which have brought buoyancy to Drumheller's economy. To the southwest of town, along **Highway 10**, you can take the 24km (15-mile) **East Coulee Drive** through the small communities left over from the heyday of coal mining. **Bleriot Ferry** marks the halfway point along the circular trail, where you can take the cable ferry across the river for free.

ⓘ 170 Centre Street
Highway 9 leads to Hanna.

Hanna, Alberta

6 This is used as a hunting ground for geese, as the giant replicas at the entrances to town signify. There are motels and restaurants in this town, whose **Pioneer Museum** on East Municipal Road recreates 19th-century pioneer life and demonstrates prairie life. To the west of Hanna, off **Highway 9**, the Handhills rise some 185m (670 feet) above the prairie; the panoramic view from the top is worth it, as this is the second highest point between the Rockies and the East.

ⓘ Highway 9, west entrance to Hanna (summer only)

*Take **Highway 36**, then **12** to Stettler.*

Stettler, Alberta

7 In this town a historic village has been re-created as a **Town and Country Museum**. It comprises 11 buildings, including a general store, blacksmith's and courthouse.

ⓘ Intersection of **Highways 12** and **56** (summer only)

Highway 56 takes you to Camrose.

Camrose, Alberta

8 Alberta calls Camrose its 'Rose City', but in reality it is a service center for the mixed farming and oil and coal industries around it. It is the base for **Byer's**, who make flour: tours of their mill (50th Avenue) can be made. The company's first mill can be seen at the **Camrose and District Centennial Museum** (53rd and 46th Streets), which also includes a restored pioneer church, a 1906 schoolhouse, an 1898 log home and fire hall. **Alberta's Littlest Airport**, about 22km (14 miles) away (on **Highway 13**, then **Kelsey Road**), has eight model runways for model aircraft. Its hobby shop is a temptation.

ⓘ West entrance to Camrose

*Look for **Highway 21** to take you back to Edmonton.*

Edmonton – Wetaskiwin	**65 (40)**
Wetaskiwin – Ponoka	**36 (22)**
Ponoka – Red Deer	**48 (30)**
Red Deer – Trochu	**88 (55)**
Trochu – Drumheller	**90 (56)**
Drumheller – Hanna	**83 (52)**
Hanna – Stettler	**128 (80)**
Stettler – Camrose	**84 (52)**
Camrose – Edmonton	**93 (58)**

BACK TO NATURE

Central Alberta's Badlands and hoodoos are the result of millions of years of life. Wildlife and wildflowers add movement and color to this part of the province, while fossils recall the long past. You don't have to move too far from a town to study nature: the **Buffalo Trail**, for example, starts in Drumheller on **Highway 576**, which travels for a couple of miles to a paddock of privately owned buffalo. **Kerry Wood Nature Center** (near Red Deer) serves as the entrance to the **Gaetz Lakes Sanctuary**.

4 days – 623km (387 miles)

LAKES & MOUNTAINS

Calgary • Canmore • Banff • Lake Louise • Rocky Mountain House • Cochrane Calgary

From the gateway to the mountains, this tour leads you to picturesque alpine country, with lofty peaks and emerald lakes. It is the route through the Rockies to Banff National Park, an Alberta highlight. Majestic scenery and year-round outdoor activities are the big attraction of this tour, which takes you past Banff National Park's splendid landmarks. This route is for nature lovers and environmentalists who enjoy the great outdoors whatever the time of year.

SPECIAL TO ...

2 There are celebrations all year round in the mountain region, but one of the main events is the **Winter Festival** held annually in January in Banff. At this time there is a variety of sports events, from tray races to the rather more grueling kind, as well as a snow golf competition. Dances and a parade add to the enjoyment. In June Banff holds a **Back to Banff Days** festival and a **Television Festival**, plus, throughout the summer, a **Festival of the Arts**. A **Mountain Film Festival** is staged here in November.

FOR HISTORY BUFFS

5 In 1881 the **Cochrane Ranch Historical Site**, on **Highway 1A**, became the headquarters of a cattle operation on a scale previously unknown in Canada. It is still in use, but also acts as an interpretive area to honor the industry and those responsible for its development. The wildlife and vegetation that made ranches possible can be experienced on the walking trails. The visitor center is open mid-May to Labor Day.

Moraine Lake and Valley of the Ten Peaks, Banff National Park. This park is right in the heart of the Rockies and has two excellent resorts, Lake Louise and Banff

ⓘ Burns Building, 237 8th Avenue South East, Calgary

*Take **Highway 1**, then **Highway 1A** through Kananaskis to Canmore.*

Canmore, Alberta

1 Canmore and Kananaskis together cover 4,000sq km (1,544 square miles) and share their facilities as one four-season resort, but if you plan a stopover you may prefer the village of Kananaskis (off **Highway 40**), which is set in a quiet alpine valley. The village offers accommodations in three well-appointed hotels. Adjacent to the village there is a 106m (350-foot) vertical drop—a night-lit toboggan run; and, as a ski alternative, a program of horse-drawn sleigh rides operate from the village. The Nakiska ski area is just up the hill from the Kananaskis hotels.

Canmore is a little like a dormitory town for Banff and is definitely a service center for the Kananaskis

The Banff Springs Hotel, a Scottish-style castle in the Rockies, has an international reputation for excellence in food, comfort and entertainment. The 18-hole golf course is one of the world's finest

area. The town, at the base of the Three Sisters Mountain, borders on Banff National Park, so it could be your base for park activities. The **Canmore Nordic Center** hosted 1988 Winter Olympic events; there are 56km (35 miles) of trails to suit intermediate and advanced skiers, and a night-lit track as well, but the area is also suitable for hiking, mountain biking and picnicking. Minutes from this former coal-mining town (established in 1883), the **Smith-Dorrien/Spray Trail** leads to the **Spray Lakes** area and **Peter Lougheed Provincial Park**, used for fishing, hiking and cross-country skiing.

As you might expect, there are a number of shops, restaurants and hotels in the Canmore vicinity, and the town itself boasts a good number of art galleries along Eighth Avenue and surrounding streets, where the work of Canadian artists is displayed.

ⓘ off **Highway 1** at west end of town

***Highway 1A** continues to Banff.*

Banff, Alberta

2 The highlight of this tour, Banff is a picturesque alpine community, a Rocky Mountain resort just west of the entrance to Banff National Park. Its famous landmark, the **Banff Springs Hotel**, looks like a castle, but there are many alternative places to stay, lots of places to eat (**Bumper's** is recommended for beef), and places to shop. Throughout the year, the hub for musical and other events is the **Banff Center** on St Julian Road. There are several museums to visit in Banff: **Luxton Museum**, on Birch Avenue, features the early life of the Canadian Indian and the area's wildlife;

the **Natural History Museum**, on Banff Avenue (in Clock Tower Mall), shows how the Rockies evolved geologically; and the **Banff Park Museum**, on the same avenue, reflects the Victorian era. Exhibitions take place at the **Banff Center** in the **Walter J Phillips Gallery**; and the **Whyte Museum of the Canadian Rockies**, on Bear Street, contains Canadian Rockies archives and an art gallery.

Glorious scenery is the obvious draw and it is easy to see it from a great height: simply take the **Mount Norquay Lift** on Mount Norquay Road, just a couple of miles from town, and you can be transported to **Cliffhouse Point**, 2,135m (7,000 feet) up, for the panoramic view of Banff and Mount Rundle.

Alternatively, take the **Sunshine Village Gondola**. A few miles west of town, the Sunshine Road leads you to the gondola for a 25-minute ride to Sunshine Meadows, then a chair lift to the peak. Even closer to Banff, the **Sulphur Mountain Gondola Lift** on Mountain Avenue takes you to an observation deck and restaurant.

Outdoor pursuits are another attraction, from river rafting and canoeing to fishing, horseback riding, helisports, golf and, in winter, skiing and other winter sports. From late June to early September, naturalist programs are given at the main campsites and in information center theaters. You may rent or buy an auto tour tape to find your own way around the park.

ⓘ 93 Banff Avenue

***Highway 93** takes you to Lake Louise.*

RECOMMENDED WALKS

2 Just north of Banff you can take an easy 45-minute walk through the ghost town of Bankhead on **Lake Minnewanka Road**. Banff Park itself is networked with hiking trails that range from 10-minute strolls to rugged backpack expeditions. Off the Bow Valley Parkway, 26km (16 miles) west of Banff, you can take the self-guided **Johnston Canyon** trail along the creek. A 5km (3-mile) walk will bring you to the **Ink Pots**, six cool, bubbling springs.

3 **Moraine Lake** and the **Valley of the Ten Peaks**, near Lake Louise, is an excellent hiking area. Don't miss the short trail from the Bow Pass parking lot uphill to the **Peyto Lake Lookout**, where a self-guided nature trail winds through subalpine meadows. The lake itself is worth the effort, its color changing with the seasons.

BACK TO NATURE

Lakes are an integral part of Banff's landscape. **Lake Minnewanka** is a favorite with fishermen and with those who like boat cruises. The **Vermilion Lakes** are also popular: a circular drive, just under 11km (7 miles) around them, allows you to see the flora and fauna common to marshland, as well as prolific birdlife.
Photographic gems north of Lake Louise include **Hector Lake**, whose green waters are half backdropped by rugged mountains and **Bow Lake**, whose glacial water perfectly reflects the surrounding snow capped peaks. Across the lake is part of the large **Wapta Icefield**. Talking of water, don't forget the **Great Divide** – the geographical point where all waters flow west to the Pacific or east to the Atlantic. You can see this phenomenon happen from the picnic area here as the creek separates midflow.
You can expect to see a variety of wildlife from all points along this touring route, especially from the Bow Valley Parkway in winter. Watch for elk, deer and sheep and maybe even a wolf.

Majestic mountains and wild flowers frame the loveliness of this view of Lake Louise

Lake Louise, Alberta

3 Sister alpine resort to Banff, this area is dominated by the **Victoria Glacier**, where the fairy-tale lakeside **Chateau Louise** is one of eight hotels. The best views of the immediate area are to be had when you take the **Lake Louise Gondola Lift**. You will be able to look over the lake, the glacier and the Bow Range of mountains. (In winter the hill becomes a major ski area.) From the top of the gondola hiking trails lead through alpine flowers.
Thirteen kilometers (8 miles) to the east of the Lake Louise access road is the **Moraine Lake** beauty spot at the base of the Continental Divide, surrounded by the **Wenkchemna Parks**. You can picnic at the Great Divide itself—follow the signs for it on Highway 1A going west.

ℹ️ Near Samson Mall, Lake Louise Village (summer only)

Highway 93 continues north until the David Thompson Highway meets the Icefield Parkway at Saskatchewan River Crossing. Continue on David Thompson Highway (11) to Rocky Mountain House.

Rocky Mountain House, Alberta

4 You will reach this community (see page 88) via one of the most scenic western routes. Along the way it passes **Bighorn Dam**, which has created Alberta's longest manmade lake, **Lake Abraham**, and **Nordegg**, at one time a thriving mining community. It also passes wilderness and recreational areas.

ℹ️ Highway 11, main intersection

Take Highway 22 south to Cochrane.

Cochrane, Alberta

5 If you have had enough of highway driving and your vehicle has the stamina, the **Ghost District Off Highway Vehicle Zone**, 13km (8 miles) west of here, is the place. This is where the **Bow/Crow Forest Reserve** provides miles of maintained trails, as well as dirt roads and unmaintained trails specifically for the off-highway enthusiast (located on Highway 1). A few miles further on Highway 1A, the **Ghost Lake Reservoir** can be used for numerous water sport activities. Heritage Days are celebrated in August.

ℹ️ Westerson Cabin (summer only)

Return on Highway 1A to Calgary.

Calgary – Canmore **105 (65)**
Canmore – Banff **31 (19)**
Banff – Lake Louise **51 (32)**
Lake Louise – Rocky Mountain House **250 (155)**
Rocky Mountain House – Cochrane **148 (92)**
Cochrane – Calgary **38 (24)**

The pavilion at the Nikka Yuko Japanese Garden in Lethbridge was built in Japan but reassembled here in these tranquil gardens

ⓘ Burns Building, 237 8th Avenue. South East, Calgary

*Take **Highway 2** to High River.*

High River, Alberta

1 The symbol of this town is a Medicine Tree, an Indian symbol of two trees joined by a large branch so that the lifeblood of one tree flows into the other. The site of the traditional Indian camp and a part of that original tree are to be seen in **George Lane Memorial Park**, through which the Highwood River, lined by cottonwood trees, flows.

Birthplace of Canada's 16th Prime Minister, Joe Clark, High River is a pleasant town with tree-lined streets and brick buildings, well worth strolling. To the west are sprawling ranches, so it is not surprising that very good saddles both mass-produced and handcrafted are made here. You may like to look for engraved belt buckles at **Olson's Silver and Leather Company**, or pick out a bronze sculpture at the **Bronze Boot Art Gallery**. In the heart of town, the **Museum of the Highwood** is a converted railroad station, whose displays reflect the area's ranching history.

***Highway 2** continues to Nanton.*

Nanton, Alberta

2 Set in the middle of some of the state's finest ranchland, Nanton's main attraction is the **Lancaster**

5 days – 819km (507 miles)

ALBERTA'S CATTLE COUNTRY

Calgary ● High River ● Nanton ● Claresholm
Fort Macleod ● Waterton Lakes National Park ● Lethbridge ● Taber ● Bow Island
Medicine Hat ● Redcliff ● Brooks ● Calgary

This southern Alberta route takes you through some of the finest of the province's ranchland. Cattle are essential to the Alberta economy and ranches (guest or working) may well be considered an essential part of the holiday experience. This tour also takes you through major farming communities, where manufacturing plants are only too happy to welcome interested visitors to their plants and show them how they have overcome the problems of irrigation. Rich in coal, and later gas and oil, this prairie region of Alberta (as you head for Medicine Hat and Redcliff) has prospered and flourished.

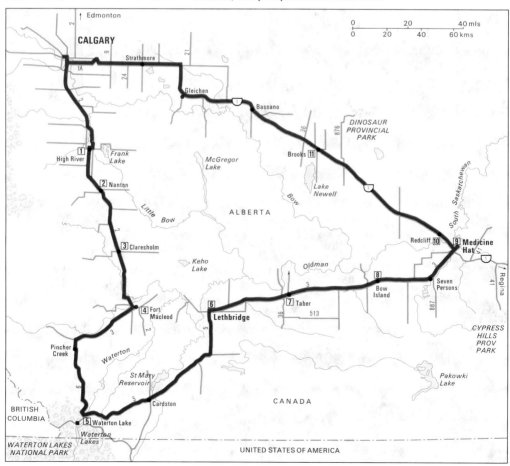

SPECIAL TO . . .

1 Almost every town has some local summer festival, very often involving the display of arts and crafts. In High River's case, there is a fine arts show and sale in June, but the town's main festive occasion takes place in August: the **North American Chuckwagon Championships** and the **Guy Weadick Rodeo**, named after the man whose entrepreneurial thoughts in the 1900s were to lead to the July Calgary Stampede. This town was also the first to hold rodeos for youngsters and this happens in May.

FOR HISTORY BUFFS

4 The **Head-Smashed-In Buffalo Jump**, 16km (10 miles) west of **Highway 2** on Spring Point Road, is North America's largest and best preserved buffalo jump (designated a World Heritage Site by Unesco). It was used by American Indians for 6,000 years to drive thousands of buffalo to their death in order to provide them with food, shelter and clothing—a unique example of commercial hunting. A multimillion-dollar interpretative center opened on the site in 1987 with its own cafeteria, film theater and gift shop, and there are short outdoor trails which are easy to walk.

FOR CHILDREN

6 It's A-Maz-Ing, on 28th Street South in Lethbridge, is a giant maze stretching over 1.6km (1 mile)—the largest and first of its kind in Canada. Getting through the puzzle of walkways and passages always seems to delight children.

9 Riverside Waterslide, in Medicine Hat, provides exciting rides for all ages who are young at heart, as several thousand gallons of water per minute sluice down smooth slides.

SCENIC ROUTES

From Calgary to Nanton you will be passing through some of Alberta's finest ranching country; then you follow the foothills to Fort Macleod. Much of the territory around Taber is irrigated farmland, while **Cypress Hills Provincial Park**, just south of Medicine Hat, stands out like an alpine oasis from the surrounding prairie. Although there is no specifically designated scenic route, this tour takes you through a wide variety of scenery.

Bomber and Nanton Air Museum, located in Centennial Park. The bomber, manufactured in Ontario, arrived in Britain too late for action. The museum will fascinate the military minded: it contains a 1600hp Merlin engine; rebuilt gun turret and many World War II items related to the Lancaster. Children can use a partly restored Anson twin-engine bomber as a hands-on playground.

*Continue on **Highway 2** to Claresholm.*

Claresholm, Alberta

3 Take a coffee or lunch stop here, perhaps combined with a visit to the **Claresholm Museum**, a former railroad station. Originally, this sandstone structure was built in 1886 in Calgary, and was rebuilt here in 1910. The town's first school and a pioneer log cabin are on site.

***Highway 2** continues to Fort Macleod.*

Fort Macleod, Alberta

4 This is southern Alberta's oldest settlement, and is a good place to stay overnight (there are several motels). The downtown historic area features a variety of wood-frame buildings from the late 1890s, as well as brick and sandstone ones from the early 1900s. The main street, in particular, is of interest: you can take a guided walk starting at the information booth next to the **Fort Macleod Museum**. The museum is representative of the original North West Mounted Police Fort, built in 1874, so naturally two of its themes are the old-style Mounties and today's Royal Canadian Mounted Police. Additionally, it explores the Indian and pioneer themes. A major attraction is the Mounted Musical Patrol rides, which take place four times every day during July and August. If you miss the real thing you can always watch the slide presentation on the ride and also on the Head-Smashed-In-Buffalo Jump.

Beside museum (summer only)

*Take **Highway 3** westwards, then **Highway 6** south to Waterton Lakes National Park.*

Waterton Lakes National Park, Alberta

5 A superb park, first established in 1895, Waterton is today recognized as a biosphere reserve. The range of sport possibilities here is a wide one, including an 18-hole golf course. Among the scenic highlights are the two-hour boat cruises on **Upper Waterton Lake**. There are 183km (114 miles) of trails to choose from, in all degrees of difficulty. If you like informative talks, attend one of the presentations given by park naturalists at the **Cameron Falls** (next to Waterton town site) or **Crandell Theater**, or join a conducted walk or wilderness hike. Drive to Cameron Lake, 16km (10 miles) from town at the foot of Mount Custer for a picnic lunch, or rent a canoe. At **Red Rock Canyon**, 17km (10½ miles) from town you will find a dramatic iron-red gorge encircled by scenic trails. The park is rich in wildlife, but the really easy way to see bison is to drive through the

Buffalo Paddock, just inside the park's northeastern boundary.

Opposite Prince of Wales Hotel (summer only)

*Take **Highway 5** to Lethbridge.*

Lethbridge, Alberta

6 This well facilitated city is a good resting place. Built at the time of the coal boom, it offers plenty to see and do. One of its major attractions is **Indian Battle Park**, in the Oldman River Valley, named after the last big Indian battle fought here between the Cree and Blackfoot tribes in 1870. **Fort Whoop-Up**, in the park, is a replica whisky-trading post. It does not dish out the malt these days, but is an interpretive center with a display gallery and slide presentation on the province's early days. Children will enjoy the wagon train tour of the river valley which leaves from here. **Henderson Lake Park** is more of a recreation area, with summer sports facilities that include a golf course, boating on the lake, bowling greens and an outdoor pool. For quiet meditation, the **Nikka Yuko Japanese Gardens** are perfect. There are a variety of trails in this park but there are also nature walks at the **Helen Schuler Coulee Center**. If you have time for a museum, make it the **Sir Alexander Galt** on First Street and Fifth Avenue: small but well done, relating to the city's early history and providing orientation to Lethbridge's River Valley Park system.

2805 Scenic Drive South

*Take **Highway 3** east to Taber.*

Taber, Alberta

7 For those who are interested in agriculture, Taber is a good spot to stop, for it is situated in one of Alberta's prime farming areas and is base to several agricultural plants. To tour plants, an appointment is usually necessary: **Empress Foods** shows how fruits and vegetables are canned and packed; **Chin Ridge Farms**, reached via **Highway 36** south and **Highway 513** east, demonstrates seed cleaning and processing specialty crops; **Taber Sugar Beet Factory**, at the junction of **Highway 3** and **Highway 36**, shows how sugar beet is processed. No appointment is necessary to visit **Shipwheel Cattle Feeders**, reached via **Highway 36** north, where 5,000 head of cattle graze on 1,214 naturally irrigated hectares (3,000 acres) of grassland. One of the top 10 Arabian horse breeding stables—**Willomar Arabians**—is also located close to Taber and will give tours on request.

***Highway 3** continues to Bow Island.*

Bow Island, Alberta

8 You are still in the agricultural belt here, so a stop is only recommended if you want more plant tours: **Alberta Sunflower Seeds** gives field tours in August, but processing can be seen October to March.

Highway 3 east (summer only)

***Highway 3** continues to Medicine Hat.*

The Calgary Tower Olympic Flame burns high above this impressive city, maturing symbol of modern Canada

Medicine Hat, Alberta

9 This is a green city oasis in the middle of the prairie. When Rudyard Kipling called it a city 'with all hell for a basement' he was referring to the area's gas fields, discovered accidentally in 1883 by a crew drilling for water. As a visitor city (Alberta's fifth largest), it offers a full range of hotels, restaurants and shops. Medicine Hat is a progressive city, as symbolized by the new architecture of its riverside **City Hall**, but it is also an old one, as a downtown walking tour will show. Here, the turn-of-the-century architecture emphasizes Medicine Hat's early prosperity. The style of southern Alberta life at that time is also illustrated by **Echodale Farm** and the **Ajax Coalmine** in Echodale Park.

The history of western Canada and pioneer and Indian artifacts are displayed at the **Medicine Hat Historical Museum and National Exhibition Center**, on Bomford Crescent Southwest. Clay-making was one of the old city industries and its history is outlined at the **Clay Product Interpretive Center** on Medalta Avenue.

Highway 1 takes you to Redcliff.

Redcliff, Alberta

10 Like other towns in this area, Redcliff was first developed as a coal-mining community. It was named after the red cliffs of the Saskatchewan River, which can be seen below the town. A good example of large, layered red sandstone boulders is to be seen on the 324-hectare (800-acre) site known as **Red Rock Coulee** (south of Seven Persons on **Highway 887**). This nature site encompasses a small badlands area, with alternate layers of sandstone and clay and hoodoos under a hard sandstone cap. Redcliff's own **museum** houses a number of industrial exhibits related to the region.

Continue to Brooks on **Highway 1**.

Brooks, Alberta

11 There is a choice of places to stay and to eat in this town, which was named after a Canadian Pacific Railway divisional engineer. One engineering achievement is the **Brooks Aqueduct**, built in 1914, which carries 18cu m (650 cubic feet) of water per second to a height of 18m (60 feet) for 3km (2 miles) over lowland. Just west of here, on **Highway 1**, the **Alberta Horticultural Center** lets you take a self-guided walk through its flower and shrub garden, and will give greenhouse and laboratory tours on request for those with a more studied interest. East of Brooks, on **Highway 1**, the **Brooks Wildlife Center**, which has a pheasant hatchery, raises ring-necked pheasants for release into the wild. Tours of the hatchery and rearing facilities are available on request.

🄸 **Highway 1**, east side of Brooks (summer only)

Return to Calgary via **Highway 1**, *then* **1A**.

Calgary – High River	58 (36)
High River – Nanton	29 (18)
Nanton – Claresholm	41 (25)
Claresholm – Fort Macleod	36 (22)
Fort Macleod – Waterton Lakes National Park	92 (57)
Waterton Lakes National Park – Lethbridge	122 (76)
Lethbridge – Taber	48 (30)
Taber – Bow Island	57 (35)
Bow Island – Medicine Hat	57 (35)
Medicine Hat – Redcliff	7 (4)
Redcliff – Brooks	96 (60)
Brooks – Calgary	176 (109)

RECOMMENDED WALKS

9 Medicine Hat's River Valley Parks comprise over 405 hectares (1,000 acres) of parkland and double that amount as an environmental reserve. There are 40km (25 miles) of regional trails and within the parks almost 16km (10 miles) of trails which are perfect for exploration on foot (though you may cycle if you prefer). Maps of the trails are available at the Tourist Information Center.

BACK TO NATURE

11 **Dinosaur Provincial Park**, 40km (25 miles) northeast of Brooks, is rather special because it protects one of the world's most extensive dinosaur fields. It is a Unesco World Heritage Site and covers 6,070 hectares (15,000 acres). Daily interpretive programs in summer, as well as self-guided walks, enable you to learn geological, natural and cultural history, and at **Field Station Visitors' Center** you may watch dinosaur fossils being prepared. Scientists have discovered some 35 species of dinosaur in the area. Much of the park is restricted because of scientific work, but some camping facilities are available.

BRITISH COLUMBIA & THE YUKON

Vancouver:
Vancouver, sparkling and scenic, nestling beneath mountains and water-fronted, is one of Canada's largest cities. From the top of Grouse Mountain, where the city is at your feet, to the tip of Granville Island, a colorful market place, Vancouver is a place for the good life; plush hotels, plentiful restaurants with all types of cuisine, sophisticated nightlife and fashionable boutiques (try **Robson Street**, picturesque **Gastown** or lively **Chinatown**).

It is a city of parks (don't miss **Stanley**, home of the Vancouver Aquarium) and of gardens such as the **Botanical Gardens** at the University of British Columbia. The shoreline beaches offer a retreat for sport and relaxation. It is a city of museums: the **Vancouver Museum**, with its historic and art displays and its **H R MacMillan Planetarium** is a must, but the UBC's **Museum of Anthropology** and **M Y Williams Geology Museum** also hold natural wonders and masterpieces. Visit, too, the **Vancouver Art Gallery**, in a 19th-century former courthouse; the **Vancouver Police Centennial Museum**; and the **Maritime Museum**.

British Columbia is not called 'Super Natural' for nothing. It is Canada's third largest province, a land of diversity and outdoor adventure, where extensive plateaux, great rivers and myriad lakes are caught between rugged mountains. Offshore, hundreds of islands (including the largest, Vancouver) mix fishing, mining, logging and city bustle with peace and quiet.

When this province became part of Canada in 1871, about a quarter of its inhabitants were native Indians. Early settlers were of British origin, joined in the late 19th century by large groups of Chinese laborers who came to work on the railroad. Today, being part of the Pacific rim, many other Far Eastern influences contribute to the British Columbia culture.

British Columbia shares the Rockies with Alberta, but it is not the only mountain range. In Kootenay country, the highway curves through the mountains, climbing to the peaks of the Valhallas. In the southwest, where the Fraser Valley is framed by peaks, roads lead to mountain resorts such as Whistler.

There are almost 400 parks in British Columbia, among them three national historic parks: Fort Langley, Fort St James and Fort Rodd Hill, commemorative of pioneer days. The Gold Rush drew many, and the trails they took can be followed now. The ghost towns they left behind have become British Columbia heritage. Gold was the magic word which transformed Yukon, the northwest corner of Canada. By 1898 everyone intent on getting rich quick was heading for the Klondike. There were many more hardships for the gold seekers than for today's motorist, who can explore Yukon's wild beauty along thousands of miles of road. The riverboats which once navigated the waterways to the Klondike now rest on the shores of rivers and lakes, and present-day voyagers can canoe, kayak or whitewater raft the rivers that lattice Yukon for fun, make alpine hikes safely, and fish for pleasure, rather than survival.

Yukon is a little out of the ordinary. In addition to its exciting sport possibilities, it offers unique mementoes, notably Indian crafts such as home-tanned moose hide moccasins or hand-crafted birch snow-shoes; and frontier-days celebrations are occasions for kicking up heels. There are cities here, but nature still dominates. As a taster, read the verse of Jack London and Robert Service, and you will be ready to take to the Alaska Highway.

Kamloops:

Kamloops, in the high country, was a meeting place for the native people long before it became the hub of the fur traders in 1812, and it has been a thriving center ever since. It is the largest city in this ranchland area, and the 200-plus lakes and streams in the surrounds are famous for their trout fishing. The city itself offers good accommodation, river beaches and water slides, and a wildlife park whose 100 species include cougar and buffalo. It has its own **museum** and **art gallery**, and features sternwheeler cruises on the Thompson River and many summer festivals. The summers can be really hot here!

Cranbrook:

Cranbrook, regional center for British Columbia's Rockies, is situated at the foot of Mount Baker in the Valley of a Thousand Peaks, not far from Fort Steele. There are plenty of facilities, including a superbly landscaped 18-hole championship **golf course** and a **children's park**. Don't miss the **Railway Museum and Gallery**, which features one of the great vintage trains, Trans Canada Ltd, restored to its 1920s elegance.

Whitehorse:

Whitehorse, Yukon's capital, grew from village to city when construction began on the Alaska Highway in 1942. It sits on the site where gold seekers' craft were destroyed in 1898 by the Whitehorse Rapids and Miles Canyon, through which you can now cruise at ease. Klondike exhibits can be seen in the **Old Log Church Museum**, along with other historic displays, and the spirit of Gold Rush Days is captured by the **Frantic Follies Vaude-ville Show**. The **MacBride Museum** is the best for an in-depth look at Yukon's past from native cultures on. Free guided walking tours of downtown Whitehorse are given daily in July and August by the Yukon Historical and Museums Association, and free escorted nature walks are offered year round by the Yukon Conservation Society. Guided evening shoreline fishing excursions operate mid-May to mid-September, and many air charter companies feature mini-flightseeing trips.

The 21st-century skyline of Vancouver's World Trade Center and Canada Place, with the city's business area behind

3 days – 574km (358 miles)

GOLD RUSH DAYS

Vancouver • Squamish • Whistler
Pemberton • Lillooet • Lytton • Yale
Hope • Vancouver

The winding **Highway 99** to Pemberton takes you on an easy-going circular tour, following beautiful Howe Sound, past bays and coves, and then passing snowcapped peaks and alpine lakes encircled by firs. The mountainous Duffy Lake Road to Lillooet was only for use in summer but should now be paved; the rest of the route can be taken (with care) year round. As you head south past the confluence of the mighty Fraser and Thompson Rivers, you can enjoy the drama of Fraser Canyon and the beauty of the Valley.

SPECIAL TO . . .

2 Whistler holds some of the liveliest celebrations, such as the two-month (July and August) **Festival of Street Entertainment**, and the June **Children's Festival**.
In May the **Fraser Valley International Arts Festival** is held at Abbotsford, a town which hosts a July **Berry Festival**, too. It is worth making a note of the June **Children's Festival** in Chilliwack; August **Logger Days**, with contests at Squamish (1); and Hope's **Brigade Days** in September (7).

FOR CHILDREN

Who can resist rockhounding and gold panning? Many precious stones have been found around Lillooet and gold panning is possible at **Cayoosh Creek Park**. You can pan for gold in Lytton too, and search the riverbanks for jade. The **Gold Panning Recreational Reserve** runs just over 5km (3 miles) along the Fraser River. More usual thrills are available at **TransCanada Waterslide** (junction of **Highways 1** and **9**, near Chilliwack), with 10 slides and bumper boats, and at **Flintstones Bedrock City**, in the same vicinity, with rides and attractions.

Summer tourists enjoying Horstman Glacier atop Blackcomb Mountain

ℹ 1055 Dunsmuir Street, Vancouver

*Head north on **Highway 99** to Squamish.*

Squamish, British Columbia

1 Situated at the head of Howe Sound, some 66km (41 miles) north of Vancouver, Squamish (named after the native people who lived here) has a natural deep-water port surrounded by restaurants, shops and comfortable accommodation. Overlooked by 2,678m (8,786-foot)-high **Mount Garibaldi**, the town is also protectively guarded by the **Stawamus Chief Mountain**— second only to Gibraltar in granite size, and a superb challenge for rock climbers. Though there is a **Squamish Valley Museum** downtown, containing items about Valley history, it is the scenic and photographic possibilities that make Squamish so popular. The nearby **Howe Sound** is popular for fishing, sailing and windsurfing; from nearby **Brackendale** nature enthusiasts will spot hundreds of eagles; and ski planes from the Squamish airport will fly you over some of North America's largest glaciers and icecaps.

ℹ 37950 Cleveland Avenue

Highway 99 *continues to Whistler.*

A mountain stream separates the fairways at the Whistler Golf Club

Whistler, British Columbia

2 This alpine, European-style resort sits amid the Blackcomb and Whistler Mountains and is as pleasant in summer as it is for winter sports. Because it is only 120km (75 miles) from Vancouver, it is much loved for snowmobiling, ice fishing and skiing for all ages; but this is a year-round resort, with a choice of accommodation from budget to the luxurious—such as **Chateau Whistler**. In addition to golf (there will soon be a second 18-hole course), mountain biking and even summer skiing on Blackcomb's **Horstman Glacier**, you can whizz to alpine meadows in 18 minutes in an express enclosed gondola. On these upper slopes, enjoy majestic vistas, a meal with a view or a guided walking tour with a qualified naturalist.

i Junction of **Highway 99** and Lake Placid Road; also at Village Square and Village Gate (summer only)

Highway 99 continues to Pemberton.

Pemberton, British Columbia

3 The seed potato capital of North America is a friendly and tiny farming community, looking rather out of place in its alpine setting. Its own **museum** on Prospects Street focuses on two cultures: the Gold Rush days of the Fraser River and the native Indians of the Mount Currie and D'Arcy communities to the north. Nearby beauty spots include **Nairn Falls** and, on the way to Lillooet, **Joffre Lakes** and **Joffre Glacier**.

i Junction of **Highway 99** and Portage Road (summer only)

Follow the **Duffy Lake Road** *to Lillooet.*

Lillooet, British Columbia

4 Locals often refer to this particular tour as 'The Nugget Route'. One reason is that this little village is at Mile 0 of the Cariboo Road: that is, what used to be the Cariboo Gold Rush Trail. The trail was first constructed in 1862 to help miners and traders reach the interior more easily. Towns and villages on the Cariboo Road incorporate mileages into their names, starting from the **Cairn Mile 0** on Main Street, part of Lillooet's Golden Mile of History. Opposite, in the **museum**, you can learn more about the good old pioneer days.

In 1863, with a population of 15,000, Lillooet claimed to be the second largest town north of San Francisco. In 1934, it claimed the liveliest newspaper in the province, thanks to snuff-snorting editor, Ma Murray, who guaranteed a chuckle every week and a belly laugh once a month or your money back. Her old **newspaper office** can be seen on Main Street.

You can pan for gold here, but you will be more certain of a catch in the lakes surrounding the village. Rockhounds should be in their element: this is one of the best areas for finding jade and agate. The **Chinese Rock Piles**, below Hangman's Park and by the old suspension bridge, were washed one by one by Chinese gold seekers hoping to recover traces overlooked by earlier miners.

i 790 Main Street (May-October)

Take **Highway 12** *to Lytton.*

Lytton, British Columbia

5 Located where the roaring Fraser and Thompson Rivers meet, Lytton is a good base for river rafters and rockhounds. Originally the site was an Indian village, Camchin, meaning 'cross mouth'; explorers referred to it as The Forks, and only in 1858 was it renamed to honor Colonial Secretary of State Sir Edward Bulwer Lytton. Today, logging is a main concern here, apart from the tourists who come to battle the rivers. For an incredible view of **Thompson Canyon**, head east on **Highway 1** to **Skihist Provincial Park**. Another side trip on **Highway 8**, northeast, takes you to **Spences Bridge**, a small settlement named after the man who built the bridge across the Thompson River.

i 400 Fraser Street (open mid-June to mid-September)

Take **Highway 1** *(the Gold Rush Trail) via Fraser Canyon to Yale.*

Yale, British Columbia

6 Reaching Yale is an exciting part of this tour: you travel via the Fraser River Canyon, just after Boston Bar, a real obstacle to travel before the days of highways and tunnels. At **Hell's Gate** there is thrilling river rafting, but it is safer today than when miners were drowned trying to navigate their rafts through this narrow gorge. The Hell's Gate Fishway helps two million salmon each year to climb to their spawning grounds. A good picnic spot, with a view of the Fraser River and Canyon, is **Alexandra Bridge Provincial Park**: the old Alexandra Bridge, built in 1926 and named after the Princess of Wales, replaced the

FOR HISTORY BUFFS

1 The **BC Museum of Mining** at Britannia Beach is a national historic site worth seeing on your way to Squamish. It used to be an enormous working copper mine, and you can still see operational equipment when you take a guided tour underground into the mountain on an electric train. The museum building houses hundreds of artifacts including a rock and mineral collection.

Fort Langley National Historic Park, on the banks of the Fraser River, was the trading post from which adventurers left for the mountainous interior in search of furs, and later in search of gold. Unofficially in those days it was a 'capital' of the province, which was inaugurated in the **Big House** here in 1858. The fort served as an administration and provision center for all Hudson's Bay Company operations in the Pacific North West. Today you will see **Kilby General Store Museum**, typical of the once familiar country stores, and the **Burnaby Village Museum**, which re-creates the scenes and style of the 1890s.

4 In the Lillooet region there are some 350 archaeological sites that show evidence of the Upper Lillooet Indians. These include the remains of villages, pictographs and other fascinating details.

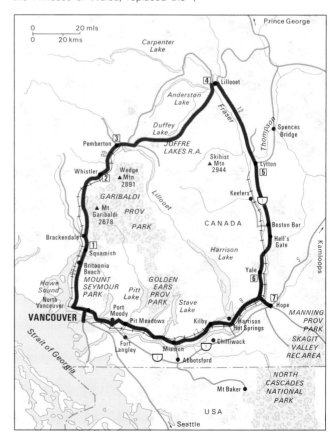

SCENIC ROUTES

The **Squamish Highway (99)**, between Horseshoe Bay and Pemberton, is a spectacularly scenic stretch along Howe Sound, with several vantage points along the way. The Fraser and Thompson Rivers are part of one of Canada's largest watersheds, and when they collide at Lytton it is quite a sight. Just under 16km (10 miles) from Hope (beyond Kawkawa Lake Provincial Park), the fantastic scenery of the gorge in **Coquihalla Canyon Provincial Recreation Area** brought Hollywood directors here to film *First Blood* (the Rambo movie) and *Shoot to Kill*, among others.

RECOMMENDED WALKS

Garibaldi Provincial Park (access signs on **Highway 99** between Squamish and Whistler) is a must for hikers. Developed trail systems lead to the five most popular areas: Diamond Head, Black Tusk/Garibaldi Lake, Cheakamus Lake, Singing Pass and Wedgemount Lake. Azure lakes, frosty glaciers and alpine meadow are good reasons to come. For an easy stroll, the 14km- (9-mile) -plus, mostly paved valley trail at Whistler (connecting the six lakeside parks here) is an excellent choice. Just south of Yale on **Highway 1** a four-hour **Cave Hiking Trail** gives magnificent views of Cascade and Lillooet Mountains.

North of **Highway 7**, **Golden Ears Provincial Park** offers 80km (50 miles) of hiking trails (some of them abandoned railroad grades), varying in difficulty. **Centennial Trail** is a good introduction—about two hours; **Incline Trail** is a steep, one-hour hike from Mike Lake; **Incline Trail** to **Hitching Rock** a two-hour walk to Lake Beautiful; **Alouette Mountain Logging Road** a two-hour walk through a research forest; **West Canyon Trail** a three-hour steep hike; and most strenuous the seven-hour hike to the top of **Golden Ears Mountain**.

BACK TO NATURE

Just north of Squamish is the home of the bald eagle: January and February, when they nest, are the best viewing times. Migrating wildfowl also make a rest stop in this area. The parks are full of wildlife, and one delightful little rodent, the hoary marmot, can be seen in the summer in **Heather Meadow**, through the west gate of **Manning Provincial Park**, 25km (16 miles) from Hope.

original suspension span of 1863, built to extend the Cariboo Wagon Road across the river. Today, there is a new Alexandra Bridge near by.

Because of the rapids, Yale, when founded as a Hudson's Bay fur post in 1848, was simply called The Falls. A natural obstruction in the shape of **Lady Franklin Rock**—a large boulder in the center of the river, which blocked steamer passage—made this the head of navigation for the Fraser River, since goods had to be unloaded here and carried on by wagon train to the Cariboo gold fields. During 1858 thousands of gold prospectors passed through the town, but by 1886 Yale's heyday was over, and today it concerns itself with forestry. It boasts the province's oldest church on original foundations—**St John the Divine**—built in about 1859 by Royal Engineers, and its pioneer cemetery, whose tombstones testify to the many losses during the gold rush era, when harsh conditions claimed many lives. Memorabilia of the times, including the building of the railway, can be seen in the **museum** on Douglas Street, which also displays an 1860–1900 bottle collection.

🛈 Highway 1 at west entrance to town (June–September)

Highway 1 continues to Hope.

No prizes for guessing the inspiration behind the name of Bridal Veil Falls in its beautiful provincial park

Hope, British Columbia

7 Like its neighboring towns, Hope relies on forestry as its main industry. Situated at the entrance to Fraser River Canyon in a natural amphitheater of mountains, it is a base for visiting several beautiful lakes and provincial parks which are nearby like Kawkawa, perfect for swimming and boating. In its **museum** on Water Street there is a gold concentrator and a ball mill which originated from a gold mill once in operation in the Coquihalla River Valley.

🛈 919 Water Street

*Take **Highway 7** along the Fraser River into 'Rainbow Country' stopping at Bridal Veil Falls Provincial Park on the way and return to Vancouver.*

Vancouver – Squamish	54 **(34)**
Squamish – Whistler	59 **(37)**
Whistler – Pemberton	35 **(22)**
Pemberton – Lillooet	85 **(53)**
Lillooet – Lytton	69 **(43)**
Lytton – Yale	82 **(51)**
Yale – Hope	23 **(14)**
Hope – Vancouver	167 **(104)**

Throughout Vancouver Island, Indian arts and crafts are celebrated and reproduced as gifts

🛈 1055 Dunsmuir Street, Vancouver

*Take **Highway 99** to the ferry and then to Sechelt on **Highway 101**.*

Sechelt, British Columbia

1 Just before you reach Sechelt, stop at the fishing village of Gibsons, an attractive hillside community used for a television series called *The Beachcombers*. On summer afternoons you can tour **Molly's Reach Café** studio on Lower Marine Drive.

Sechelt itself has the Strait of Georgia on one side and, on the other, the Sechelt Inlet: only a narrow sandbar connects it to the mainland. The coastline all around here is suited to watersports, and there are several salmon farms off the inlet.

*Continue on **Highway 101** via a 45-minute ferry ride from Earls Cove to Saltery Bay to Powell River.*

Powell River, British Columbia

2 At the northernmost end of Highway 101, Powell River is just over 30km (19 miles) from Saltery Bay and its provincial park, and Lang Bay, where country farmers raise sheep and cattle. Like many towns in this region, it grew up around a pulp and paper mill. The river is noted for its salmon, and there are several marinas close to the city, as well as some 30 lakes within easy reach, where you can cast a line for cutthroat trout or take the family canoeing.

The **Powell Forest Canoe Route** is ideal for all ages: it begins at Lois Lake, little more than 14km (9 miles) south of the river, and connects 12 lakes. The shortest route is around 50km (31 miles), but this can be extended to over 145km (90 miles). Head for Haslam Lake, then Duck Lake Road, and follow the signs for **Lang Creek Hatchery**, and you can see cohos being raised (adults September–November, young April–September). In the **historic museum** on Marine Avenue you can learn more of the area's history.

If you choose to stay in Powell River, you could take an excursion by ferry to **Texada Island**, first charted by Spanish explorers, now home to over 1,000 people, and noted for its 'flower rocks', which look as if they have white flowers embedded in them, and are used for jewelry.

🛈 6807 Wharf Street

Cross by ferry from Powell River to Comox—a one-hour 15-minute ride.

Comox/Courtenay, British Columbia

3 These sister cities in the Comox Valley are surrounded by farmland and overlooked by mountains, a combination that can mean skiing and golf in the same day! You arrive in Comox harbor, where you can visit the old **Lorne Hotel**, built in 1878 on Comox Avenue, and drive along to **Filberg Lodge** (1890), constructed of local

3/4 days – 528km (328 miles)

THE SUNSHINE COAST

Vancouver ● Sechelt ● Powell River
Comox/Courtenay ● Qualicum Beach
Nanaimo ● Duncan ● Victoria ● Vancouver

Use this gentle coastal route to explore Vancouver Island's inlets, ports and coves overlooking the Strait of Georgia, and its scattered islands. Called the Sunshine Coast, this coastline is blessed by good weather and colorful underwater seascapes, with a rich marine life. You will also see mountains on the island itself – Mount Golden Hinde, at the center, is 2,200m (7,218 feet) – with cascading waterfalls, spruce and fir forests.

materials and including a petroglyph, in one of the fireplaces. Nearby **Kye Beach** is long and sandy, well suited to families and still a bit of a secret.

Downtown Courtenay has plenty of accommodation and many boutiques. Its **District Museum**, on Cliffe Avenue, is an old log building that features logging equipment (an industry important to this area) and native artifacts.

SPECIAL TO . . .

7 Victoria has the **Victorian Days** festival and parade in May, and a late June **Folkfest**.

Jazz festivals and craft fairs frequently take place throughout the Island, and sailing and canoe races and fishing tournaments are also specialties.

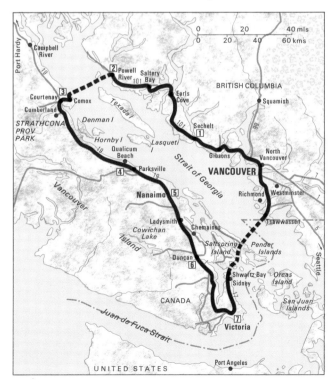

FOR HISTORY BUFFS

5 **The Bastion** in Nanaimo is part of an original Hudson's Bay fort. As well as being an architectural landmark it contains a collection, including guns and insignia, that focuses on the 1850–1880 period and also holds the archives of military records and personal documents. Daily, in summer, 20 guardsmen dressed in 1850s naval uniform are piped to the Bastion, where they perform the Noon Day Gun ceremony—elaborately cleaning, loading and firing the cannon over the harbor in salute to visitors.

FOR CHILDREN

7 Victoria is a good holiday center for children's attractions. The **Royal London Wax Museum** on Belleville Street displays models of royals, and next door, below the harbor's causeway at **Undersea Gardens**, you can descend beneath the sea for a peek at marine life. Car buffs should enjoy the **Classic Car Museum** on Douglas Street. On Beach Drive at Oak Bay Marina, **Sealand of the Pacific's** killer whales, seals and sealions perform for visitors. **Miniature World**, on Humboldt Street, is where a host of hand-carved toy soldiers portray a range of scenes. A large outdoor collection of animated figures may be seen at **Fable Cottage Estate**, on Cordova Bay Road.

SCENIC ROUTES

7 The **Marine Scenic Drive** in Victoria starts at the foot of Douglas Street on the waterfront at Dallas Road, following the waterfront for some 29km (18 miles) plus to the southern end of Saanich Peninsula. From Beacon Hill Park this lovely route passes mansions, gardens and beaches such as Gonzales Bay, Shoal Bay, Willows Beach and Cordova Bay, and continues to Ten Mile Point and Mount Douglas Park. As you travel you will have a constant view of the Olympic Mountains.

The stretch of **Highway 1** between Victoria and Nanaimo has viewpoints and parks along the way, and **Highway 17A** between Victoria and the Swartz Bay terminal is a picturesque alternative to the main road, **Highway 17**.

⌂ 2040 Cliffe Avenue, Courtenay

*Take **Highway 19** south to Qualicum Beach.*

Qualicum Beach, British Columbia

4 The fishing has always been good at Qualicum Beach, which is why the Indians named it 'the place where the dog salmon run'. Have a cup of tea in the village tearoom or browse the shops: **The Old School House Gallery and Art Center** welcomes visitors to its craft studios on Fern Road West. You could visit a fish hatchery—**Little Qualicum River Fisheries**, just north of Little Qualicum River Bridge, encourages tourists. In **Horne Lake Caves Provincial Park**, a few miles north off **Highway 19**, two caves are open year round for self-guided tours: bring your flashlight and common sense. In summer you can tour caves with an experienced guide.

Not far south, Parksville is an established resort community with a sandy seashore. Take a look at the log church of **St Anne's** (1894) or go

---

'Little' Qualicum Falls actually drops dramatically over three giant steps to the river below

to the **Little Mountain Lookout** on Bellevue Road for the view. A foot-passenger ferry travels from French Creek to Lasqueti Island, a 45-minute cruise halfway across the Georgia Strait. The island is largely undeveloped.

⌂ In town on **Highway 19**, marked by a totem pole, Qualicum Beach; at south entrance to Parksville on Highway 19

***Highway 19** continues to Nanaimo.*

Nanaimo, British Columbia

5 The cluster of Indian villages called Snenymo ('great and mighty people') is now Vancouver Island's second largest city and a major port. The waterfront is always busy with freighters, tugs, barges and fishing boats, and redevelopment projects have replaced foundries and mills with seafront walkways and gardens. Among Nanaimo's historic buildings are the **courthouse** (1896) and the **Palace Hotel** (1899), and historical artifacts are displayed in **Centennial Museum** on Cameron Street. A coal mine, pioneer town, Chinese gallery and reconstructed miner's cottage are also featured in adjacent **Piper's**

A thunderbird and a bear figure on a typical totem pole. Native art contributes to the richness of Canadian culture

Park. There are some 24 parks, from the central **Bowen Park**, with plenty of recreational facilities, and **Georgia Park**, dedicated to the first Indian tribes, to **Morrell Wildlife Sanctuary** for birdwatching and **Newcastle Island Provincial Marine Park** (reached by foot-passenger ferry) in the harbor, for picnicking, hiking and deer-spotting.

Among the many day trip possibilities is a ferry ride from downtown Nanaimo to the pretty island of **Gabriola**, whose country roads are good for cycling and whose high bluffs are the nesting place for seabirds.

🛈 7 Commercial Street

*Take **Highway 1** via Ladysmith, south to Duncan.*

Duncan, British Columbia

6 The main center for the Cowichan Valley's farming and forestry industries is home to British Columbia's band of Indians. The Cowichan Indian heritage is noticeable everywhere in Duncan, from the knitted garments they make to the

totem poles along the highway and downtown. Though these are new, they have earned the town the nickname 'City of Totems'. Look in at the **Khowutzun Arts and Crafts Gallery** and you · will find a choice of Cowichan sweaters, traditionally made from raw fleece and bearing family crest designs or geometric patterns.

The **BC Forest Museum** 1.6km (1 mile) north, near Somenos Lake, explains the forest industry through indoor and outdoor displays. Enjoy the natural beauty of **Lake Cowichan**, to the west, or sample some of its trout, cooked in a restaurant at Cowichan Bay, a peaceful village near the mouth of Cowichan River. The energetic can hike up Mount Sicker to see the ghost town: at one time the copper mines carried promise of huge profits, but in the end they played out too soon.

Chemainus, about 26km (16 miles) north on Stuart Channel, has become a major art center, and 24 enormous murals depict the area's history on downtown walls.

🛈 381 Trans-Canada Highway **(1)**, center of town

*Continue on **Highway 1** to Victoria.*

RECOMMENDED WALKS

1 Since vehicles are not allowed, **Sechelt Inlets Provincial Marine Recreation Area** is ideal for walkers. Take the road to **Porpoise Bay Provincial Park**, a couple of miles out of town, and you will find water access to the area.

3 **Strathcona Provincial Park**, within easy reach of Comox, is a hiker's paradise, with its challenging alpine meadows, peaks and forests. Within its boundaries are the island's highest mountain, Golden Hinde, and Canada's highest waterfalls, the Della. The two most popular areas are Forbidden Plateau and Mount Washington, and there is a lodge which offers programs in wilderness skills.

BACK TO NATURE

Because of the abundance of salmon in this region's waters, bald eagles are an added attraction. Late autumn is a good time to spot them from the **Mount Valentine Viewpoint** at Powell River, reached via a 20-minute hiking trail and rocky staircase. Eagles and seabirds may also be sighted on **Denman Island** and **Lasqueti Island**, as well as on **Gabriola Island**'s high bluffs. (Nature tours operate out of Nanaimo.) **Somenos Flats**, just north of Duncan, is a noted nesting area for a large variety of waterbirds, including mute swans and blue-winged teal. Whales are the other attraction here: you should be able to see them from a variety of coastal points and islands, but certainly on two to three-hour cruises from Victoria.

Victoria, British Columbia

7 Victoria, capital of the province, is situated at the southernmost tip of Vancouver Island. It was the island's first settlement, established as a Hudson's Bay fort in 1843, and is now a seaside city and a garden city, with floral displays in **Butchart Gardens**, and on the streets from spring to autumn. Named in honor of Queen Victoria, the city has always had strong links with Britain and shows numerous Old-World connections within walking distance of the harbor. It is only a few miles from the US, whose Olympic Mountains (in Washington State) across the Juan de Fuca Strait, make an attractive backdrop.

The bustling inner harbor, watched over by the grand old **Empress Hotel** (have an English afternoon tea here), is a good place to start sightseeing. Cruise around the harbor, join a fishing trip or a whale-watching cruise. Look over the **Parliament Buildings** above the harbor, where tours are given, or hop on a double-decker bus or a horse and carriage, which leave from near by for tours of the city.

At the heart of the Old Town is **Bastion Square**, site of the original Fort Victoria, where saloons and warehouses have been converted to restaurants and art galleries. Near the harbor, at **Market Square**, pre-1900 architecture has been restored. Look for antiques along **Antique Row**,

Where business and pleasure meet: Victoria's elegant Parliament Buildings—finished in 1898—form a backdrop to the busy harbor, a haven for all sorts of craft

a stretch of Fort Street up from the waterfront, or visit Victoria's own **Chinatown** from Government Street, where you can explore the artists' studios in narrow **Fan Tan Alley**.

In good weather a quiet spot in the middle of downtown is **Beacon Hill Park**, complete with cricket pitch, and totems and native carvers can be viewed in **Thunderbird Park**. The **Royal BC Museum**, on Belleville Street, renowned for its native Indian artifacts, also incorporates a pioneer town, sawmill, fish cannery, coal mine, train station and Captain George Vancouver's ship, the *Discovery*. Another excellent museum is the **Maritime**, on Bastion Square, an impressive turreted structure that houses many nautical items associated with the city's past.

ℹ️ 812 Wharf Street

Return to Vancouver via ferry.

Vancouver – Sechelt	**60 (37)**
Sechelt – Powell River	**98 (61)**
Powell River – Courtenay	**40 (25)**
Courtenay – Qualicum Beach	**73 (45)**
Qualicum Beach – Nanaimo	**35 (22)**
Nanaimo – Duncan	**51 (32)**
Duncan – Victoria	**61 (38)**
Victoria – Vancouver	**110 (68)**

Ripe for the picking: a mouth-watering apple harvest at Kelowna in this fruit-rich province

ℹ️ 10 Tenth Avenue, Kamloops

*Take **Highway 5** from Kamloops to Merritt.*

Merritt, British Columbia

1 In the midst of ranchland at the confluence of the Nicola and Coldwater Rivers, Merritt is surrounded by numerous good fishing lakes. The most dominant landmark is the **Coldwater Hotel**, built in 1908 and named after the river which flows through the Coquihalla Pass. It continues to be the social hub for locals, and it is worth dropping into its large brass and oak bar for a beer. Nicola Valley history is explained at the local **Nicola Valley Museum**, on Jackson Avenue.

ℹ️ At the junction of **Highways 5** and 5A

*Take **Highway 5A** to Princeton.*

Princeton, British Columbia

2 Within 19km (12 miles) of this small town there used to be bustling mining settlements, now silent witnesses to the days when there really was gold in them thar hills. You need a lot of imagination to figure out where all the saloons and shops used to be in **Granite City**, even though it was once British Columbia's third largest city, but the **Coalmont Hotel** in the semi-ghost town of Coalmont, where train robber Billy Miner used to hide out, is still operating.

Princeton, like Merritt, is a base for lake fishing—there are 48 lakes for trout within an 80km (50 mile) radius. The **Princeton District Pioneer Museum** on Vermilion Avenue shows how much of a role the Chinese played in the early days of mining and railroad development. Ask at the museum for directions to the **Dewdney Trail**, where unmarked pictographs—animal symbols and hieroglyphics—appear on the rock bluff at about eye level.

ℹ️ 167 Vermilion Avenue (open May-September)

*Take **Highway 3** to Hedley.*

Hedley, British Columbia

3 This tiny community was once famous for its **Nickel Plate Gold Mine**. Make a coffee stop in the **Nickel Plate Restaurant**, right on Highway 3, take a short stroll around town, and drop into the modern cultural center, **Heritage House**, for a look at the mining displays. Visitors can try panning for gold in the **Similkameen River** or **20 Mile Creek**, but nobody can promise any great finds.

***Highway 3A** continues to Keremeos.*

Keremeos, British Columbia

4 On a hot day this mountain-surrounded village is the perfect stop for a glass of freshly squeezed fruit juice from any of the 25 or so wayside stands. Keremeos has one

Orchards near Keremeos in the Similkameen River Valley

5 days – 643km (399 miles)

FRUIT-FLAVORED ROUTE

Kamloops • Merritt • Princeton • Hedley Keremeos • Osoyoos • Penticton Summerland • Peachland • Kelowna Vernon • Salmon Arm • Kamloops

You start this tour in what Canada calls its High Country, but much of the route takes you to the Okanagan-Similkameen area—British Columbia's sunshine valley, where the fruit grows in abundance. The climate is as good for grapes as for apples, so there are several wineries in the region. Heavily populated, the area contains three main cities. The scenery along the route is varied: Cascade Mountains west of Princeton, arid territory south of Osoyoos, and lake country in the center.

SPECIAL TO ...

In the fruit-growing country are several fruit-flavored celebrations. One of the biggest and best is the late September **Okanagan Wine Festival**, which takes place throughout the Valley, but the April and May **Blossom Festivals** in Summerland and Penticton are the prettiest. Osoyoos' **Cherry Fiesta Days** in early July and Penticton's **Peach Festival** in mid-July are fun, and most of the towns have an autumn fair in September. May is a good month for rodeos, in Vernon, Kelowna, Princeton and Keremeos.

FOR HISTORY BUFFS

9 **Father Pandosy Mission**, southeast of Kelowna's city center at the corner of Benvoulin and Casoro Roads, is the site of the Valley's first vineyard and orchard. Founded by Father Charles Pandosy in 1859, the Mission served both the Okanagan Indians and the white settlers. This historic center was declared a World Heritage Site in 1983, after the priest's grave was discovered in a nearby cemetery. The restored Mission, log buildings, chapel and schoolhouse show what Valley life was like over a century ago.

of the longest fruit-growing seasons in the province: look for summer cherries, peaches and apricots and autumn apples and grapes, but visit the **St Lazlo Vineyard Estate Winery**, less than 1.6km (1 mile) east on **Highway 3**, any time of the year. You might plan a picnic at **The Grist Mill**, beside Keremeos Creek, whose grounds are among shady orchards. The mill was established here in 1877 to produce flour from Okanagan wheat, serving the pioneer community until the turn of this century. The restored waterwheel continues to drive the mill machinery and, in the Visitor Center, hands-on exhibits tell you how technology worked in the 1880s. Guided tours are given May to September but the site is open year round.

There are two small local **museums**, but the surrounding parks and scenery will have greater appeal. You can go fishing in local waters, horseback riding at a nearby ranch, golfing or rockhounding.

ⓘ Main Street in Memorial Park (open May–October)

Highway 3 continues south past Spotted Lake to Osoyoos.

Osoyoos, British Columbia

5 Just north of the US border, Osoyoos has an Indian name which basically means 'narrowing of the waters', a good description of its location on both sides of narrowing Lake Osoyoos. The architecture seems Spanish; red-tiled roofs, white stucco and wrought iron; and the re-created windmill was built and is lived in by a Dutch couple. Unique Osoyoos visitor attractions include Canada's only **banana farm**, Okanagan Valley's **pocket desert**

(which can be explored on a guided horseback tour), and popular borderline **Haynes Point Provincial Park**, where the country's tiniest bird, the Calliope hummingbird, likes to flitter about.

ⓘ On **Highway 3** at the junction with **Highway 97**

Take Highway 3A or alternatively Highway 97 past Oliver and Okanagan Falls to Penticton.

Penticton, British Columbia

6 This city, which sits on a delta between the Skaha and Okanagan Lakes, could well be your choice for an overnight stop. It is a major tourist destination, the region's second largest urban center, with a number of lakeside resorts and motels perfect for families. In spring; when the orchards within the city limits are in bloom, Penticton is at its loveliest, but with a particularly warm, dry climate it is a favorite summer retreat. City sights include the SS *Sicamous*, a sternwheeler that plied Okanagan Lake until early this century; the **Art Gallery of the South Okanagan**, on Ellis Street; and the **Penticton Museum**, on Main Street. Several wineries within easy reach of the city can be toured in an afternoon, or you can relax on the lake beaches.

ⓘ 185 Lakeshore Drive

Highway 97 continues to Summerland.

Summerland, British Columbia

7 There are plenty of tourist facilities at this major fruit-processing center at the head of three valleys. Tours may be taken of **Beaven's Orchard Cannery**, the **Federal Agricultural Research Station** and the **Provincial Trout Hatchery**, as well as **Summerland Sweets** (which produces syrups and jams) and the **Sumac Ridge Estate Winery**. For the best view of this town, named after its fine summery weather, drive to the top of **Giant's Head Park**. Giant's Head Mountain looks like the profile of a man and used to be an active volcano. From the park there is a spectacular panorama of vineyards, orchards and lakeshore beaches. Okanagan Lake is said to be the home of the mythical Ogopogo monster, depicted in drawings by the Indians many moons ago. Travel north of Summerland through Okanagan Mountain Provincial Park and you will come to **Ogopogo's Home** lookout, overlooking Squally Point (on the east side of the lake). You may just sight the friendly sea serpent adopted by Lake Country as its symbol; in any case, you will have a good view of both Penticton and Kelowna.

ⓘ Summerfair Shopping Center on **Highway 97**

Highway 97 continues to Peachland.

Peachland, British Columbia

8 This fruit-growing town faces Okanagan Lake with rocky bluffs behind it. There was an early logging industry here, and there are well-posted directions to the **Silver Lake Forestry Center**, to the west of

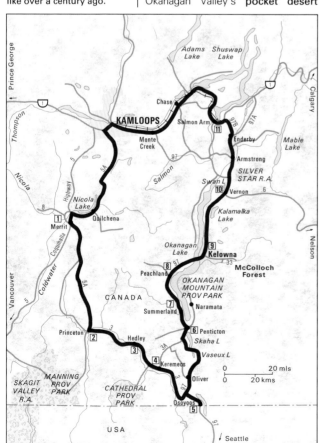

Highway 97. Here you will find the old Brenda copper mine and an excellent **museum** that features logging exhibits. It is the orchards and pine trees which give Peachland its attractive appearance. Pictures of orchard development are on show in the local **museum**, housed in a former Baptist church built of wood in 1910. British Columbia's first winery, **Chateau St Claire**, is located a few miles north (tours and tastings Easter to Thanksgiving).

🛈 Museum, 5890 Beach Avenue (summer only)

Highway 97 *continues to Kelowna.*

Kelowna, British Columbia

9 The largest city in Okanagan-Similkameen is a hub of activity on a par with Kamloops. The name derives from the Indian word for grizzly bear, which in fact referred to the grizzled appearance of an early settler, not the animal. Situated at the center of Okanagan Lake, Kelowna gives access to a full range of watersports, from windsurfing to parasailing, houseboating to cruising on a paddlewheeler. Equipment and boats may be rented from several marinas.

Serious shoppers will head uptown to the area's largest mall, Orchard

This working Dutch windmill, also a family home, is one of the many unique features of Osoyoos. The millstones are on the upper floor

Park Mall, but boutique browsers will prefer Bernard Street, which leads to the *Sails* sculpture at the entrance of shoreside City Park. In the **Kelowna Centennial Museum and Art Gallery**, on Queensway, exhibits include a reconstructed Salish Indian pit dwelling, an 1861 trading post and a large collection of local art.

There are four wineries close to the city, including the Valley's largest, **Calona** on Richter Street, and hilltop **Mission Hill Vineyards** in Westbank. However, several other product tours are available: **Sun-Rype**, on Ethel Street, which processes fruit, is the most popular with families; **Western Star Trucks**, on Enterprise Way, does not accept under-5s; **Fletcher Challenge Mill** and plywood plant gives tours on request for those over 11. Take the car for a self-guided tour of **McCulloch Forest**, which begins on McCulloch Road and links up with **Highway 33**: you will need about two hours.

🛈 544 Harvey Avenue on **Highway 97**

Highway 97 *continues to Vernon.*

FOR CHILDREN

10 Water thrills are the obvious treat for children in this region. Not far from Swan Lake, near Vernon, the **Atlantis Waterslide** is one of the man-made attractions, and **Okanagan Bobslide** (north of Swan Lake Junction), with its Olympic-style bobslides is another.

9 Wild 'n' Wet Waterslides are a Kelowna favorite, next door to **Flintstones Bedrock City**, which has several amusements for children.

SCENIC ROUTES

Highway 5A from Kamloops to Merritt is a charming alternative to the freeway, especially the first section, with its vistas of giant dry hills. Scenic **Highway 97** is a beautiful drive, as it passes through lake and orchard country into dairy country around Vernon. One interesting backroad loop may be made just north of Okanagan Falls at the Kaleden junction, if you turn southwest off **Highway 97**.

RECOMMENDED WALKS

4 Just west of Keremeos, **Cathedral Provincial Park** is a hiker's dream. There are 40km (25 miles) of wilderness trails, including a section of the Centennial Trail to Manning Provincial Park. (Note the gravel access road is not suited to motor homes.) A short but steep and hot hike takes you to **Keremeos Columns Provincial Park** (northeast), and since the route is on private land, permission from residents is required. If you have the stamina, the views of these high volcanically formed column-like basalt cliffs are worth it.

8 You can only hike or boat into **Okanagan Mountain Provincial Park** on the east side of Okanagan Lake, opposite Peachland (access from Peachland by boat, via secondary roads from Naramata or Kelowna). There are 24km (15 miles) of trails here.

BACK TO NATURE

There is a rich diversity of wildlife within the Okanagan-Similkameen region: mountain goats in the Hedley-Keremeos area are best spotted in April and late October; winter sightings of California bighorn sheep are more than likely south of Penticton. The valley is an important resting place for migratory birds, including snow geese and loons, and you should be able to watch myriad species from most points along the tour.

The parks are all excellent for nature enthusiasts: keep an eye out for golden eagles, hawks and mule deer in **Cathedral Provincial Park**; and the calliope hummingbird and yellow-bellied marmots in **Haynes Provincial Park**. The **Federal Ecological Reserve**, or pocket desert, not far north of Osoyoos, is home to many rare plant and animal species. Watch for turkey vultures, burrowing owls and the timid Northern Pacific rattlesnake. Further north at Vaseux Lake, the **Federal Migratory Bird Sanctuary** is a rest stop for almost every migratory bird, and at the **Vaseux Wildlife Center** you will see the province's largest herd of bighorn sheep.

Vernon, British Columbia

10 At the northern end of Lake Country's fruit belt, this well-equipped city is surrounded by three lakes—Okanagan, Kalamalka and Swan and within easy driving distance of over 90 more, so fishing around here is a choice occupation. Naturally, there are beaches (try **Kin Beach** and **Kalamalka Beach**) and good watersports. For the best view of Kalamalka Lake, 'a rainbow lake of many colours', takes a hike or mountain bike ride to **Kalamalka Lookout**, just south of the city. There are various places to stay, from b&bs to the Village Green Inn resort complex; plenty of restaurants, pubs and shops, and dozens of fruit and vegetable stands, as well as a Farmer's Market for picnic purchases. Settlement history from the time of the Indians to that of the miners and ranchers is illustrated at the **Greater Vernon Museum**, in the Civic Center Complex, while product tours include the **Okanagan Spring Brewery**. A favorite trip takes you a few miles north to **O'Keefe Ranch**, one of the first in the area, founded in 1867, which became a major cattle empire. Restored buildings include a church and general store.

A recommended side trip is to **Silver Star**, 22km (14 miles) away. Although it is best known as a ski resort, with night-lit trails and accom-

Incomparable fishing is to be found in McGuire Lake Park

modation styled to the 1890s, summer cyclists and hikers enjoy it too. A chairlift operates to the top of Silver Star Mountain.

☑ 3700–33rd Street

***Highway 97B** leads to Salmon Arm.*

Salmon Arm, British Columbia

11 The route now returns to the High Country in a city on the flood plain of the Salmon River at the end of one of the arms of Shuswap Lake. The early settlers needed nothing more than a pitchfork to hook the salmon which swam up the creeks in such numbers that they were used for fertilizer. Fishing remains one of the outdoor pursuits, along with boating and hiking and nature observation. You need go no further than the **Waterfront Park and Pier** to view foreshore birds and waterfowl.

☑ 7 Hudson Street

*Return on **Highway 1** to Kamloops.*

Kamloops – Merritt **95 (59)**
Merritt – Princeton **85 (53)**
Princeton – Hedley **37 (23)**
Hedley – Keremeos **30 (19)**
Keremeos – Osoyoos **46 (29)**
Osoyoos – Penticton **52 (32)**
Penticton – Summerland **20 (12)**
Summerland – Peachland **30 (19)**
Peachland – Kelowna **28 (17)**
Kelowna – Vernon **47 (29)**
Vernon – Salmon Arm **60 (37)**
Salmon Arm – Kamloops **113 (70)**

Takakkaw Falls in Yoho National Park: the name means 'It is wonderful' in Cree—and speaks for itself

ⓘ 2279 Cranbrook Street North, Cranbrook

*Take **Highway 95A** to Kimberley.*

Kimberley, British Columbia

1 Like a number of other towns in the area, Kimberley has always been connected with mining. Much of that heritage can be seen at the **Heritage Museum**, on Spokane Street, and if you wish to take a tour of an operating mine, **Cominco's Sullivan Mine**, ask at the Information Center in town. Minutes from downtown, via Gerry Sorensen Way, a train previously used in an underground mine now takes tourists on a short scenic ride.

Kimberley may remind you of Bavaria; it is one of Canada's highest cities and is noted as a wintersport center. When you sit in the pedestrianized downtown shopping area known as the **Platzl**, listening to an outdoor band and hear the giant cuckoo clock strike the hour, it is easy to believe you are in an alpine town!

ⓘ 295 Wallinger Street

*Take **Highway 95A** then **95** via Fairmont Hot Springs to Invermere.*

Invermere, British Columbia

2 You might say the first tourist to this town, on the shores of Windermere Lake, was fur trader and explorer David Thompson, who crossed the Rockies in 1807 and traveled down the Columbia River to this point, where a trading post was built. Today's visitors come because of the lake's summer activities and the ski slopes of **Panorama Resort**. Both **Athalmar Provincial Beach** and **Kinsmen Beach** are within walking distance of town and the lake is popular for water sports. The hot springs—**Fairmont** to the south and **Radium** to the north—are simple to reach.

ⓘ Seventh Avenue and 5A Street (open June–September)

***Highway 95** continues north to Golden.*

Golden, British Columbia

3 Not named for any great gold strike, but merely to outshine Silver City, Golden is situated where the Kicking Horse River joins the Columbia River. This could be a base for a visit to **Yoho National Park**, whose entrance is 24km (15 miles) east on **Highway 1**. Scenically, the park's name—Kootenay Indian for 'awe'—expresses it exactly. It will delight campers and hikers and you may well see moose, deer and black bear near the highway.

ⓘ Highway 95, downtown Golden

*Take **Highway 1** west to Glacier National Park.*

Cascade Lakes, West Hungabee Mountain, Yoho National Park. The park offers natural hot spring baths, angling, sailing, climbing— and peerless scenic beauty

4/5 days – 846km (526 miles)

CANADA'S ALPS

Cranbrook • Kimberley • Invermere • Golden
Glacier National Park • Revelstoke
Nakusp • New Denver • Kaslo
Ainsworth Hot Springs • Balfour • Creston
Cranbrook

Mountain scenery, wilderness, glacial lakes—all are features of the British Columbia Rockies, a region which embraces the Purcell range, and is best admired in and around Yoho and Kootenay National Parks. It is fine land for nature lovers and sport enthusiasts, so bring cameras, binoculars and a sense of adventure. But it can be gentle, too, with small villages and plush resorts around the Kootenay Lake area; and relaxing, with hot springs at Nakusp, Ainsworth, Fairmont and Radium.

FOR CHILDREN

9 Little is specifically designed for children on this route, but nature's own appeal is evident. One suggestion is **Cody Caves Provincial Park**, access by gravel road off **Highway 31** near Ainsworth Hot Springs. A 20-minute trail leads to the caves, which, except for a ladder or two, are as Henry Cody found them almost a century ago. Guided tours are available in summer. If you go on your own, take a flashlight, rope and rainwear.

SCENIC ROUTES

Scenery is the key to this route. Some would say that **Highway 3A**, along Kootenay Lake, is the most impressive, with the majestic combination of sky, water and snowcapped mountains; and a magnificent vista appears with every bend in the road during the 80km (50-mile) stretch between Kootenay Bay and Creston. One of the most scenic mountain roads anywhere is the **Rogers Route**, through Rogers Pass.

RECOMMENDED WALKS

2 **Purcell Wilderness Conservancy** can be reached via Toby Creek Road which will lead to the **Earl Grey Pass Trail**: for experienced hikers only, this is probably a three-day hike. This route was used by the Shuswap Indians, Canada's Governor General, Earl Grey and later by miners.

3 In **Yoho National Park** there are many hiking trails around **Emerald Lake**. A few miles from the park entrance, just across the Kicking Horse River, a short but steep trail (summer use only) will bring you to some strangely formed sandstone hoodoos, created by erosion.

BACK TO NATURE

The wilderness parks are home to black and grizzly bears, bighorn sheep and caribou, which could well be sighted in **Mount Revelstoke, Kokanee Glacier** or **Valhalla Parks**. One of the better places to sight bald eagles is at **Windermere Creek** (south beyond Fairmont Hot Springs, on the the east of Windermere Lake), for they are attracted by the spawning landlocked salmon in autumn. More than 250 bird species are at home in **Creston Valley Wildlife Management Area (Highway 3**, just north of town), a waterfowl refuge where snow geese gather and ospreys nest: telescopes and binoculars available.

Glacier National Park, British Columbia

4 The scenery here, in the northern ranges of the Selkirk Mountains, is spectacular: glaciers, rain forests, emerald lakes, waterfalls and jagged peaks. For centuries this was an insurmountable natural barrier, avoided by Indians and explorers until the Canadian Pacific Railway managed to build through the Rogers Pass at the summit. Building the highway was another challenge, and even now snowsheds protect the road in avalanche conditions; the road may sometimes be closed in winter. Summer visitors come to hike, camp, fish and explore, stopping first at the Lodge and Information Center at Rogers Pass, where films are shown and nature programs given.

Highway 1 continues to *Revelstoke.*

Revelstoke, British Columbia

5 If you want to see a Glacier or Revelstoke site, this town at the northern end of Upper Arrow Lake is the best base. Named after British banker Lord Revelstoke, the town tends to emphasize winter activities, including snow-cat and heli-skiing at **Mount Mackenzie** and **Durrand Glacier**. The latter also offers summer mountaineering and hiking. You can canoe on **Upper Arrow Lake**

and **Lake Revelstoke**, both reservoirs, providing you study topographical maps first to find places to land if it is windy. Locally popular for summer swimming is **Williamson Lake**, and **Columbia View Provincial Park** (north off **Highway 1** to **Highway 23**) is a scenic setting for picnics. Revelstoke's own **museum**, on First Street, shows transportation achievements, and the **art gallery** above it portrays the work of local artists.

The highway runs through **Mount Revelstoke National Park** and a winding gravel road travels about 26km (16 miles) to the summit.

ⓘ 199 Connaught Avenue

Take Highway 23 to Nakusp.

Nakusp, British Columbia

6 This peaceful town, huddled between mountains by the Upper Arrow Lake, was first established during the mining boom in the Slocan Valley. Local history is chronicled in the **museum** at **Nakusp Village Hall** and increased tourism has given the town a **marina** and an assortment of restaurants. The main attractions are the **hot springs**, a mile or so north, whose two steaming pools are thoroughly invigorating and open year round.

ⓘ 88 Sixth Street

Take Highway 6 to New Denver.

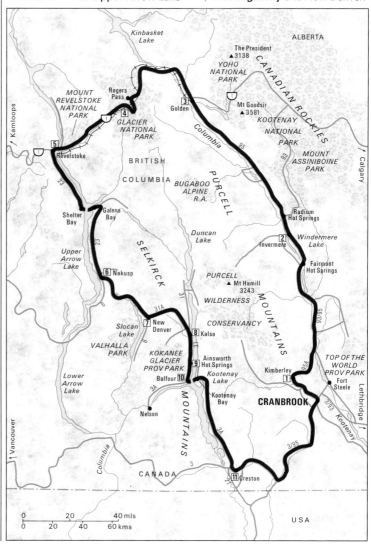

Scale:
0 — 20 — 40 mls
0 — 20 — 40 — 60 kms

A winter view of the Trans–Canada Highway at the summit of Rogers Pass, Glacier National Park

New Denver, British Columbia

7 New Denver gives the impression of being a sleepy village. Actually, it is a busy service center for hunters, hikers and sportsmen on the shore of Slocan Lake below Idaho Park and across the lake from Valhalla Provincial Park. It was originally a winter camp for silver prospectors, whose history is told in the **Silvery Slocan Museum**, at the corner of Sixth Street and Marine Drive. Very much a walkers' base, New Denver's trails range from the easy Molly Hughes trail along the lakeshore to the hard trail up Reco Mountain.

ℹ️ Museum (June–August)

Highway 31A continues to Kaslo.

Kaslo, British Columbia

8 Canada's 'Little Switzerland' is situated at sheltered Kaslo Bay on Kootenay Lake, between the Selkirk and Purcell Mountains. Kaslo can offer accommodations, restaurants and marinas. A favorite attraction is the SS *Moyie*, beached on Front Street: BC's last commercial stern-wheeler, now housing a **museum** with a collection of photographs and artifacts concerning local history. Launched in 1898, the vessel plied this lake for over five decades. Another landmark is the **Langham Cultural Center** on A Avenue, formerly a handsome boom-town hotel (1883) and now a performing arts center for the West Kootenays.

ℹ️ SS *Moyie* (open mid-April to mid-October)

Take Highway 31 to Ainsworth Hot Springs.

Ainsworth Hot Springs, British Columbia

9 Thanks to the natural springs and the views of the Purcell Mountains across Kootenay Lake, this is a pleasant resort, with a pool that opens year round and is in a horseshoe-shaped cave. This was a mine shaft, abandoned when the drillers discovered there was more hot water than ore. A little way north is the **Woodbury Resort** complex, which offers a tour of **Woodbury Mining Museum**, where you may try gold panning.

Highway 31 continues to Balfour.

Balfour, British Columbia

10 This small resort community is the western terminus for the ferry across Kootenay Lake, said to be the world's longest free ferry ride; ferries leave hourly in tourist season from Balfour across the lake to Kootenay Bay, giving a marvelous view of Kokanee Glacier Provincial Park. Balfour is also a great place to fish. Giant Gerard rainbow trout often weigh more than 15kg (33lb) and the Kootenay Lake can reward you with Kokanee salmon over 4kg (8lb).

Cross to Kootenay Bay via the ferry and continue on Highway 3A to Creston.

Creston, British Columbia

11 Imagine a prairie town in a mountain setting and you will have some idea of Creston. It overlooks the Kootenay River, meandering between the Selkirk and Purcell Mountains on its way to Kootenay Lake, and the broad lush valley serves up a fat harvest of fruits and vegetables, from asparagus to cherries and pumpkins. **Creston Valley Museum** is more unusual than most local museums. It features both indoor and outdoor displays, among them animated life-size pioneer figures, which tell the story of Creston Valley. Several product tours are available in town: the **Columbia Brewing Company** on Erickson Street will show you around in July and August; the **Candle Factory** on Northwest Boulevard gives tours from mid-May to October; and **Cresteramics** on Railway Boulevard demonstrates local talent in its workshop.

On the eastern outskirts of town, pause at **Wayside Garden and Arboretum**, a soothing flower-filled oasis with mountain and orchard views.

ℹ️ 1711 Canyon Street, Highway 3

Return to Cranbrook via Highway 3.

FOR HISTORY BUFFS

Fort Steele (**Highway 93**, just north of junction with **Highway 3**) is a living museum. Located at the confluence of the Kootenay and St Mary Rivers above Wildhorse Creek, it should have been the region's main city: accident, or the era's politics, left it abandoned while it was still young when the railroad bypassed it. What you will see today are 40 restored buildings from the original town and Mountie camp. You can get a souvenir copy of an old newspaper at the Prospector Printing Office, buy pioneer goods in Kershaw's Family Store, take a stagecoach ride and watch demonstrations of wheel making, quilting and horseshoeing. Most of the activities and special events take place between June and September.

SPECIAL TO . . .

The high country holds winter fests around January and February—at Kimberley and Golden; for example. In the lake country, fishing derbies and logging contests are frequent. Kaslo's August **Arts Festival** is one of the region's best (8) and several of the small Kootenay towns hold fall fairs. One of the most delightful celebrations is Creston's annual **Blossom Festival** in May, when the long weekend's events include chuck wagon races, parades and a fiddlers' contest (11).

5 days – 831km (517 miles)

THE GREAT OUTDOORS

Whitehorse ● Takhini Hot Springs
Haines Junction ● Burwash Landing
Haines, Alaska ● Skagway, Alaska
Carcross ● Whitehorse

Yukon is about outdoor living: it is a vast territory, so don't expect this tour to take you through anything more than a mere portion. This is purely a taste of the region, incorporating tiny segments of two notable highways: the Alaska Highway, which starts out in British Columbia and ends up in Alaska (US) 2,233km (1,388 miles) later, and the Klondike Highway, which roughly follows the Gold Stampede Trail of 1898. It also encompasses a portion of Haines Road, which climbs from tidewater up the Chilkat Pass and skirts the border of the St Elias Mountains. Yukon has spectacular scenery, but cannot promise five-star accommodation. Check the necessity for a US visa: you will be crossing into Alaska and back.

The people of the Yukon: an Inuit girl dressed for the weather in Canada's most demanding climate

ⓘ 302 Steele Street, Whitehorse

*Take **Highway 1**, then an access road to Takhini Springs.*

Takhini Hot Springs, Yukon

1 Use this as a stopping place on the Klondike Highway (just off the main Alaska Highway route), to the north of Whitehorse. Here, natural mineral hot springs that are maintained at 36°C (96°F) are surrounded by mountains for scenic and restorative swimming. Walks and horseback riding are also possibilities in this area.

*Return to the **Alaska Highway (1)** and continue to Haines Junction.*

Haines Junction, Yukon

2 This is the headquarters for the Kluane National Park; the visitor reception center is in the middle of the village. Residentially, this is only a small community at the base of the St Elias Mountains, dominated by Mount Logan. As its name suggests, the village marks the junction of the Alaska and the Haines Highways and boasts some small motels and restaurants, well-maintained RV (recreational vehicle) parks and campsites and other visitor services. It is an obvious staging point for outdoor activities, and at the visitor center you can find out everything you

The Yukon takes its name from an Indian word meaning 'clear water'—nowhere more evident than here in Kluane National Park (pronounced kloo-ah-nee)

need to know about the park and watch an award-winning audio-visual presentation which describes it.

Much of Kluane remains inaccessible unless you are a mountaineer, so the environment has not changed much since the Southern Tuchone Indians hunted the valleys for caribou and fished its waters for salmon. Miners rushed to the area in 1903 in search of gold, but most left disappointed, and only the ruins of their mining camps are to be seen, gradually being swallowed up by the surrounding wilderness. From Haines Junction you may make an overnight trail ride into the park or book a seat for a helicopter tour that flies over Canada's highest mountain, Mount Logan.

ℹ Km post 1635

*Continue north on the **Alaska Highway** via the ghost town of Silver City and Destruction Bay village, to Burwash Landing.*

Burwash Landing, Yukon

3 From this tiny Indian lakeside community you will find a panoramic view of Kluane Lake; it also has one of the best wildlife displays in the Yukon at the **Kluane Museum of Natural History**. Some of the exhibits are in diorama form; some interpret native origins with artifacts and costumes. At the **Burwash Landing Resort** (where you may wish to stay) you can make bookings for flightseeing excursions over the park's icefields and as near as possible to Mount Logan, or have

The prospect of gold lured thousands to the Yukon. Many dreams died here

a go at gold panning in Yukon creeks. The trout fishing is superb in **Kluane Lake**.

*Retrace your route to Haines Junction and continue south on the **Haines Road (3)** via Kathleen Lake Viewpoint. After crossing into British Columbia you will come to Chilkat Pass, highest point on the Highway at almost 1,215 (3,986 feet), shortly before reaching the international boundary between Canada and the US. After customs, continue to Haines, Alaska.*

FOR HISTORY BUFFS

6 The Yukon's history is a young but exciting one. Reminders lie in the riverboats that once plied the waterways to the Klondike, and now rest on the shores of rivers and lakes. Remnants from gold mines often lie where they were left by creeks, and abandoned ghost towns are becoming overgrown with weeds. Not far from Carcross, **Robinson Roadhouse** is one such old town site, constructed in the early 1900s for gold prospectors, and **Venus Mine**, on the way to Carcross, was once an active silver and gold ore-crushing mill in the early 1900s.

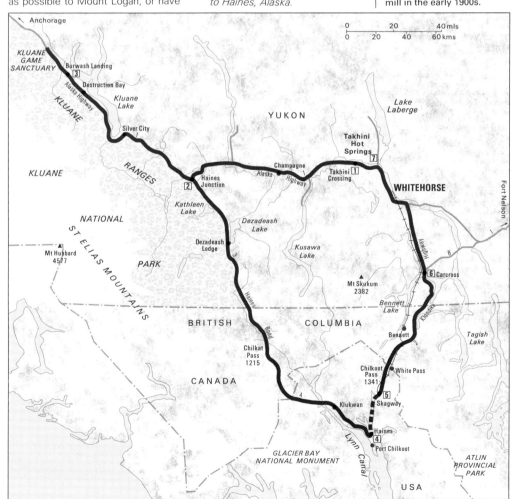

FOR CHILDREN

Like many places in Canada, the thrill of the outdoors far outweighs anything man could devise. Rivers, for example, are the roads to adventure: such as the Yukon, whose headwaters are in **Lake Bennett**, and whose tributaries in summer are ideal for novice canoeists. Sightseeing by air over Kluane's glaciers is an adrenalin-pumping experience for all ages, and learning about the Yukon Indians from the museums or choosing a souvenir from their craft shops is an interesting education.

SCENIC ROUTES

This circular tour is one big scenic route, with many viewpoints along the way such as **Bear Creek Summit** and **Boutillier Summit** on the way from Haines Junction to Destruction Bay and Kluane Lake Viewpoint, a scenic overlook of the lake. The trip between Haines and Skagway in Alaska is breathtaking and continues to be so as the Klondike Highway climbs through the Skagway Valley, lush and silvered with waterfalls. Once it has reached the summit, it descends to the southern lakes on the way to Carcross and, beyond, the glimmer of **Emerald Lake**.

RECOMMENDED WALKS

The **Chilkoot Trail** is the most famous of hikes, starting at Dyea, not far from Skagway, and winding through rain forests, alpine meadow, and over talus rock to the pass itself, 1,341m (4,400 feet) high. Along the way there is much evidence of those 'Sourdoughs' (people who spent one or more winters in Alaska) who rushed to the Klondike almost a century ago. The trail then descends to a series of lakes: **Crater**, **Deep**, and **Lindeman** near Bennett. It is well marked, regularly patroled and runs in total for 53km (33 miles), taking an average hiker three to five days, but be warned: it isn't easy.

In the **Kluane National Park** there are 249km (155 miles) of trails, some suited to one-day hikes, some leading to more remote areas. They range from easy trails to those needing serious backpacking experience. During summer, scheduled guided hikes are given by park services.

Off the Haines Road, **St Elias Lake Trail** winds through sub-alpine meadow for 6km (4 miles); you may spot mountain goats on this easy hike. The 15-minute self-guided walk along the **Rock Glacier Trail** will give you an excellent view of Kluane country.

Haines, Alaska, US

4 Haines was the starting point of the historic **Dalton Trail**, a toll road hacked out of the wilderness by gold rush entrepreneur Jack Dalton to lead over Chilkat Pass to the Klondike goldfields. The **Haines Highway**, which you have just followed, parallels much of that earlier Dalton Trail, which was the principal route into the Yukon's interior until 1898, when the passes near Skagway and Dyea became the more normal routes in to Canada.

Surrounded by mountains, islands and waterways, this pleasant city has a blend of Indian culture and pioneering history best seen at **Fort William E Seward** and its associated **Chilkat Indian craft shops**—Chilkat Indian dancing may be watched in the restored **Raven Tribal House** in Totem Village on the grounds of the former fort, and at the **Sheldon Museum**, which displays many Indian and gold-rush artifacts, including interesting Tlingit Indian beadwork and basketry.

ⓘ 2nd and Willard Streets

Take the ferry through the Lynn Canal to Skagway, Alaska.

The Watson River, near Carcross, shining beneath the Yukon sky. In the background, the Gray Ridge of the Coastal Mountains

Survivor of gold rush days, the Caribou Hotel in Carcross. 'The Duchess' is another reminder of those wild frenzied times

Skagway, Alaska, US

5 Situated in a majestic setting at the northernmost point of the Lynn Canal, this port-of-call for cruise ships, start of the Klondike Highway, is the northern terminus of the Inside Passage. Skagway was a famous gold-rush town and its first granite building, dating from the boom days of 1898, now houses the **Trail of '98 Museum**. A visit here is a must, for there is a treasure trove of memorabilia, some of which you would hardly believe the prospectors could attempt to carry over the trail. In many of the shops along the main thoroughfare, **Broadway**, there are also items relating to the gold rush period and entertainment is often Klondike style. Skagway's historic district has been designated **Klondike Gold Rush National Historic Park**.

*The **Klondike Highway**, which you now take, roughly follows the trail of the 1898 gold stampeders via Chilkoot and White Pass. You will pass through customs, re-entering Canada and on to Carcross.*

Carcross, Yukon

6 This scenic village is situated between Bennett and Nares Lakes, where the lake steamer *SS Tutshi* sits beached on the narrows. Guided tours of the old sternwheeler, launched in 1917 and in service until 1971, are given mid-May to mid-September. In the early days this was a major hunting area, hence the name, which is an abbreviation of Caribou Crossing. Much later it became a main depot for the White Pass and Yukon Route railroad, and a supply center for the Conrad Mine on Windy Arm of Tagish Lake, as well as the shipment point for goods going to the gold rush town of Atlin. The old **train depot** is these days a gift shop and snack bar; the old warehouse, a luncheon theater.

One popular excursion is to take a cruise from Carcross to **Bennett**, where you will be given a guided walking tour to the old **log church**. Fishing trips are another possibility (The lake yielded the world's second largest trout.)! Five kilometers (2 miles) north of Carcross the **Museum of Yukon Natural History** displays animal exhibits in authentic diorama settings.

ℹ beside SS *Tutshi* (open mid-May to mid-September)

Continue to Whitehorse on the ***Klondike Highway (2)***.

Whitehorse – Takhini Hot Springs **27 (17)**
Takhini Hot Springs – Haines Junction **97 (60)**
Haines Junction – Burwash Landing **127 (79)**
Burwash Landing – Haines, Alaska **383 (238)**
Haines, Alaska – Skagway, Alaska **30 (19)**
Skagway, Alaska – Carcross **90 (56)**
Carcross – Whitehorse **77 (48)**

BACK TO NATURE

A great variety of wildlife lives on the edge of Kluane Park's icefields, including moose, mountain goats and snowy-white Dall sheep. Stop in at the **Sheep Mountain Interpretive Area and Visitor Center** on the Alaska Highway (towards Burwash Landing), which has a spotting scope and informed staff to answer questions about the Dall sheep.

In Alaska, naturalists will find a major winter rookery not far from Haines, where hundreds of bald eagles alight in October and November, drawn by the late run of salmon in the Chilkat River.

Glacier Bay brims with wildlife—harbor seals, mountain goats, whales, bears and over 200 species of bird. **The Glacier Bay National Monument**, reached from Haines, is one of the wonders of the modern world: a 12,950 sq km (5,000-square-mile) reserve of active tidewater glaciers, iced bays and rain forests. It is particularly well known for the humpback whale, which feeds here in summer.

INDEX

References to captions are in italic.

A

Abernethy 82
accidents on the road 6
African Lion Safari and Game Reserve 43
Ainsworth Hot Springs 113
Alaska 116
Alberta 84, 86–97
        tour maps 86, 90, 93, 95
Alexander Bridge Provincial Park 101–2
Alexander Graham Bell National Historic Park 12
Algonquin Provincial Park 55–6, *56*, 57
Alma 20
Almonte 57, *57*
Annapolis Royal 14, *15*
Antigonish 12
Asessippi Provincial Park 67
Assiniboia 80
Athabasca Glacier *87* 88
Aulac 20
Avalon Wilderness Reserve 25
Avonlea 80

B

Baddeck 12
Badlands 89, 90, *91*
Baie-du-Fêvre 39
Baie-Saint-Paul 34, 35
Baie-Sainte-Catherine 34, 35
Balfour 113
Bancroft 56
Banff 92, *92*, 93
Banff National Park *92*, 93
banks 5
Bannock Point 61
Barrie 46
Bastion 104
Batiscan 37
Batoche *75*, 75–6
Battleford 77
Battleford National Historic Park 77
BC Museum of Mining 101
Beaupré 34–5
Bécancour 39
Beloeil *31*, *33*, 33
Blackcomb Mountain *100*
Blackstrap Provincial Park 74
Blaine Lake 77
Bon Echo Provincial Park 56
Bow Island 96
Bow Valley Parkway 93
Bow/Crow Forest Reserve 94
Brampton 49
Brandon 68
breakdowns 6
Bridal Veil Falls *102*
Brigus 23
British Columbia 98, 100–13
        tour maps 101, 103, 108, 112
Brooks 97
Bruce Trail 44, 49, 51
Brudenell 17
Burwash Landing 115

C

Cabot Trail 12
Calgary 85, 92, 95, *97*

Campobello Island 21
Camrose 91
Canada's Wonderland 50
Canmore 92–3
Cannington Manor Historic Park 82
Cap-de-la-Madeleine 38
Cape Breton Highland National Park 12
Cape Breton Island 11–12
Cape St Mary Seabird Sanctuary 25
car rental 7
Carbonear *23*, 24
Carcross *116*, 117, *117*
Carlyle 82
Cathedral Provincial Park 110
Cavendish 18
Chambly 31
Champlain 37
Charlottetown 9, 16, *16*
Chemin du Roi 38
Chester 13
Cheticamp *10*, 12
Chicoutimi 36
Claresholm 96
Clear Lake 67
Cochrane 94
Cochrane Ranche Historical Site 92
Cody Caves Provincial Park 112
Collingwood 49–50
Comox 103
Coquihalla Canyon Provincial Recreation Area 102
Courtenay 103
Cranbrook 99, 111
credit cards 4
Creston 113
Crystal Farm Battlefield Park 54
currency 4
customs regulations 4
Cypress Hills Provincial Park *78*, 79, 80, *80*

D

Dauphin 59, 67
Deer Island 21
Devil's Punch Bowl 42
Dinosaur Provincial Park 97
Drumheller *89*, 90–1
Drumheller Dinosaur and Fossil Museum 89
Drummondville 31, 32
Duck Lake 75
Duck Mountain Provincial Park 67, 68, 69
Duncan 105
Dundas 42, 44, 45
Dundas Valley Conservation Area 44

E

Eastend 80
Economy 10
Edmonton 84–5, *85*, 86, 89, *89*
Eldon 16
Elkhorn 67
Elora *50*, 51
emergencies 4
entry documents 4
Eriksdale 65

F

Falcon Lake 61
Father Pandosy Mission 108
Fenelon Falls 48, *48*
Ferryland 25
Fisheries Museum of the Atlantic 14
Flesherton 51

Flower Pot Rocks 20
fly/drive 7
Foam Lake 74
Fort Anne *15*
Fort Anne National Park 14
Fort Beausejour 20
Fort Carlton Historic Park 75
Fort Chambly National Historic Park 32
Fort Erie 43, 44
Fort George National Historic Park 43
Fort Henry 53
Fort Langley National Historic Park 101
Fort Macleod 96
Fort Qu'Appelle 82–3
Fort Steele 113
Fort Walsh National Historic Park 80
Fort Wellington 53
Fortress of Louisbourg National Historic Park *10*, 11
Fredericton 22, *22*
Frontenac Provincial Park 54
Fundy National Park *21*, 22

G

Gananoque 53, 54
Garibaldi Provincial Park 102
Gatineau Hills *28*
Georgetown 17
Georgian Bay Islands National Park 48, *51*
Gibsons 103
Gimli 64, 65
Glacier Bay National Monument 117
Glacier National Park 112, *113*
Golden 111
Golden Ears Provincial Park 102
Good Spirit Lake 74
Granby 31, 32, 33
Grand Manan Island 21, 22
Grand Marais 63
Gravenhurst 46, 47
Gray *83*
Great Divide 94
Greenwater Lake Provincial Park 74
Grenfell 82
Grist Mill 108
Guelph 49, 50, 51
Gull Harbor Resort and Conference Center 65

H

Haines 116
Haines Junction 114–15
Halifax 8, *9*, 10, 13
Hamilton 42
Hanna 91
Harbor Grace 23–4
Haynes Point Provincial Park 108
Head-Smashed-In Buffalo Jump 96
health insurance 4
Heart's Content 24
Hébertville 35, 36
Hecla Provincial Park 65
Hedley 107
High River 95, 96
Hinton 86
Hope 100, 102
Hopewell Cape 20
Hull *4*, *28*, 29–30, *30*

I

Icefields Parkway *86*, 88
Ingonish 12

ACKNOWLEDGEMENTS

The Automobile Association would like to thank the following photographers, libraries and associations for their help in the preparation of this book:

MICHAEL DENT   69 Riding Mountain.

GOVERNMENT OF NEWFOUNDLAND & LABRADOR DEPT OF TOURISM 23 Stationers Festival Carboneau.

MANITOBA INDUSTRY FOR TRADE & TOURISM   67 Clear Lake, Minnedosa Valley.

MILLER COMSTOCK INC.   1 Niagara Falls (E Otto), 4 Quebec Can Mus Civilization (W Wittman), 5 Peggy's Cove (R Chambers), 7 Bas-Saint Laurent (E Otto), 8/9 Halifax (G Hunter), 10 Acadian Cultural Centre (W Gordon), 10 Fortress of Louisbourg (E Otto), 13 Oak Island (K Wright), 13 Peggy's Cove (R Chambers), 14 Lobster Traps Lunenburg (W Griebeling), 15 Fort Anne Annapolis, 16 Charlottetown, 17 King's County, 18 Malpeque (G Hunter), 19 Summerside (M Saunders), 20 The Rocks Hopewell (E Otto), 21 Fundy N T Park, 22 Fredericton (Malak), 23 Nr Pouch Cove, 25 St John's, 26/7 Chat Frontence Old Quebec, 28 Gatineau Hills (E Otto), 30 Hull Mus of Civilization, 32 Melbourne St Francoise River (G Hunter), 34 Sainte Anne de Beaupré (E Otto), 34 Tadoussac (W Griebeling), 36 North Malbaie (K Sommerer), 37 Presbytere Deschambault, 39 North shore St Lawrence (W Griebeling), 40 Toronto (E Otto), 42 The Owl & Pussycat, 43 Stoney Creek Mon (W Griebeling), 45 Niagara Falls (E Otto), 46 St Marie Among Huons, 47 Martyr's Shrine (W Griebeling), 48 Fenelon Falls (B Hoferichter), 50 The Elora Gorge, 51 Georgian Bay, 52 Church at Manotick (E Otto), 52/3 Kingston Roy Milt College (R Chambers), 54 Ottawa (E Otto), 55 N Gall of Canada (G Hunter), 56 Smoke Lake, 57 Mill of Kintail (E Otto), 58/9 Parliament Building, Winnipeg (Malak), 60 Mennonite Vill (W Griebeling), 61 Legislative Building, Winnipeg (B Hoferichter), 62 Grain Elevators, Manitoba (W Griebeling), 63 Church Angusville, 64 Bull Riding Selkirk, 65 L Winnipeg, 66 Lower F. Garry, 71 Saskatoon, 77 N Battleford, 78 Cypress Hills (E Otto), 79 Regina (Malak), 80 Conglomerate Cliffs (E Otto), 81 Elevator siding & sunset (G Hunter), 81 Qu'Appelle Valley (E Otto), 83 Great Regina Plain (G Hunter), 85 Edmonton, 86 Icefield Parkway (E Otto), 87 Snowcoach Athabasca Glacier (T Dietrich), 88 Rocky Mountains (G Hunter), 89 Dinosaur Display (M Shewchuk), 91 Drumneller (G Hunter), 92 Moraine Lake, 92 Banff Springs Hotel, 94 L Louise (E Otto), 95 Nikka Yoko Jap Gardens (G Hunter), 97 Calgary (E Otto), 98 Vancouver, 100 Horstman Glacier, 100 Whistler/Blackcomb Golf Club (G Hunter), 102 Bridal Veil Falls (R Hall), 104 Little Qualicum Falls (Malak), 105 Stanley Park (G Hunter), 106 Victoria (R Hall), 107 Similkameen River Valley, 109 Windmill Lower Okanagan (G Hunter), 110 McGuire Lake (B Rose), 111 Takakkaw Falls (W Griebeling), 111 Cascade Lakes (E Otto), 113 Rogers Pass (G Hunter), 114 Inuit Girl (M Beedell) 114 Kluane N Park (E Otto), 115 Gold (Comstock Inc), 116 Watson River & Gray Ridge, 117 Carcross Loco (G Hunter).

MINISTRY OF TOURISM ONTARIO   49 Alpine Skiing.

SASKATCHEWAN ECONOMIC DIVISION & TRADE   72 Saskatchewan River, Western Red Lily, 73 Rodeo, 74 Fishing, 76 Bison.

TELEGRAPH COLOUR LIBRARY   28 Mt Trèmblant, 32 Beloeil Patate-Ville, 38 Tobacco Farm Joliette.

THE STOCK MARKET PHOTO AGENCY INC.   33 Beloeil.

ZEFA PICTURE LIBRARY UK LTD   Cover Maligne Lake, 3 Maligne Lake & Jasper N P, 75 Saskatchewan Batoche.